Rhetoric and Representation in Nonfiction Film examines the basic theoretical issues that ground any in-depth study of nonfiction film and video. Exploring the legitimacy of the distinction between fiction and nonfiction, Carl Plantinga here characterizes nonfiction film in a new way. He surveys the functions of moving images in visual communication and shows how nonfiction discourse presents information through structure and style, among other topics. Plantinga also examines several fundamental philosophical issues that are at the heart of nonfiction representation and communication, including the nature and functions of objectivity, reflexivity, and truth-telling. *Rhetoric and Representation in Nonfiction Film* takes a "critical realist" perspective on these issues and offers an alternative to the dominant postmodernist and poststructuralist theories of nonfiction film.

RHETORIC AND
REPRESENTATION IN
NONFICTION FILM

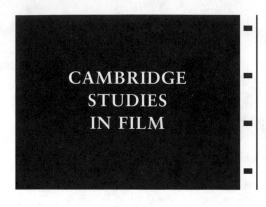

CAMBRIDGE STUDIES IN FILM

GENERAL EDITORS:

William Rothman, *University of Miami*
Dudley Andrew, *University of Iowa*

OTHER BOOKS IN THE SERIES:

Another Frank Capra, by Leland Poague
Film and Phenomenology, by Allan Casebier
Film at the Intersection of High and Mass Culture, by Paul Coates
Inside Soviet Film Satire: Laughter with a Lash, Andrew Horton, editor
Projecting Illusion: Film Spectatorship and the Impression of Reality, by Richard Allen
Russian Critics on the Cinema of Glasnost, Michael Brashinsky and Andrew Horton, editors
Theorizing the Moving Image, by Noël Carroll

RHETORIC AND REPRESENTATION IN NONFICTION FILM

CARL R. PLANTINGA
Hollins College

CAMBRIDGE
UNIVERSITY PRESS

PUBLISHED BY THE PRESS SYNDICATE OF THE UNIVERSITY OF CAMBRIDGE
The Pitt Building, Trumpington Street, Cambridge CB2 1RP, United Kingdom

CAMBRIDGE UNIVERSITY PRESS
The Edinburgh Building, Cambridge CB2 2RU, United Kingdom
40 West 20th Street, New York, NY 10011-3211, USA
10 Stamford Road, Oakleigh, Melbourne 3166, Australia

First published 1997

Printed in the United States of America

Typeset in Sabon

Library of Congress Cataloging-in-Publication Data

Plantinga, Carl R.
    Rhetoric and representation in nonfiction film / Carl R.
  Plantinga.
      p.   cm. – (Cambridge studies in film)
    Includes bibliographical references and index.
    ISBN 0-521-57326-2 (hc)
    1. Documentary films – History and criticism.   2. Experimental
  films – History and criticism.   I. Title.   II. Series.
  PN1995.9.D6P56   1997
  070.1'8 – dc20   96-45968
                                                            CIP

*A catalog record for this book is available from
the British Library.*

ISBN 0–521–57326-2 hardback

For Cynthia

Contents

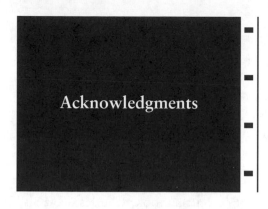

Acknowledgments

Many persons provided help and encouragement during the writing of this book. If any go unacknowledged, I apologize. *Rhetoric and Representation in Nonfiction Film* originated as a Ph.D. dissertation at the University of Wisconsin–Madison. I'd first like to thank the members of my committee: Donald Crafton, Donald Crawford, Vance Kepley, Jr., and J.J. Murphy. Special thanks go to David Bordwell, who directed the project and generously offers his advice and support to this day. Many teachers, friends, and colleagues offered education, encouragement, and advice. Among them are Edward Branigan, Noël Carroll, Allan Casebier, Darrell William Davis, Dirk Eitzen, Kevin Hagopian, Denise Hartsough, Elizabeth Keyser, Irvin Kroese, Jacques Le Fleur, Stephen Prince, Murray Smith, Kristin Thompson, and Bill White.

Thanks to Beatrice Rehl, Fine Arts Editor at Cambridge University Press. Members of the Hollins College Faculty Writing Workshop saw pieces of this book in earlier drafts, and offered useful suggestions. In addition, my work benefited from several Hollins Travel and Research Grants, plus a Cabell Fellowship for 1994–95. Hollins College was flexible and generous in granting me the leave of absence that enabled me to complete this book. Thanks are due to various archivists who made available many of the nonfiction films I viewed while preparing this book: Maxine Fleckner-Ducey and the staff of the Wisconsin Center for Film and Theater Research, and Charles Silver at the Museum of Modern Art. I also thank the Wisconsin State Historical Society for access to primary documents on the documentary television series *The Twentieth Century*, essential for my examination of journalistic objectivity in the concluding chapter.

Sections of the first chapter are taken from "Defining Documentary: Fiction, Non-Fiction, and Projected Worlds," in *Persistence of Vision 5* (Spring 1987), 44–54. I thank Noël Carroll for originally soliciting that essay. Elements of the second chapter derive from "The Mirror Framed: A Case for Expression in Documentary," in *Wide Angle* 13, 2

(April 1991), 40–53. Thanks to Jeanne Hall for publishing the piece, to the current editor, Ruth Bradley, for permission to reprint parts of it. Part of Chapter Five is taken from "Roger and History and Irony and Me," *Michigan Academician* 24, 3 (Spring 1992), 511–520, and a portion of the sixth chapter appeared in "Blurry Boundaries, Troubling Typologies, and the Unruly Nonfiction Film," *Semiotica* 98, 3/4 (1994), 387–396.

I owe several persons special acknowledgment. Thanks to Bill Nichols for reading and commenting on the book; Charles Wolf also carefully read the manuscript, and offered invaluable suggestions for revision; Bill Rothman's close reading caused me to examine many of my assumptions and clarify the argument at several key points. This is a much better product for their efforts. Still, of course, any mistakes may be attributed only to me.

Nicholas Wolterstorff, who taught at Calvin College while I was an undergraduate there, made the study of aesthetics and philosophy fascinating and encouraged my initial explorations of classical film theory. I thank my parents, Alvin and Kathleen Plantinga, for a lifetime of education, encouragement, and good cheer. To Cynthia Kok I offer thanks for consistent support and for enduring the personal trials that accompany any project such as this. To her I dedicate this book.

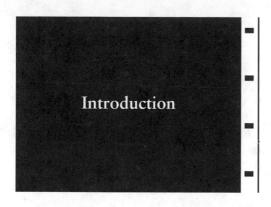

Introduction

Moving picture nonfictions, typically called documentaries or nonfiction films and television, are a diverse lot. Those I examine in this book include independently-produced features (*American Dream, Brother's Keeper*, and *The Lovely May* [*Le Joli Mai*], journalistic documentaries (*See it Now* with Edward R. Murrow, *Frontline*), government-sponsored films (*The River, Song of Ceylon, Why Vietnam?*), anti-war, anti-government films (*Far From Vietnam, Hearts and Minds*), public television programs (*The Civil War, Eyes on the Prize*, and *Nature*), network news "magazines" (*CBS 60 Minutes, 20/20*) , compilation films (*The Fall of the Romanov Dynasty, Victory at Sea*), and poetic and experimental work (*Manhatta, Valentin de las Sierras*).

Rhetoric and Representation in Nonfiction Film works toward a *pragmatics* and a *rhetoric* of moving picture nonfictions. Nonfiction film pragmatics is the study of how nonfictions are used to perform various social tasks. Erik Barnouw implicitly acknowledges the rich variety of nonfictions in his history of the genre in section headings alluding to the diverse purposes of their makers: explorer, reporter, advocate, poet, promoter, observer, guerrilla, etc.[1] Michael Renov describes four functions of nonfiction films as (1) to record, reveal, or preserve, (2) to persuade or promote, (3) to analyze or interrogate, and (4) to express.[2] The purposes of the nonfiction film are limited only by the breadth of human communication itself.

It has been argued that images can perform many of the actions for which language is used – warning, asserting, identifying, informing, ridiculing, critiquing, etc.[3] When we broaden the study of speech acts to encompass actions performed through the presentation of entire nonfiction texts, and to images and sounds used *within* texts, the matter becomes quite complicated. Instead of the simple utterances of a language user, we have a complex meld of images and sounds, in a work playing in some cases longer than two hours (consider *Shoah* or *The Civil War*, for example). Moreover, the sentence is typically uttered

1

by an individual, often for a discernible purpose, whereas a work of nonfiction is a group project which, after its initial release, can be used for a variety of purposes depending on the context of exhibition.

One of the tasks of the nonfiction student or scholar is to investigate how producers, distributors, exhibitors, and audiences employ films and videos in the realm of human action. However, if the uses of nonfiction films are as varied as the films themselves, theory alone cannot circumscribe the work's possible uses, or determine *a priori* the ideological effect of a text or genre. History and criticism must place movements, filmmakers, and individual films in their contexts. Theory, at best, supplies conceptual tools.

To contribute to such a pragmatics, we must first explore central philosophical issues. The first four chapters of this book examine two issues fundamental to all theoretical explorations of nonfiction film. The first – the nature of nonfiction and the nonfiction film – has proven to be utterly baffling to generations of filmmakers and scholars. The second issue – the semantics of moving picture photography – is no less central, and the scholarly discussion every bit as contentious. While emphasizing the historical nature of the genre, these chapters propose a characterization of nonfiction moving pictures that distinguishes fiction from nonfiction, accounts for the diversity of nonfiction films and videos, and accounts for expressive techniques, often mistakenly called "fictional," in nonfictions.

A pragmatics of nonfiction moving pictures must deal with the semantic issues of photographic realism and reference. It must also explore the rhetorical uses of images and sounds. Sometimes those who endorse a qualified realism of the image, as I do here, are claimed to hold all types of fantastical beliefs, ranging from the "presence" of the photograph's referent, to confidence that the photograph *automatically* guarantees unproblematic evidence about its referent, to a belief in magic. Photographic realists are also claimed to have various shortcomings of a personal or psychological nature. At various times, they have been called philistines, narcissists, or fetishists. In *The Burden of Representation*, for example, John Tagg writes that Roland Barthes' assertions about photographic realism must be considered in light of "the death of his own mother, his reawakened sense of unsupportable (sic) loss, and his search for 'a just image' and not 'just an image' of her," and implies that Barthes' claims stem from a desire for "the repossession of his mother's body."[4]

Although Barthes may in fact have had this problem, and other realists may hold various naïve beliefs, it is nonetheless possible to make a more sophisticated case for photographic realism. In the third and fourth chapters I do so, drawing on diverse sources to argue that as iconic and indexical signs, still and moving photographs (and recorded sounds) can refer to the profilmic scene in ways that account for its unique informative power. However, the iconic and indexical aspects of the image are never automatic, guaranteed, or unproblematic. Moreover, images and sounds also have connotative and symbolic aspects, and point forward, so to speak, to their rhetorical functions.

This book is also meant to contribute to a rhetoric of nonfiction moving pictures. I mean "rhetoric" not in the relativistic sense of Stanley Fish. Fish makes rhetoric into an all-encompassing phenomenon, claiming as irrelevant and misleading all notions of truth, evidence, or reason. Fish's project calls first for a debunking of orthodoxies and "arrangements of power," a recognition that everything is rhetorical. Second, for a loosening or weakening of "the structures of domination and oppression that now hold us captive."[5] These forces he identifies with rhetoric, arguing that we must counter the power of rhetoric and liberate ourselves from its hegemony. However, if all is rhetoric, then our debunking is itself just more self-serving drivel (with no grounding in truth, evidence, reason). Why should anyone be persuaded by it?[6]

Nor do I mean by "rhetoric" merely the realm of persuasion. I take the word in a broader sense, as the study of the richness, complexity, and expressiveness of nonfiction discourse, and the means by which it is structured to have influence on the viewer. To this end, the fifth chapter describes nonfiction discourse in general terms, then examines the means by which it fashions its representation – through selection, ordering, emphasis, and what I call "voice." The sixth chapter discusses the means others have used to talk about subgenres of nonfiction, from Bill Nichols' modes of documentary to divisions based on categorical, rhetorical, and narrative form. Then it further expands on the concept of voice, showing the formal means by which nonfiction texts claim or disavow levels of authority, and describing what I call the "formal" and the "open" voices. The seventh and eighth chapters examine structure, style, and technique, in each case not as elements of a "free-floating play of signifiers," but of an expressive discourse that makes reference to the actual world. In the ninth chapter I explore an alternative to the formal and open voices, the "poetic voice," manifesting itself in poetic documentaries, avant-garde nonfictions, metadocumentaries, and parodies.

Chapters 5–9 emphasize the formal, syntactical qualities of nonfiction moving pictures. Yet it would be inaccurate to describe my project as formalist. As I said above, I'm interested in studying the place non-fictions occupy in the social world, and in the morality and ideology of discourse. A valuable way to contribute to such a study is to investigate the formal workings of texts, since their structures influence how texts can be used and what effects they may have. I want to avoid the bold and general, but misguided, claims some theorists make about "the" ideological effect of nonfiction films.[7] For example, Brian Winston argues that the photograph is invested with such an aura of science that despite all disavowals by filmmakers, spectators always take the image as unproblematic and transparent truth.[8] This misleading "scientifici-ty" is allegedly built into the photographic apparatus, an outcome of its historical association with scientific instruments. Yet Winston doesn't believe in the automatic veracity of the photographic image. Is it right for Winston to impart a universal ideological effect to the photograph from which he is exempt? My contention is that ideological effects cannot be posited at such a broad level of generality, but instead must be determined in reference to specific texts, events, contexts, and audiences. If this makes it more difficult to determine ideological effect apart from history, then so be it. History, criticism, and theory must have a symbiotic relationship.

I make no general claims about *the* historical meaning of nonfiction moving pictures, or their *central* ideological effects. They have none. It seems to me that nonfictions occupy a central place in Western culture, but that their importance is manifested in infinite variations. Moreover, nonfiction moving pictures, like photography in general, have no unitary ideological effect, central function, or singular purpose, but a multitude of effects and purposes, depending on use, context, audience, and other factors. Rhetorical, text-based studies can contribute to the overall pragmatics of nonfiction film by examining how texts make meaning and use persuasive techniques. A fuller understanding of the uses of films, however, requires serious historical and critical investigation.

The final chapter of *Rhetoric and Representation in Nonfiction Film* considers some broad issues raised by nonfiction discourse. There I examine the strengths and weaknesses of the formal and open voices and their alternatives, showing how each is suited for specific purposes. I question and evaluate concepts such as objectivity, balance, and fairness in relation to historical or journalistic documentaries, and show how these concepts play out in an historical compilation documentary,

The Twentieth Century. I discuss filmic illusion and reflexivity as they apply to the nonfiction film spectator. Finally, I conclude with some remarks about truth-telling and the ethics of nonfiction discourse.

This book integrates theory and philosophy with criticism. "Theory" here means the systematic investigation of issues central to nonfiction moving pictures. I am primarily concerned with understanding the nature and functions of nonfiction film, and thus with analysis rather than prescription. The book is also criticism, because it provides extended analyses to show how individual works exemplify particular issues. It adheres to no well-defined school or program, but approaches issues with reference to a broad spectrum of sources, from film theory, philosophy, cultural criticism, narratology, psychology, art theory, and of course, nonfiction film scholarship.

Rhetoric and Representation in Nonfiction Film does not cover all relevant issues. Although it deals with the ethical responsibilities of the film maker toward the audience, it does not examine the rights of persons used as documentary subjects, a topic explored quite thoroughly elsewhere.[10] The same is true for ethnographic and anthropological films, a discussion of which is better left to those more familiar with particular problems raised by those fields. Neither does this book deal extensively with the dramatic documentary, or docudrama. This topic has *not* been sufficiently explored, and someone should begin that project soon.

Moreover, *Rhetoric and Representation in Nonfiction Film* does not claim the last word on the subjects it *does* cover. It is rather part of a collaborative project in film studies, media studies, and other disciplines. I care less about whether I am right in all cases than about the contribution this work makes to discussion, synthesis, and perhaps even controversy – to that collaborative conversation which, we hope, leads to better understanding and perhaps beyond that to more tangible benefits. I take issue with many scholars throughout these pages, and in turn, welcome their criticisms, corrections, and questioning. Too often in film and media studies, carping and defensiveness take the place of constructive discussion and debate. We often take defensive postures toward criticism of our work, and allow debate to degenerate into personal animosity. We can and should disagree with each other openly.

When I first cite a film within the text, I give its date of release. For historical information about the films, see Richard M. Barsam's *Nonfiction Film: A Critical History* (Bloomington: Indiana University Press, 1992) or Erik Barnouw's *Documentary: A History of the Nonfiction*

Film (New York: Oxford University Press, 1993). These books also include bibliographies of works on specific nonfiction films and film makers. This work is not a history of nonfiction moving pictures, though it does assume a basic familiarity with that history. The better the reader's historical grounding, the better she will be able to test my claims against specific films and the historical record.

The past few years have witnessed a marked increase in the scholarly attention paid to nonfiction moving pictures. An annual conference, "Visual Evidence," is devoted to the subject. Many significant books have been published, and a book series is planned on the topic.[11] To existing theoretical paradigms – William Guyn's semiological-psychoanalytic model, narrowly derivative of Metz, in *A Cinema of Nonfiction* (1990); Bill Nichols' "discourse of sobriety," with roots in anthropology and information theory, in *Representing Reality* (1992); Michael Renov's Derridean-inflected "modalities of desire" in documentary poetics in *Theorizing Documentary* (1993); and Brian Winston's postmodern skepticism in *Claiming the Real* (1995) – this book offers a distinct alternative.

Rhetoric and Representation in Nonfiction Film provides a philosophical discussion of the central issues of nonfiction discourse. In its integration of philosophy, theory, and criticism, it contributes to a pragmatics of nonfiction film. It develops a rhetoric of nonfiction, exploring the diverse means – structure, style, discourse, and voice – through which moving picture nonfictions represent the world.

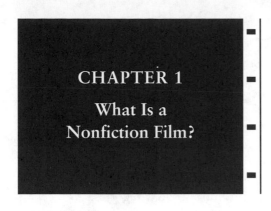

CHAPTER 1

What Is a Nonfiction Film?

Why bother to define the nonfiction film?[1] Some might say that we already know one when we see one. Others may wish to avoid definitions because "defining" film genres may degenerate into academic pigeon-holing, that pedantic exercise whereby scholars assign films to synthetic categories, only to find that actual films exceed and escape those categories. Furthermore, definitions sometimes become a search for nonexistent essences. Defining then becomes a prescriptive attempt to promote a preferred characteristic as "essential" under the guise of a merely descriptive definition.

If all of these objections bear an element of truth, why not forgo discussion of definitions altogether? My contention is that characterizing nonfiction film, when properly approached, is indispensable for a study such as this. Questions about the nature and function of nonfiction and documentary infuse *all* of the theoretical debates about the genre. Every emerging style and many of the films that capture national attention give rise to similar questions about the nature of nonfiction film in relation to issues such as objectivity, the forms and purposes of nonfiction, and the uses and effects of photography and sound recording.

Roger and Me (1989), for example, caused intense controversy in the United States press. The debate centered on whether director Michael Moore's rearrangement of the film's chronological order of events constituted deceitfulness, or was acceptable documentary practice.[2] Much of the confusion stemmed from different conceptions of nonfiction film. We can usefully discuss these issues only after we have either (1) come to a mutual agreement about what nonfiction films are, or (2) acknowledged differences in our uses of the terms "nonfiction" or "documentary."

Why Categories, Definitions, and Distinctions?

To organize entities into analytic categories is sometimes called "Aristotelian," a word none too complimentary in contemporary film studies. The spirit of the age, which in film studies is at present postmodernist, points us toward intertextuality, dispersion, and diffusion. Among its other claims, Derridean deconstruction has challenged the ease with which we make linguistic distinctions. A basic element of postmodern thought squarely contests fitting films into broad categories.

Postmodern theorists criticize the imposition of artificial categories onto the world as though they were natural and discovered. The postmodernist argument often proceeds from a rejection of the objectivist, classical notion of categories, which holds that all categories can be defined by an essential property or properties common to their members, to a wholesale dismissal of categories and categorization as means of discourse and thought. However, the postmodern emphasis on dispersion, diffusion, and intermixture goes too far if it denies the value of categories altogether. As George Lakoff writes, categorization is fundamental to the way we make sense of experience.[3]

Although the classical conception of categories fails for many types of categories, most of our words and symbols designate categories; understanding language depends on categorization. Categories are fundamental to thought, perception, action, and speech. When we see something as a kind of thing, we are categorizing. Categories also enable reasoning. With an unclear understanding of the categories we use, we risk confusions of thought and talking at cross-purposes. To reject categorization is to reject communication, understanding, and meaningful experience. A more prudent course would be to operate with a more subtle and complex understanding of how categories function. If we do this, the characterization of nonfiction film becomes suggestive and enlightening, rather than artificial and controlling.

We must also take definitions seriously, because defining the documentary is often connected with issues of power and control. Definitions often promote preferred uses of nonfiction film, or foreground characteristics thought to be desirable or "proper." What various groups think nonfiction films *are* determines in part which films are funded, find distribution, and receive recognition. The case of *Roger and Me* is again illustrative. When the film failed to receive an Academy Award nomination for Best Feature Documentary in 1989, 45 filmmakers (including Pamela Yates, Spike Lee, and Louis Malle) circulated an "Open Letter to the Film Community" in which they express "outrage" at the omission. Yates claims that the nominating committee "seems to have a very narrow-minded approach to what documentary films are. They can only be quote unquote objective reportage."[4] In 1992 a group of well-known nonfiction filmmakers again assailed the Board of Governors of the Academy of Motion Picture Arts and Sciences for passing over what the filmmakers considered to be the finest examples of the genre. The films not nominated were the documentaries that won notoriety and/or some measure of successful distribution: *Paris is Burning, 35 Up, Hearts of Darkness: A Filmmaker's Apocalypse, A Brief History of Time, Empire of the Air*, and *Truth or Dare*.[5]

At issue here is not the value of Academy Awards, but the nature of nonfiction film, and what constitutes not only excellence, but *proper uses* of the genre. The definition of nonfiction film, and more narrowly of the documentary, is often hotly contested and is negotiated through the relationships between discourse and practice.

Nonetheless, we still know a nonfiction film when we see one. Or do we? If this means that we can all pick out films that are clear examples of the nonfiction category, then it is true but trivial. On the other hand, if the statement, "We already know what a nonfiction film is," means that understanding the nature of the category of nonfiction is easy, then it couldn't be more wrong. I may be able to pick out *Harlan County, U.S.A.* (1976) as a nonfiction film, but still have little idea of what makes it nonfiction. In fact, recent discussions of nonfiction show that we differ about what a nonfiction film is.

If we think of nonfiction film as any film not fictional, we need an understanding of the nature of fiction. If we attempt to find positive characteristics of nonfiction film, we must find a means to relate films as diverse as *The Man With the Movie Camera* (*Chelovek s kinoapparatom*, 1929), *High School, Glass* (*Glas*, 1958), *Sans Soleil* (1982), *The Thin Blue Line* (1988), and *CBS Sixty Minutes*. It turns out that the issues here are quite complex. We don't easily come to know what nonfiction film is, but only tentatively, and provisionally, after careful consideration.

Fiction and Nonfiction: Notes on a Distinction

A common position among both film scholars and nonfiction filmmakers is that the distinction between the fiction and nonfiction film is illicit. John Grierson, the British filmmaker and producer who did so much in the 1930s to define what the documentary would be for future generations, called the documentary the "creative treatment of actuality." In contrast, those who deny the distinction between fiction and nonfiction think of nonfiction film, by definition, as somehow "unmanipulated," and seemingly define nonfiction films as the "transparent," rather than "creative," treatment of actuality. Jean-Louis Comolli, in an essay on cinéma verité, equates manipulation of filmic materials with a tendency toward fiction:

[An] automatic consequence of all the manipulations which would mold the film-document, is a coefficient of "non-reality"; a kind of fictional aura attaches itself to the filmed events and facts. From the moment they become film and are placed in a cinematic perspective, all film-documents and every recording of a raw event take on a filmic reality which either adds to or subtracts from their particular initial reality . . . , un-realizing or sur-realizing it, but in both cases slightly falsifying it and drawing it to the side of fiction.[6]

Comolli assumes that although manipulation is associated with the fiction film, in nonfiction reality is represented transparently, as a pristine and untouched re-presentation of the real. Comolli implicitly invokes the realism of André Bazin, who argued that the photograph is a phenomenon of nature, and ideology becomes mixed with the cinema only when the photograph is manipulated or put into a context foreign to it. For Comolli, when a filmed event or "fact" is manipulated, it loses its natural purity and takes on an aura of fiction.

Several filmmakers have similarly equated manipulation of nonfiction material with fiction. The direct cinema filmmakers Albert Maysles and Frederick Wiseman, for example, see editing as a "fictionalization" of their materials.[7] Maysles says: "I'm interested in fictional technique as it relates to factual material . . . [I]n a sense, editing is a fiction, really, because you're putting it together, you're taking things out of place."[8] Wiseman has claimed that "reality-fictions" is a more accurate word for his films than "documentaries," and that what he is doing is similar to the novelist's reporting on events.[9]

The arguments of Comolli, Wiseman, and Maysles function as an important countermeasure to the claim that nonfiction offers pure, unmediated truth. Yet their common mistake, in my opinion, is to equate the manipulation of materials with fiction, as if only a film that lacked any manipulation of the "pristine" photographic document could qualify as nonfiction. Those who deny the distinction between fiction and nonfiction film – Jacques Aumont et al., for example, say (after Christian Metz) that "every film is a fiction film"[10] – incorporate a very broad spectrum of devices as fictional. Among the qualities thought to render a film fictional are that it offers representations and not reality itself, that it shows objects that have symbolic and connotative meaning, that it represents ideas and not simply visual objects, and that it makes use of stylistic and narrative techniques also used in the fiction film.

This type of argument proceeds questionably, first by defining fiction in such a broad fashion that it is difficult to imagine any discourse that is nonfiction, and second by proposing impossible requirements for nonfiction. As Noël Carroll writes, "It posits the celluloid reproduction of a *ding-en-sich* as the goal of nonfiction, notes the impossibility of the task and declares all film fictional."[11] Thus, if we consider anything that manipulates its materials as fiction, all films become fiction films. For how could any film present reality transparently, or offer reality *itself* rather than a representation of reality? If that is our requirement for nonfiction films, then we must admit that none exist.

However, conflating fiction with nonfiction confuses the issues, and leaves many important questions unanswered. Were we to collapse the distinction, we would still need a means of differentiating films such as *The Wizard of Oz* (1939) and *Harlan County, USA*. As I will argue below, fictions and nonfictions such as these perform distinct social functions,[12] and are viewed by spectators with reference to a different set of expectations and conventions. If both manipulate their filmic materials through structure, style, etc., then perhaps we must look to the distinction between fiction and nonfiction films elsewhere than in filmic manipulation.

Another common argument against the distinction is based on the absence of clear boundaries between fiction and nonfiction films.[13] For example, Haskell Wexler's *Medium Cool* (1969) uses footage of actors and actresses at the actual 1968 Democratic convention in Chicago, and also incorporates footage of the actual riots that occurred there. If no clear boundaries exist between fiction and nonfiction, and if this film and others are not clear members of either camp, doesn't this make the distinction itself questionable? But this is to take a simplistic view of the nature of categories. Some categories are clearly demarcated, such as "Queen of England." By convention, British society limits the membership of this category to one. With other categories, however, membership is more difficult to discern. We would all agree that a three-year-old child is young, and a ninety-year-old man old. However, in regard to a 35-, 50-, or 65-year-old, we are less certain. It does not follow that the categories are therefore illicit, and that we are unjustified in thinking of some people as old or young.

Some categories have fuzzy boundaries. This may be the case with nonfiction film, where certain films fit the category only uncomfortably. This bodes no problem for the distinction itself. As John Searle notes, "It is a condition of the adequacy of a precise theory of an indeterminate phenomenon that it should precisely characterize that phenomenon as indeterminate; and a distinction is no less a distinction for allowing for a family of related, marginal, diverting cases."[14]

Past Attempts at Definition

Some attempts at definition fail to distinguish nonfiction film – any film not fiction – from the less inclusive "documentary." Many characterizations of nonfiction film or documentary have searched for necessary and/or sufficient conditions.[15] But all of these attempts have run into problems. Some have been too broad in scope, defining the documentary in so general a way that it fails to distinguish films of the genre from those of other genres. Second, other definitions have too narrowly defined the nonfiction, such that many films normally thought to belong to the genre are excluded, seemingly arbitrarily.

Among the broad ones, we find John Grierson's oft-quoted characterization of the documentary as "the creative treatment of actuality."[16] In requiring creativity of the documentary, Grierson hoped to distinguish it from the tedious information film, and to recognize the need for dramatization in representing social issues. Thus for Grierson, not all nonfiction films are documentaries; they must first satisfy requirements of dramatization and "creativity." That the treatment in a documentary must be of *actuality*, rather than of the staged facsimile, is one of Grierson's first principles: "We believe that the original (or native) actor, and the original (or native) scene, are better guides to the screen interpretation of the modern world [than actors and sets]."[17]

Though Grierson's phrase is remarkably suggestive, it needs further development. As it stands it is too broad. Does not fiction also explore actual political, religious, and personal issues? Filmmaker Satyajit Ray sums up this objection most eloquently:

[T]he question that immediately arises from the definition is: What is reality? Surely it is not only what constitutes the tangible aspects of everyday existence.

Subtle and complex human relationships, which many of the best fiction films deal with, are also as much a part of reality as those other aspects generally probed by documentary makers. Even fables and myths and fairy tales have their roots in reality. Krishna, Ravana, Aladdin, Cinderella, Jack the Giant Killer – all have their prototypes in real life. Therefore, in a sense, fables and myths are also creative interpretations of reality. In fact, all artists in all branches of non-abstract art are engaged in the same pursuit that Grierson has assigned exclusively to the makers of documentary films.[18]

More serious problems arise when we attempt to narrow definitions of the documentary further; the usual outcome is to exclude films normally thought to be documentaries. Raymond Spottiswoode correctly notes that on the question of definition, writers on the documentary have been "distressingly vague." He calls Grierson's definition "as embracing as art itself," but the definition he proposes suffers from the opposite malady. "The documentary film," he writes, "is in subject and approach a dramatized presentation of man's relation to his institutional life, whether industrial, social, or political; and in technique, a subordination of form to content."[19] Spottiswoode's definition excludes the "lecture" film because it is not sufficiently dramatized; the nature film and "personal" film, since they are not primarily concerned with institutions; and the "film symphony" because it fails to subordinate subject to technique. According to Spottiswoode's definition, then, Disney's *Beaver Valley* (1950), the Maysles brothers' *Showman* (1962), D.A. Pennebaker's *Don't Look Back* (1966), and Walter Ruttman's *Berlin: Symphony of the City* (*Berlin: die Sinfonie der Grosstadt*, 1927) could not be called documentaries. A definition such as this seems overly prescriptive, even if it is meant to apply to documentaries and not to nonfiction films generally.

Several current scholars define the documentary as a film that makes an argument rather than entertains or diverts. Bill Nichols recognizes that the documentary is a protean institution, consisting of texts, a community of practitioners, and conventional practices, which are subject to historical change. Nonetheless, he writes that the documentary film requires "a representation, case, or argument about the historical world,"[20] and that documentary spectators work with "a pattern of inferences that helps us to determine what kind of *argument* the text is making about the historical world . . ."(my emphasis).[21]

Of course, many documentaries do make arguments. However, writers such as Nichols clearly mean their claims to apply to a broad spectrum of nonfiction films. Is argument central in Joris Ivens' *Rain* (1929), which explores visual patterns of rain in Amsterdam? We could ask the same question of *Sherman's March* (1986), *Berlin: Symphony of a City*, and many more. One might respond that every film has political implications, and thus every film makes an "argument" about reality. If every film has political implications, however, this is true of fiction as well as documentary. Moreover, if we think of argument as an ordered series of premises leading to a conclusion, then many nonfiction films have little to do with argument.

Why Traditional Definitions Fail

To better understand past failures to define the documentary, it is useful to look at unsuccessful attempts to define art. Philosophers, critics, and artists have been attempting to define this elusive concept for over 2000 years, dating back at least to Plato and his finding the essence of art in its "imitation" of life. Thinkers have defined art as "significant form," as the expression of emotion, as "emotion recollected in tranquillity," as an iconic symbol of the forms of feelings, as the interplay of forms, and so forth.[22] None of these definitions have been satisfactory, perhaps because there is no essential characteristic of art, no necessary and sufficient condition.

In an influential essay, Morris Weitz argued that "art" is an "open concept," has no essence, and cannot be defined in the traditional sense.[23] In making this argument, Weitz draws on the work of Ludwig Wittgenstein, who claims that for open concepts, such as "game," there is no property that members of the category all have in common. Rather than an essence, we can find "a complicated network of similarities overlapping and criss-crossing," or what the philosopher calls "family resemblances."[24] For example, while games such as chess or tag are competitive, others are not. Children will sometimes "play house," for example. We can say that being competitive is not essential to games, but a "family resemblance" that some, but not all, games share.

In Weitz's view, thinkers have failed to find the elusive essence of art, because there is none. We can find family resemblances, but no intrinsic property common to all works of art. This does not imply that past attempts to define art are worthless, for as Weitz points out, though they fail to find an essence to art, they nonetheless succeed in drawing attention to important properties of works of art we may not otherwise have noticed. It is plausible to contend that "nonfiction" and especially "documentary" are open concepts too. If so, a traditional attempt to define the documentary is bound to fail, since the concept has no essence, but rather a braid of family resemblances.

George Lakoff claims that many categories have fuzzy boundaries, and are best thought of in relation to prototypes with a spreading wave of less central examples. The prototypical example of a category possesses all of the properties thought central to the category, whereas a more peripheral member (and here the status of "membership" may be unclear) might contain only one or some of those characteristics. *Vietnam: A Television History* (1983), for example, might be considered a prototypical documentary, because it has many of the central family resemblances (as I argue below). It makes truth claims about the historical world, maintains a seriousness of purpose, and couches its claims in a conventionally structured, unified text, making use of documentary storytelling techniques – such as voice-over narration – from an authoritative perspective. Chris Marker's *Letter from Siberia* (1957), on the other hand, might be said to occupy the margins of the genre. Although it presents itself as a travelogue, its voice-over narration claims that it is a "letter from Siberia," it engages more in witty word-play than in the presentation of information, and the film includes not only footage of Siberia, but animated "advertisements" and whimsical homages to the woolly mammoth.

Lakoff calls his theory of categories "prototype theory."[25] Many categories (or what Lakoff calls "fuzzy sets") have gradations of membership, such that for certain examples of the category, one cannot say finally whether it is a member or not. In the case of other examples – prototypical examples – membership is more certain. If we characterize the documentary from the standpoint of prototype theory, we will find prototypical examples and learn from them what our culture considers most central. And we will see how prototypical examples change with history.

Indexing and the Assertive Stance

A useful characterization of nonfiction film must have marked explanatory power, but must simultaneously account for marginal and borderline examples of the genre. It must recognize the historical, continuously evolving nature, not only of nonfiction practices, texts, and practitioners, but of the very notions of "nonfiction" and "documentary."

We may find nothing intrinsic in a film or book that clearly marks it as fiction or nonfiction. The distinction between fiction and nonfiction is not based solely on intrinsic textual properties, but also on the extrinsic context of production, distribution, and reception. The idea that we should explore context has been in circulation for some time. Perhaps the first attempt to describe the extrinsic nature of nonfiction film is Noël Carroll's 1983 theory of indexing.[26] Carroll writes that viewers usually know if the film they see is fiction or nonfiction, because producers, writers, directors, distributors, and exhibitors index the film; they publicly identify it usually as either fiction or nonfiction. The spectator's response to the film generally depends on this indexing. In the case of nonfiction, Carroll claims, we respond by mobilizing "objective standards" and gauging the representation according to standards, norms, and routines of evidence.[27] When a film is indexed as nonfiction, it encourages a special type of spectator activity.

Indexing occurs through credits and titles, explicit mentions of the film as nonfiction in advertising, press releases, interviews, word of mouth, and numerous other means. Textual cues normally also index the film as fiction or nonfiction. Prototypical documentaries such as *Frontline* or segments of *CBS 60 Minutes* feature the voice-over narration of an on-screen journalist who provides information and authority. Various types of nonfiction films have conventional characteristics, as do fictional genres, and these conventions are sometimes sufficient to index the film for the spectator. (These conventional cues can also be used to intentionally "trick" the spectator, as in *No Lies* (1973) or *Daughter Rite* (1978), in these cases for the purpose of foregrounding documentary conventions and the ease with which the spectator can be misled).

In a 1987 essay, I offered a related account of the distinction between fiction and nonfiction.[28] There I made reference to Nicholas Wolterstorff's theory of "projected worlds."[29] Wolterstorff's theory is closely related to speech act theory in certain respects. Speech act theorists argue that through language humans act in the world; to communicate verbally is not simply to "make meaning" but to perform actions: reporting, admitting, congratulating, promising, thanking, announcing, asserting, warning, admonishing, and so forth. A corollary is that the meaning of a linguistic message becomes clear (to the extent that it ever *does* become clear) only in the context in which it is uttered, written, or otherwise presented.

For example, the sentence, "There once was a woman of Paris" can be uttered in a variety of ways and in a variety of contexts, each of which would constitute a different *action* and imply a different meaning. Were I to utter the sentence *assertively*, for example, I would be making the claim that there once was an actual woman of Paris. According to Wolterstorff, I can also utter the sentence *fictively*. Were I to present this sentence within the context of a fictional novel, I would not be claiming that there was an actual woman of Paris, but instead would be inviting you to *consider* a certain state of affairs as an imaginative fiction.

For Wolterstorff, just as speakers perform actions (speech acts) through utterances, artists perform actions through works of art. One action characteristically performed with *representational* works Wolterstorff calls "world projection." The "world" of a representational work, be it a film, novel, or painting, consists of an often complex web of states of affairs.[30] The states of affairs that make up the world can be explicitly mentioned, implied, or shown. When Truman Capote, in *In Cold Blood*, writes of the Clutter residence, "As for the interior, there were spongy displays of liver-colored carpet . . . ," that state of affairs – that there were spongy displays of liver-colored carpet – is explicitly mentioned. In the cinema, of course, a voice-over narrator may verbally project states of affairs, but typically they are shown or heard through moving photographs and sound.

According to Wolterstorff, worlds are projected in conjunction with various *stances*. Within a sociocultural context, the text's writer or producer(s) may take an assertive, interrogative, optative (expressing a wish or choice), or imperative stance toward the projected world. The typical stance taken toward a novel or fiction film is the *fictive stance*. As Wolterstorff explains, "To take up the fictive stance toward some state of affairs is not to *assert* that the state of affairs is true, is not to ask whether it is true, is not to *request* that it be made true, is not to *wish* that it be true. It is simply to invite us to consider that state of affairs."[31] In the nonfiction film, on the other hand, the typical stance taken is *assertive*; the states of affairs represented are asserted to occur in the actual world as portrayed.[32]

For films, the distinction might be made as follows. The stance taken toward the world projected in Dreyer's *Vampyr* (1932) is fictive. We are not meant to take the events depicted in *Vampyr* as having actually occurred. If a spectator exits the theater and roams the countryside, searching for the character David Gray, one would say that he had profoundly misunderstood the function and intent of the film as fiction. As a fiction film, it merely invites us to *consider* the states of affairs it presents (for whatever reasons people watch and enjoy fiction).[33] Dreyer and *Vampyr*'s producers were not misleading the public in representing David Gray and the chateau, for they never asserted that they actually exist, apart from the world projected through the work.

Nonfiction film operates in a different manner. The stance taken toward states of affairs in the television series *Vietnam: A Television History*, for example, is assertive, not fictive. When the spectator determines that the film has been indexed as nonfiction, and that the stance taken toward the states of affairs presented is assertive, she or he takes its claims as truth claims or assertions of actual fact, and its images and sounds as historical portrayals. We take the filmmaker to be asserting that the states of affairs presented in the nonfiction occur(red) in the world. The French occupied Vietnam before the Americans. American soldiers were unprepared for the confusing guerrilla war they found in Vietnam. In representing the events of the Vietnam War, the series makes claims about the actual world, and about the accuracy of its representations of that world.

What I claimed in that 1987 essay, then, is that nonfiction films are those that assert that the states of affairs they present occur(red) in the actual world. Perhaps a clearer way to put it is to say that nonfictions assert a belief that given objects, entities, states of affairs, events, or situations actually occur(red) or exist(ed) in the actual world as portrayed.[34] This distinction between nonfiction and fiction stems from two forms of discourse found in most societies, corresponding to two fundamental purposes. On the one hand, we use discourse to make explicit claims about reality – to inform each other about occurent states of affairs. On the other, we use discourse to present fictional stories (consisting of states of affairs that do not actually occur). Although we may use fiction and nonfiction for similar purposes, for example to warn each about the dangers of strong drink, they nonetheless constitute different means to that same end.

Note that this conception of the nonfiction film assumes no necessary realism or resemblance between the nonfiction work and actuality. As I argue in following chapters, the moving photograph and recorded sound, under special circumstances, have a special status in relation to the recorded scene, of an order different from a verbal description. However, this status is also common in the fiction film, and thus cannot distinguish nonfiction from fiction. My argument is that the fundamental distinction comes via the *situation* of the film in its sociocultural milieu – its indexing and the spectator response this cues, and not according to an ostensible imitation or recording of the real.

Moreover, when I say that a film takes an assertive stance toward what it shows, this is shorthand for a series of more complicated activities. Actually, it is the filmmakers (and perhaps others who use the film) who take the stance, and who make assertions (and perform a variety of other actions) through the text. By indexing a film as nonfiction, and by taking an assertive stance toward what they present, the filmmakers cue the spectator to understand and evaluate what is shown as a nonfiction. When we gauge that a film has been indexed as nonfiction, we take its explicit claims for assertions; even its implications have a force of assertion. Obviously, I do not mean "assertion" here to apply only to linguistic declarations; in its broader sense, one can make assertions not only with language, but with (nonlinguistic) pictures and sounds as well.

Edward Branigan writes that seeing a film as nonfiction, as opposed to fiction, cues the spectator to make use of a different "*method* or *procedure* for making decisions about assigning reference."[35] Branigan offers a sophisticated theory of what it means to comprehend a film nonfictionally, and he rightfully points out that we can view any fiction film nonfictionally, as, for example, when we see *The Wizard of Oz* as an example of Judy Garland's performance style, circa 1939.[36] However, we must distinguish between what Branigan calls "nonfiction comprehension" and the nonfiction artifact. The film's index is not merely an inference by the spectator, but a property or element of the text within its historical context. The domain of indexing is more social than individual. The spectator must *discover* how a film is indexed, and she or he is capable of being mistaken. Were I to call *The Wizard of Oz* a nonfiction film, I would be making a false claim about its conventional use.

Consider, for an analogous example, that common household appliance, the toaster. The toaster's conventional function is to toast bread, but it may have other, unconventional uses. Ray may use the toaster as a weapon to ward off an intruder in his home. But if Ray were asked what artifact he used to cause such cuts and bruises to appear on the intruder's head, he would answer, "a toaster," although he had *used* the toaster as a club. The point is that human artifacts are often named according to their conventional functions, and an unconventional use of an artifact does not require that we change its name.[37]

Similarly, Jane is free to approach (and use) *Rear Window* (1954) as a documentary study of Grace Kelly's portrayal of the fictional Lisa, and Jack may see *The Battle of San Pietro* as fictional because he believes that no such battle actually occurred. In both cases, however, if they were to identify *Rear Window* as nonfiction, and *The Battle of San Pietro* as fiction, their identifications would be mistaken. Indexing, like the naming of objects generally, lies within the domain of social convention. Jane and Jack are free to use these films for whatever purposes they like, and this is neither a question of denying the importance of alternative readings and unconventional uses, nor of restricting them. But unconventional uses do not make *Rear Window* nonfiction, any more than they make Ray's toaster a club. At the same time, it must also be noted that no index is indelible; all may change with time, since social conventions change. The point is that *indexing is a social phenomenon, and to a degree is independent of individual uses of the film.*

This appeal to reception is perhaps the most recent approach to the nonfiction/fiction distinction. Thus Brian Winston argues that the best means to distinguish the documentary from fiction is by an appeal to different modes of reception; the documentary is all in your head.[38] Dirk Eitzen writes that rather than say that documentaries make assertions, we should say that they are *perceived* to make assertions. We must then see the documentary "not as a kind of text but as a kind of reading."[39] Although it is certainly useful to chart the differences in ways spectators approach fiction versus nonfiction texts, as Branigan does, it is only confusing to deny an objective distinction between fiction and nonfiction films, *when* such a distinction can clearly be made. If I perceive *Red Dawn* (1984) to be making assertions about an historical Soviet invasion of the United States, am I merely comprehending the film nonfictionally, or making a preposterous mistake? Similarly, were I view *Night and Fog* (1955) as though it were making no assertions about the holocaust, you could legitimately claim that I had misunderstood the function and intent of the film. The fiction/nonfiction distinction is not merely in your head, but in films and in the cultural and historical context in which they are produced and viewed.

Although the assertive stance often distinguishes nonfiction from fiction, it does not imply assertion in the sense of an argument. Filmmakers may perform a variety of acts with nonfiction texts – interrogating, hinting, implying, exclaiming, ridiculing, observing, and so forth – either in addition to or through asserting that the states of affairs presented occur in the actual world.[40] Nonfictions can be incredibly rich, and my suggestion that nonfictions present states of affairs in a certain way should not be taken to imply that this is *all* that nonfiction films are doing.

Ambiguity and Indexing

Characterizing nonfiction as I have thus far raises problematic issues. For one, as Allan Casebier notes, the "indexing/assertive stance view by itself . . . makes it look too much like there are simply two types of film, nonfiction and fiction films, whose different status has its locus in purely conventionally grounded characteristics of the film and its publicity."[41] Casebier claims that other factors are essential in describing indexing, including our independent knowledge of the subject of the nonfiction and our common sense beliefs about the world.

If indexing were purely a matter of publicity, for example, one could argue that any film whatsoever could be successfully indexed as nonfiction. But I don't think this is true. For example, suppose that David Lynch had seriously attempted to index *Eraserhead* as nonfiction, or that Ed Wood, Jr., had valiantly done the same with *Plan 9 from Outer Space*. Clearly, audiences would take the films as fictional despite the producer's intentions. Indexing cannot be wholly determined by the producer/distributor/exhibitor, but also depends on that index being taken up by the audience. As I said above, indexing is a social phenomenon, as much determined by what audiences will accept as nonfiction or fiction as by the intentions of those who handle the film.

Moreover, indexing lacks the clarity I have so far implied. Some films unproblematically indexed as fictions nonetheless make assertions about the actual world, thus mixing the fictive and assertive stances. Consider *El Norte* (1983), a fiction film chronicling the flight northward of two persecuted Guatemalen young people. We have no trouble seeing the film as fiction in one sense; its story events are presented fictively, as are the major characters, Rosita and Enrique Xuncax. However, part of *El Norte's* purpose is clearly to represent the actual social conditions of Guatemala as manifestly repressive. Although it is plausible to say that many fiction films make few assertions about the actual world, others – parables or explicitly political films – assert that various represented states of affairs actually occur. Although a text may be indexed as fiction globally, its setting and the timeliness of its political concerns, for example, may cue us to take its representations to make reference to the actual world. It becomes a kind of allegory that presents some states of affairs as fictive, yet through that fictive presentation makes assertions.

Some nonfiction films, on the other hand, incorporate clearly fictional or staged scenes in a similar hybrid fashion. *The Thin Blue Line* not only replays scenes from the television series *Boston Blackie*, but uses staged reenactments of the policeman's murder and Randall Adams' interrogation. The *Boston Blackie* scenes are not used to make assertions that what they depict actually occurred, but to suggest some of the fantasies of a particularly unreliable witness. Again, a film may be globally indexed as nonfiction and nonetheless incorporate what are normally considered "fictional" elements. Many types of filmic material can be used to assert, imply, interrogate, and so forth.

Between fiction and nonfiction also lies that hybrid genre we call dramatic documentary or docudrama, which seems to be enjoying such a resurgence in television "reality programming." These typically take the form of television series making use of reenactments, such as *Rescue 911* or *Unsolved Mysteries*, or epics about historical events, for example the recent *Gettysburg* (1993). The discursive community typically allows more artistic license to these sorts of works than it will to journalistic documentaries. Most historical epics, for example, mix the assertion of historical truth claims with more speculative accounts of narrative events. Programs such as *Rescue 911*, similarly, mix the assertion of claims about what actually occurred during some crime or disaster, with a staging or reenactment of the event. In general, dramatic documentaries imply a global stance of *assertive analogy*, in which assertions are made by analogy (staging, reenactment) rather than directly. But what makes the genre so messy is that in the midst of this global stance, dramatic documentaries may also, at the local level, make the direct assertions of the nonfiction film, or present purely imaginative speculations in a manner closer to fiction.

Of fiction, nonfiction, and dramatic documentary, the latter is the murkiest, standing halfway between documentary and fiction, its status as a discourse most potentially confusing to audiences. Critics often consider the docudrama to be a cheap exploitation of usually prurient or violent historical events; it is considered to be a genre halfway between art and information, fulfilling neither function well. We might suspect that some audiences attain a sense of history from such historical films. Thus the docudrama – rightly or wrongly – is typically relegated to the trashheap of media kitsch along with soap operas and game shows.

Some films escape the conventional notions of fiction, nonfiction, or dramatic documentary, and for those films, indexing may be ambiguous or even nonexistent. Oliver Stone's *JFK* (1991) is a particularly striking example. For this film about the Kennedy assassination, Stone blends genres in interesting ways. He combines the Zapruder film of the assassination and other archival footage with staged footage on Super-8, 16 mm, and video. The staged footage is designed to resemble newsreel footage and the Zapruder film. *JFK* mixes this footage in a jumbled collage that makes it impossible for the typical viewer to discriminate between reenactments and archival material.

More importantly, *JFK* continually mixes the assertion of historical fact with what Stone freely admits is speculation. *JFK* begins much like a traditional documentary, with voice-over narration introducing shots of Eisenhower warning us about the powerful military-industrial complex, then moving to a brief history of the Kennedy presidency, accompanied by the relevant archival material. The film then subtly begins to incorporate staged scenes, beginning with black and white footage of a woman dumped from a car and her warning that "They're going to kill Kennedy," to characters in a New Orleans bar viewing news footage of the actual assassination. Thus the film initially establishes a framework for the assertion of truth claims (characteristic of nonfiction), and gradually incorporates the stagings and reenactments more common to docudrama and the fiction film.

Just as the viewer might wonder which footage is staged and which is actual archival footage, neither is the spectator sure what to take as hypothetical speculations and what to take as truth claims. This ambiguity is mirrored in what Stone himself has said about the film and about his intentions in making it. On the one hand, Stone claims that he means the film to function as counter-myth rather than an account of the literal historical truth. Only a small percentage of the American people believe the hypotheses of the Warren Commission, that Kennedy was shot by a lone assassin, Oswald. Nonetheless, this has been the official government version of the events of December 22, 1963, ever since that report emerged. In suggesting that *JFK* serves as counter-myth, Stone implies that his myth, although on the same speculative plane as the Warren report, is more politically useful. In substituting one myth for another, Stone hoped to encourage people to question authority and to be more suspicious of covert right-wing operations in the government.

Other evidence, however, implies that Stone means us to take the film as more than myth-making, and closer to a literal historical account. Although Stone freely admits that the film contains speculations, he nonetheless hired researchers to find as much evidence as possible to back up his assertions. He hired Jane Rusconi, a Yale graduate, as research coordinator. Zachary Sklar, coauthor with Stone of the *JFK* screenplay, says the research was necessary because "we wanted to make sure we were on solid ground with the facts in this case because it touches so many raw nerves. . . . Of necessity we had to speculate in some places, but we didn't want any flying saucers in there that people could latch onto and say, 'Oh, look, they put this in, so we can discredit the entire film.'"[42]

The question remains about the effects of such ambiguous or nonexistent indexing on the audience. Speculation ranged from a pessimistic *New York Times* editorial claiming that the "children of the video age" will "swallow *JFK* whole,"[43] to Art Simon's claim that the film will create "alert viewers" because its structure mirrors the complexities of the search for historical truth.[44] The point is that in this postmodern age, such intermixtures have become increasingly common.

Clearly, then, in specific films the distinction between fiction and nonfiction will sometimes be fuzzy at best. In some cases, it may be impossible to classify a film as fiction or nonfiction. However, we should remember that the index/assertive stance view holds for clear cases of nonfiction and fiction. The fact that not all films *are* such cases bodes no problem for the distinction itself. A distinction with fuzzy boundaries is no less a distinction; central examples of the separate genres still exhibit the differences on which the distinction is based.

Showing and Asserting in Nonfiction

One might respond to my claims about the assertive stance by countering that my view is too beholden to linguistics. After all, nonfiction films communicate largely through images, not merely by the direct assertions of voice-over narrators or printed intertitles. In fact, the observational documentary, for example, forwards few direct assertions, if an assertion be defined as a linguistic act. Trevor Ponech instead forwards the notion of "showing that" as characteristic of the nonfiction film. As he writes, "A filmmaker 'shows that' something is the case when she intends for the viewer to come to have particular perceptions, impressions, beliefs, or pieces of knowledge as a result of viewing some motion picture footage."[45]

The index/assertive stance view has not so far dealt adequately with the pictorial nature of nonfiction film, and Ponech's claims are a necessary and important corrective to that (as are the third and fourth chapters here). However, my view is that the filmmaker(s) take an assertive stance toward what they present, but that making assertions need not be linguistic. Ponech uses observational documentaries such as Wiseman's *Titicut Follies* (1967) to make his case, because observational films make "showing that" more central than other kinds of nonfiction. But nonfiction films – including Wiseman's – make assertions, and/or imply an accurate portrayal of their subject, in a number of ways: often through the direct linguistic assertions of a narrator; through editing; through music and sound effects; at times through interviews together with their placement in the text; and, of course, by showing moving photographs. What these all have in common, in nonfiction, is that they are used to make assertions about the actual world. Showing and "showing that," while important elements, are anterior to the assertive stance that is the defining characteristic of nonfiction.

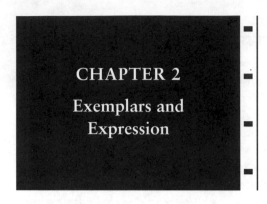

CHAPTER 2
Exemplars and Expression

Scholars often distinguish between the nonfiction film and the documentary, as the latter often denotes a narrower range of texts than the former. If nonfiction includes every film not fictional, then the term "documentary" is reserved for a particular group of films – more than mere nonfictions. As Richard Meran Barsam writes in the 1973 edition of his history of nonfiction film, "All documentaries are nonfiction films, but not all nonfiction films are documentaries."[1] Barsam reserves the term "documentary" for the Griersonian "social" documentary, but others have used the term to designate other subgenres of nonfiction, for example the modern journalistic documentary.

We might assume that a category such as nonfiction film should have a prototype, some film or type of film that clearly represents what most would take to be the best example of the genre. This isn't the case, however. The history of nonfiction clearly shows that public assumptions about the prototypical nonfiction film change. Moreover, at any given time, we sometimes find differences about what constitutes a prototype for the genre. For example, while some take the journalistic documentary, with its implication of objectivity and its journalist-narrator, to be the central kind of nonfiction film, others take the observational film (the films of Frederick Wiseman, for example) as a better example of a "pure" documentary, since it ostensibly attempts to "record" actual scenes and events. Rather than seeking a prototype, we should describe exemplars, or in other words, types of films that some have thought to be central examples of nonfiction.

The Griersonian Documentary

The term *documentaire* was widely used in France in the 1920s, and Edward S. Curtis used the terms "documentary material" and "documentary works" in relation to moving picture nonfictions as early as 1914.[2] Nevertheless, John Grierson is widely thought to have been the first to use the term "documentary" in English in relation to Robert Flaherty's *Moana* (1926) in 1926.[3] The word began to regularly appear as a noun in the English-speaking world by the thirties, by which time it had begun to designate a "higher" order of nonfiction cinema in which, as Grierson writes, "we pass from the plain (or fancy) descriptions of natural material, to arrangements, re-arrangements, and creative shapings of it."[4]

The phrase describing the documentary as "the creative treatment of actuality" is most famously associated with Grierson, but his stipulations about the proper function of the documentary film – the so-called "first principles" – have been especially influential. First, Grierson claimed that the documentary must be dramatic, not merely instructional, in order to promote a common pattern of thought and feeling among audience members. Second, and most importantly, the documentary is best used for "propaganda." For Grierson, the documentary must have a social purpose, educating the masses and enabling them to better understand their place in society and the public institutions that organize their lives. Grierson called for a form of "realist documentary" that would harness the aesthetic for the social. It would make "poetry where no poet has gone before it, and where no ends, sufficient for the purposes of art, are easily observed."[5]

Grierson considered his silent film, *Drifters* (1929), to be an example of this new realist cinema of a higher order. The film is about the sea and fishermen, an "adventure of the herring fishery."[6] It details the work of the fisherman, from the preparations for the trip, to the process of fishing with nets and floats, to the unloading and selling of the fish. In its editing and accumulation of detail, it well represents the rhythm of the sea, the monotony of the work, and the skill and professionalism of the workers. As Grierson writes (in his characteristic bravado), "if you can tell me a story with a better crescendo in energies, images, atmospherics, and all that make up the sum and substance of the cinema, I promise you I shall make my next film of it forthwith."[7]

Grierson's directives have influenced the course of documentary filmmaking, and have in part determined what many observers, critics, and filmmakers have thought nonfiction film *should* be. His influence never extended to France, however. As Noel Burch notes, with a few exceptions the French tend toward highly-stylized, aesthetic exercises, rather than the "serious" social analyses fostered by the Griersonian tradition. Rather than remain "faithful" or "true" to their material,

French documentary filmmakers have often seen the documentary as an opportunity to make art, and have transcended their subjects rather than reported on them. Although Jean Rouch is arguably a documentarist in the Anglo-American sense, Agnes Varda, Georges Franju, Chris Marker, and Alain Resnais, for example, have produced highly expressive documentaries that Grierson would likely critique for lack of the "hard-headed" social concern he advocated.

In the Anglo-American tradition, however, the Griersonian documentary has long been an exemplar. As such, the Griersonian documentary separates itself from other nonfiction films such as nature and science films, instructional films, poetic nonfictions, and experimental films. One of Grierson's chief claims is that the documentary must have a serious social purpose; for Grierson, that meant dealing with present social problems. Though Grierson praised Robert Flaherty and called him the "father of documentary," he chided the explorer for making films about the past rather than the present, and for his interest in the theme of "humans versus nature" in lieu of the more pressing issues of a mass industrial society. Grierson thought that the beauty and workings of the natural world, for example, or the cultural practices of the past, were not sufficiently important topics for the documentary. Of Flaherty he writes: "In his heart he prefers a sailing barge to a snub-nosed funnel-after, and a scythe to a mechanical reaper."[8] For Grierson, this was sentimental escapism. The only legitimate topic, for Grierson, seemed to be the relation of "modern man" to contemporary mass industrial society.

Grierson's prescriptions for documentary filmmaking live on today. Indeed, many prominent scholars have repeated the claims for one function – serious social analysis – as the legitimate purpose of the documentary. Paul Rotha, in what was long the standard history of documentary, writes that one of the primary requirements of the documentary is "the expression of social analysis"; William A. Bluem says that "there must be a social purpose"; Lewis Jacobs calls for a "clear social purpose"; Michael Rabiger, in his handbook on directing the documentary, argues that a genuine documentary "invites the spectator to draw socially critical conclusions." Bill Nichols, in his recent *Representing Reality*, finds "argument" to be central to the documentary, and calls the genre a "discourse of sobriety."[9]

Suppose a theorist claimed that nonfiction writing must have a clear social purpose, and that it consisted of the making of arguments. Unless we can gerrymander these stipulations to fit biographies, diaries,

travel and nature literature, correspondence, essays on non-social topics, creative essays, instruction manuals, self-help manuals, journalism,
works on philosophy, history, biology, physics, and so forth – we
would consider them needlessly prescriptive. Unless some quality of
nonfiction *film* or *video* makes it peculiarly suited only to the purposes Grierson outlines, then we may find his prescriptions needlessly
prescriptive, too. Society uses nonfiction film and video for hundreds
of purposes; we can no longer think of one as its sole legitimate function.

Objectivity and the Journalistic Documentary

One exemplar of nonfiction film is the Griersonian social documentary.
Television has produced another – the journalistic documentary, such
as *CBS 60 Minutes, See It Now, Frontline,* or *Dateline NBC.* The Griersonian documentary assumed two essential characteristics – a serious
social purpose, and the creative treatment or dramatization of actuality.
The journalistic documentary maintains the serious social purpose, but
emphasizes a rhetoric of objectivity and the requirements of evidence
over the creative presentation favored by Grierson.

Today's media critics in the popular press tend to fix on such concepts as "objectivity," with the result that explicitly subjective and expressive nonfiction films become problematic. For if we define the nonfiction film as "objective," we marginalize those films for which objectivity, by whatever definition, is irrelevant, and limit our understanding
of how actual nonfiction films, in all their diversity, function.

Perhaps the most obvious example of the suppression of nonfiction
expression is the lack of recognition accorded certain recent films by
the Academy of Motion Picture Arts and Sciences, as I mentioned earlier. In its nominations for Academy Awards, the Academy has for the
past several years ignored many of the most important nonfiction films
of the past few decades. *The Thin Blue Line, Gates of Heaven* (1978),
Sherman's March, and *Roger and Me,* to name just a few, have all been
neglected in the nominations for Best Feature Documentary.[10] Ironically, these are also the films that have played commercial theaters, drawn
sizable audiences, and generated impressive media attention.

Perhaps the Academy Awards shouldn't be taken seriously as meaningful gauges of quality or interest. But the official snubbing of these
films is a symptom of implicit assumptions about the nature of the documentary that have important practical implications for nonfiction film

makers – who, whether for good or ill, need recognition and grants. As Pamela Yates puts it, the Academy nominating committee ". . . seems to have a very narrow-minded approach to what documentary films are. They can only be quote unquote objective reportage."[11]

Although many nonfiction films are obviously not intended to be journalistically "objective," discussions of the genre inevitably become stalled in debate about this notoriously ambiguous concept. Some critics operate on the assumption that objectivity is desirable; others maintain that it is impossible; still others claim that even to attempt it is reprehensible. An objective representation is sometimes thought of as that which is from no point of view, free of subjective biases, from a god-like perspective (or to use a less lofty analogy, from the perspective of a disinterested and unnoticed fly on the wall). Critics of this notion of objectivity point out that every film has a point of view both literally (the point of view of the camera) and figuratively (the point of view of the film's narration). Because no film can be free of point of view, they argue, objectivity is impossible. The problem, of course, is that "objectivity" can't sensibly be thought of as meaning "that which is perfectly free of subjectivity."

We might think of objectivity not as a representation free of point of view, but as one that takes conflicting positions into account in a balanced fashion, to be fair to "both sides" of an issue. Critics of this notion point out that the need for this sort of balance delimits the political arena by positing conflict as within conventional boundaries, as in debates between Democrats and Republicans. Too often such attempts at balance and fairness narrow political discourse by excluding the "marginal."

Noël Carroll has suggested that objectivity should not be associated with point of view (or the lack thereof), but with "patterns of reasoning, routines for assessing evidence, means of weighing the comparative significance of different types of evidence, and standards for observations [and] experimentation . . . shared by practitioners in that field."[12] This conception of objectivity defines it not according to any correspondence (actual or presumed) with "the real," but in relation to the practices of discursive communities.

My aim here is not to choose among these competing conceptions of objectivity, nor, indeed, to pose an alternative. My claim is that objectivity, in whatever sense, has no *necessary* connection to the nonfiction film. If the nonfiction film is defined as objective in any of these senses, it is unsurprising that eccentric and personal films such as *Gates of*

Heaven and *Paris is Burning* (1991) become problematic. None of these notions of objectivity should be taken as defining (or even necessarily desirable) features of nonfiction as such.

Consider Carroll's conception of objectivity; how is it supposed to apply to the nonfiction film *qua nonfiction*?[13] No doubt the practice of television journalism (for example) operates according to the particular conventions of "objectivity" that have developed through years of network practice. The field of the nonfiction film *in general*, however, is too diverse to admit the application of those standards of research and evidence-gathering to all nonfiction films. Why assume, for instance, that all nonfiction films present evidence in making an argument? Might not some nonfiction films have other functions?

Take Ross McElwee's *Sherman's March*. This is a self-absorbed film diary of the director's life while making the film, but it stretches in other directions as well. The film traces the Civil War path of Union General Sherman's march of destruction through the South and gauges its lingering effects. McElwee, who frequently appears before the camera and whose voice-over accompanies much of the film, talks often of the General and visits various war memorials, battlefields, and monuments. The film's subtitle, however, is "A Meditation on the Possibility of Romantic Love in the South During an Era of Nuclear Weapons Proliferation." This hints at some of the other directions in which the film meanders.

What seems more important than retracing the General's steps is the series of romantic interludes McElwee enjoys while on his journey. The young filmmaker strays from the General's path to follow an aspiring actress to an audition in New York and to visit a former lover in a nearby city. The film wanders in other directions as well, investigating McElwee's insecurities, his insomnia, his fear of nuclear apocalypse, and his unsuccessful attempts to film Burt Reynolds. *Sherman's March* is finally a film about all these things and also about its own making.

Can we plausibly think of such a film as an attempt to marshal evidence for some conclusion? I think not; at every turn *Sherman's March* stresses uncertainty and hesitation rather than the "objective" discourse of a more journalistic film.[14] It seems clear that the attempt to apply standards of objectivity to a film such as *Sherman's March* is ill-conceived. As is true for many nonfiction films, "objectivity," by any definition, is beside the point. Consider poetic films such as Joris Ivens' *The Bridge* (1928) and *Rain*, Bert Haanstra's *Glass*, and Paul Strand and Charles Sheeler's *Manhatta* (1921). These films are as far from journalism as are poetry and fiction. But as critic John Hartl notes with respect to the 1980s Academy "shut-out" of innovative documentaries:

In other categories, filmmakers are encouraged to be creative, to find new ways of treating familiar subjects and expressing themselves. In this [documentary] category, unfortunately, the rules seem designed to suppress all that's best in the form.[15]

One could argue that objectivity, as Carroll defines it, is central to the journalistic documentary. But the journalistic documentary is one exemplar among others. Objectivity, by whatever definition, is not central to all of these exemplars of nonfiction film.

Nonfictions as Photographic Records

Restrictive notions of "objectivity" are not alone in narrowing our thinking about nonfiction film. Those who consider observational cinema to be the prototypical nonfiction film, rather than one exemplar among many, take the primary directive of the observational film – the photographic and aural recording of a subject or event – to be the proper function of nonfiction. The contemporary distaste for staging and reenactment in part stems from the notion that the documentary film must record an unmanipulated profilmic event. From this it is a small, though fatal, step to claim that an essential characteristic of nonfiction is that it eschews manipulation of materials altogether.[16]

John Grierson's characterization of the documentary as "the creative treatment of actuality" succinctly embodies two major theoretical issues raised by the nonfiction film. On the one hand, nonfictions make direct references to actual events or entities and are intended to portray their subject accurately; many see this as a *recording* function. But like the fiction film, nonfictions are rhetorical constructs, fashioned and manipulated and structured representations. In fact, this seeming contradiction between the documentary as "record" and its need for structure has prominently been taken to be the central problem of the nonfiction film.[17] If the nonfiction film is a record or re-presentation, then what of its use of some of the manipulative techniques also common to the fiction film?

Consider first those who think of documentaries as having a formal correspondence to reality, as a sort of imitation or record. Richard Barsam, for example, claims that the realist impulse at the heart of documentary hopes to "record life as it is": "Nonfiction film is the art of *re*-presentation, the act of presenting actual physical reality in a form that strives creatively to record and interpret the world and be faithful to actuality."[18] This view also becomes apparent when one examines textbooks about documentary film production. W. Hugh Baddeley's *The Technique of Documentary Film Production*, for example, wholly ignores questions of the structuring and composition of documentary discourse. The likely assumption is that the structure of the nonfiction film will arise according to a natural correspondence with the subject matter. In practice, however, when filmmakers take structure for granted, the result is less an imitation of the presumed forms of reality than an unconscious appeal to conventional structures of representation.

Most film theorists recognize the problematic nature of claims for re-presentation and for the nonfiction film as an unproblematic record of the real. But contemporary theory yields problems of its own. Theorists such as Christian Metz and Jean-Louis Comolli have proposed simplistic antinomies between fiction and nonfiction, claiming that any work that transparently re-presents the real is nonfiction, and any mediated representation is fiction. Though Comolli rightly points to the manipulations inherent in any film, he errs in assuming that the nonfiction film must be a pristine copy or perfect re-presentation of reality. The distinction between fiction and nonfiction should not be based on a presumed correspondence to reality (nonfiction) versus mediated representation (fiction), but according to the stance taken toward the projected world of the text and the text's indexing.

Some theorists claim that the nonfiction claim to absolute correspondence with "the real" is a false pose, but nonetheless a pose that the nonfiction film takes via various (duplicitous) persuasive devices. Chief among these persuasive devices is the moving photograph itself, which, Brian Winston claims, bears the imprint of a science that demands and receives reverential acquiescence by the "public." Cowed by the weighty epistemic force of the photograph and its scientific veracity, the public will believe everything it sees, because "the camera never lies." As Winston notes, "All the filmmakers' off-screen denials of objectivity, all off-screen protestations as to their own subjectivity . . . , are contained and, indeed, contradicted by the overwhelmingly powerful cultural context of science."[19] William Guynn claims that discourse about the nonfiction film seeks to overcome nonfiction's need for structure and manipulation "by covering over the traces of its relation to the dominant form of cinema (fiction)."[20] For theorists who practice forms of the "hermeneutics of suspicion," derived from 1970s apparatus theory, it is as though the institutions of nonfiction filmmaking – in a kind of massive ideological scam – are themselves duplicitous, because the very apparatus on which they depend carries within it the duplicitous claims of science. The nonfiction film not only makes truth claims, but poses as a re-presentation of phenomenal reality. Furthermore, this posing as re-presentation is what is thought to separate nonfiction from fiction.

In several respects these claims are misleading. Nonfiction filmmakers attempt to tell (and show) what they take to be the truth. But this is not necessarily more duplicitous than reporting on a day's activities to a spouse, or writing an essay about one's summer vacation for an elementary school class assignment. Of course, nonfiction films can be deceptive; they are not deceptive *by definition*. Contemporary theorists often define the nonfiction film by its use of "unmanipulated" moving photographs, and assume that their placement in a structured, expressive, rhetorical context is *fictional* and not a normative nonfiction technique. This conception of nonfiction favors the observational cinema and its avoidance of expressive techniques, but ignores the long history of inventiveness and originality in nonfiction filmmaking, from the creative work of John Grierson, Robert Flaherty, and Humphrey Jennings (with their routine staging of action) to contemporary films by Ross McElwee, Michael Moore, Chris Marker, Barbara Kopple, and Errol Morris.

In short, thinking of the nonfiction film as primarily or merely a recording of the real is untenable; it cannot deal with the fact that, as John Grierson pointed out from the very beginning, nonfiction film is the *creative*, not the *imitative*, treatment of actuality. It also favors the observational film, as if it were the prototype for nonfiction, rather than one exemplar among many. Most importantly, if the nonfiction film is fundamentally imitation or re-presentation, then any attempt at the manipulation of the materials of representation pulls the film away from the genre and toward fiction. In the theory of nonfiction film, nothing could be more misleading.

Robert Flaherty and Arranging Scenes

I have argued that rather than seeking prototypical documentaries, we should look to *exemplars* of nonfiction. I have identified three such exemplars, each with its particular means of representation, and of effecting the assertive stance characteristic of nonfiction. Each exemplar, or kind of nonfiction film, has more or less common characteristics, or family resemblances. As the institutions of nonfiction filmmaking change, some of these family resemblances recede into the background, whereas others once thought peripheral emerge as paradigmatic. A family resemblance typical in 1930s documentary can fall out of favor and become antithetical to the 1960s documentary, then weakly reemerge in the 1990s. Such is the case with the practice of reenactments and staging in the production of nonfiction films.

The historical nature of the categories "documentary" and "nonfiction film" is striking when one considers the films of Robert Flaherty. Flaherty is often considered a pioneer of the documentary film. Most historical and theoretical studies of the documentary grant the filmmaker a central position in the history and development of the genre. However, if Flaherty were to make his films within the context of today's media institutions, we would almost certainly not call them documentaries, but docudramas or "dramatic documentaries." Flaherty's collaborator, Helen Van Dongen, claims that, like a fiction filmmaker, Flaherty always began shooting with a story line already crystallized: "Facts were interpreted and adapted by him and molded into elements of a world created by him, a world entirely his own."[21] Flaherty's subjects and themes are well known; he was an explorer in a sense, but aside from the particulars he showed, what he found was remarkably similar from culture to culture and from film to film: the familiar themes of humans versus the elements, of the beauty and severity of nature, of the return to the past, and of the importance of the family. In this sense he was similar to a fiction filmmaker who explores recurring themes within the context of a personal oeuvre.

In addition, the profilmic event in Flaherty films is usually arranged and/or staged for the camera. In *Nanook of the North* (1922), for example, Flaherty had the Eskimos engage in a Walrus hunt with harpoons, a practice they had abandoned when the white man introduced rifles. Flaherty's films are also cast; for *Man of Aran* (1934) he auditioned various islanders to find those who most fit his ideal. The family is played by actors unrelated to each other except for their common geographical and ancestral heritage. In *Louisiana Story* (1948), the cast is listed in the opening titles with both character names and actual names. Flaherty takes care to use actual Cajuns in this film set in the swamps of Louisiana, but these Cajuns are nonetheless actors playing scripted roles. The boy, Joseph Beaudreau, plays a character called Alexander

Napoleon Ulysses Latour. Van Dongen goes so far as to say that of all Flaherty films, only *The Land* (1942) is a "true" documentary.[22]

Flaherty's films differ from today's nonfiction exemplars in several respects. His use of staging and reenactment, however, stands out as an archaic documentary practice. With the influence of observational film in the 1960s, audiences and filmmakers became less likely to accept reenactment and staging as nonfiction techniques. Some contemporary critics discredit instances of reenactment as inauthentic; others distinguish documentary from fiction or docudrama on the basis of the degree of manipulation of the profilmic event. But although it is a manipulation, the use of reenactment and arranged scenes has a long and illustrious history in the nonfiction film, both in the United States and abroad. There is even evidence that arranging scenes was once considered a central and normative documentary technique.

American newsreels, for example, are notorious for their reenactments, which were often fraudulent. According to Raymond Fielding, every major news film producer in the period 1894–1900 faked news film as a matter of habit.[23] Reenactment also became an integral component in the films of the *March of Time* series. For example, scenes of official ceremonies were often staged using the officials who had participated in the original event. But when actual participants weren't available, common practice allowed for the use of actors.[24]

One might argue that newsreels never enjoyed central status as nonfiction films, and thus cannot be used as evidence to support the claim that staging was a prototypical technique. After all, Grierson distinguished newsreels from the documentary, disparaging the peacetime newsreel as "just a speedy snip-snap of some utterly unimportant ceremony."[25] However, most of the films produced under Grierson's tutelage, and indeed, many British documentaries of the 1930s and 1940s made use of actors and/or were composed almost wholly of arranged scenes. Humphrey Jennings' *A Diary for Timothy* (1945), for example, takes the form of a diary directed toward the fictional baby Timothy Jenkins. In chronicling the end of WWII and in looking toward the future, the film follows several characters, cross-cutting between them in a fashion reminiscent of Robert Altman's fictional *Nashville* (1975). Bill, the engine driver, and Peter Roper, the injured British flyer, actually play themselves, but they still appear in scenes wholly devised by the filmmakers.

The list of nonfiction films incorporating staging techniques is long, and it includes many documentaries thought to be central examples.

But although reenactment and staging were thought for years to be prototypical documentary techniques, today many critics and filmmakers think of them as improper for the documentary, and reserve staging for the kitchy ranks of "reality" television and the less prestigious docudrama. Even the innovative Errol Morris, who staged the policeman's murder (from several different perspectives) for *The Thin Blue Line*, felt the need in interviews to justify their use, and to establish that the reenactments were illustrations of the testimony of witnesses to the murder, not the film's assertion of what actually occurred.

This shift in documentary practice no doubt stems from the new technologies available to filmmakers in the early 1960s, and the rise of filmmaking practices established by observational film. With the development of lightweight, portable cameras and sound equipment, nonfiction filmmakers were able to film events with a freedom and spontaneity previously unknown in filmmaking. This new equipment contributed to an enthusiasm for filming the unmanipulated scene and recording natural sound – to observe rather than to teach, argue, or create. Any manipulation for dramatic or rhetorical effect tainted this supposed purity of purpose, and arranging scenes began to seem impure, dishonest, and dramatically unsatisfactory. As Fred Wiseman says, "the whole effort in documentary is to capture certain aspects of reality and not to manipulate it. If you are interested in telling people how to act, then you should work with actors."[26]

Today it is clear that the influence of observational film is waning, and many nonfiction filmmakers are again resorting to voice-over narration, nondiegetic music, and other explicitly rhetorical techniques. However, most filmmakers still balk at the overt staging of action, and find it to be a contradiction of the presumed *recording* function of documentary, or at the least, an aesthetic *faux pas*. The history of staging in nonfiction shows that the set of features, or family resemblances, we associate with nonfiction film constantly recede and expand, as practices gain and lose acceptance. In light of this, it is most fruitful to think of nonfiction not in terms of unchanging or universal intrinsic properties, but as a socially constructed category that is fluid and malleable; it changes with history.

Expression, Not Imitation; Rhetoric, Not Re-presentation

Nonfiction films are not imitations or re-presentations, but constructed representations. Consider the sentence, "Then he kicked me pretty hard in the backside, and that was the end of my engagement as an open-air entertainer." In a novel the sentence could be fictional. However, the very same words, appearing in a diary, news report, or other nonfictional context, could express claims about the actual world. Neither the words themselves nor their formal arrangement make the first instance fictional and the second nonfictional. Rather, it is the context in which the words appear. The same is true of nonfiction films.

If we think of the nonfiction film in this fashion, few of the techniques of the fiction film remain problematic for it. A film's photography may or may not carry with it the presumption of accurate portrayal. But not only is the use of photography more complex than simple recording, but nonfiction discourse is far more than the sum of its moving pictures. The nonfiction film asserts that the states of affairs it presents actually occur(red). It may also explore abstract issues and ideas much like fiction film. It may make use of expressive sound, editing, photography, conventional structures of ordering information (narrative, rhetorical, expositional), and so forth. If we see the nonfiction film as fundamentally a genre of rhetoric rather than one of imitation (or a pretense thereof), then whether its representations are embodied in a stylistically spare and "objective" discourse or an expressive and "subjective" discourse is irrelevant to its status as nonfiction film. A nonfiction film doesn't first and foremost "catch" reality; through the assertive stance taken toward its representata, it expresses and implies attitudes and statements about its subject.[27] Nonfiction film makes no claim to *reproduce* the real, but rather makes claims *about* the "real," just as any nonfiction communication does.

Nonfiction films encompass a limitless variety of discourses about the world. Thinking of nonfiction as expressive (or as Grierson claimed, "creative"), and in relation to indexing and the assertive stance, has several advantages. For one, it allows us to initiate our discussion of nonfiction without descending into the confusions raised by notions of objectivity and realism. Nonfictions are rhetorical, not primarily re-presentations. We can also see that nonfiction assertions and implications can be housed in the most subjective, stylistically expressive nonfiction films. We need not think of the music of Benjamin Britten in *Night Mail*, for example, as a diversion from nonfiction filmmaking practice. On this theory, it shouldn't be surprising that filmmakers choose to give musical form to their thoughts about their film's subjects. This emphasis on expression expands the boundaries of mainstream nonfiction to include innovative work not as a violation of the presumed dictates of nonfiction film making, but as work that in its creativity and innovation shows us what the nonfiction film can do at its best, pointing to new means for the exploration of personal, historical, and social issues. As Errol Morris says, "There's no reason why documentaries can't be as personal as fiction filmmaking and bear the imprint of those who made them. Truth isn't guaranteed by style or expression. It isn't guaranteed by anything."[28]

CHAPTER 3
Moving Image Icons

Given my claims above, the reader might legitimately wonder why I devote this and the following chapter to the function of the moving photographic image in nonfiction. I have so far claimed that the difference between the fiction and nonfiction film lies not in a distinction between manipulation and imitation, not in imagination versus copying, but in the fact that nonfiction films present their states of affairs assertively rather than fictively. Thus the distinction (however fuzzy) between the fiction and nonfiction film does not depend on any particular relationship between the image and the profilmic scene (since even animated images can be nonfiction images), but on a kind of social contract, an implicit, unspoken agreement between the text's producer(s) and the discursive community to view the film as *nonfiction*. I also claimed that theorists have overemphasized the imitative, copying function of nonfiction film, implicitly denying the creative expression and assertion fundamental to the genre. To think of any film as a pure copy or imitation of anything makes little sense.

All this is true; nevertheless the moving photographic image still holds obvious importance for nonfiction and fiction film. In fact, determining the implications of the use of cinematography and the photograph in film has been *the* central problem of film theory, especially in relation to debates about film realism and spectator effects. What is the relationship of the moving photographic image to the profilmic scene? Is it one of arbitrary convention? Of likeness between image and referent? How does the use of machines in motion picture photography – in other words, the "automatic" nature of photography – affect the way we see moving images? Can the nonfiction film's photographic images ever constitute evidence for the claims made by the film? How do images function within the general context of nonfiction communication? Does the recent development of digital imaging techniques radically alter the way in which we must view the evidential force of photography in the nonfiction film and elsewhere? Such questions are central for the study of the nonfiction film, and are the subject of this and the following chapter.

More specifically, these chapters will examine the use of photographic images as icons and as indices. I use these terms in the technical sense developed by Charles Sanders Peirce, whose tripartite division of signs was introduced to film theory by Peter Wollen.[1] Any entity – be it a word, gesture, image, or style of clothing – can be a sign when it has *meaning* for someone. Peirce devised an elaborate and complex classificatory scheme for signs. The typology that interests us here, the tripartite division of signs into icons, indices, and symbols, is based on the sign's relationship to its referent. The iconic sign resembles or is a likeness of its referent; the index – a sundial, for example – is related to its referent by proximity or causality; the symbol – for example, the word "umbrella" – bears a relationship of arbitrary convention to its referent. Photographs, Peirce thinks, are typically iconic, indexical, *and* symbolic, incorporating meanings determined by likeness, causality, and arbitrary convention within the same representation. This makes photographs highly complex representations.[2]

Icons, Anti-Art, and Bourgeois Ideology

The nature of the photographic image has recently been the locus of a good deal of contentious debate. Those who claim for the photographic image a special status find in photography the ability to produce representations that (1) are likenesses – icons – of the scene before the camera, and (2) are produced "automatically" by machines, thus providing veridical images of the world. Opponents of these claims deny that special status of photographic communication, maintaining instead that still and moving photographs, like verbal language, are constructed of conventional, arbitrary marks on a page (for photographs) or intensities of light on a screen (for movies), and that photographs must be "read" just as the words or symbols of natural languages are.

Those who deny the special status of photography are often motivated by an interest in defending photography as an expressive art form, or concern with the "illusory" ideological effects of photographs. Photography theorists, sensitive to the charge that photography is inferior as art because it "mechanically reproduces the world," go to considerable lengths to emphasize the creative work of the photographer in making a photograph; some go as far as to deny any "automatic" likeness between image and referent in the photographic process. Although the documentary filmmaker is often interested in using the camera as a recording device, the photographer as artist downplays recording in favor of artistic expression. If photography is mere imitation or recording, what room is there for art? W.J.T. Mitchell, for example, links the view that some images are realistic or naturalistic with "a modern, secular idolatry linked with the ideology of Western science and rationalism." Mitchell uses terms such as "hegemony," "the tyranny of the image," and "fetishism" to describe beliefs in the special nature of photographs. "The real miracle," he writes, "has been the successful resistance of pictorial artists to this idolatry, their insistence on continuing to show us more than meets the eye with whatever resources they can muster."[3]

Such rhetoric is needlessly defensive. If images can function as icons, this hardly threatens photography as an art. Those who favor the artistic use of photographic images need not deny their special relation to the visual world, nor the mechanical nature of the camera. The salient point is that the uses of photographs are nearly as diverse as those of verbal language. Words can be used to describe an incident more or less accurately; they can also tell a fictional story. To claim that photographs can be used to record the look of a scene is not to deny that they can also be used to create highly expressive, nonveridical representations.

The second motivation for denying the iconic possibilities of photography is central to Marxist/psychoanalytic film theory, and stems from the belief that in its use of Renaissance perspective, photography disseminates bourgeois ideology. Jean-Louis Baudry claims that in response to Galileo and the end of geocentrism, artists produced *perspectiva artificialis*, a new mode of representation ensuring "the setting up of the 'subject' [the self] as the active center and origin of meaning" and in its illusory nature hiding the work involved in its production. In addition, photography (and Renaissance perspective generally) creates a "hallucinatory reality," lays out "the space of an ideal vision," and "assures the necessity of transcendence."[4]

For the sake of argument, suppose we grant him his contention that photography was invented to serve a specific ideological end, to render a false sense of centeredness to the bourgeoisie, who had lost that security with the downfall of geocentrism. Even if this is so, there is no reason to believe that now, 100 years later, in a very different world, all photography and all of cinema share this ideological effect. Ideological effect depends on use and context as much as on origins. Despite his reference to historical origins, Baudry assumes a universal, ahistorical ideological effect for the motion picture apparatus.

The Referent and the "Ideology of the Visible"

To claim that the image in nonfiction can function as an icon squarely contests another current in critical theory, a denial of the importance of the referent, what the image represents. However, the study of the nonfiction film becomes sterile when it denies referentiality. For example, critics charged that director Michael Moore deceptively rearranged the chronology of events for his film *Roger and Me*. What interests us here is not only the film's stylistic and structural arrangement, but its representations in relation to the actual history of Flint. The 1975 *CBS Reports* episode "The Guns of Autumn," similarly, roused the ire of hunters all over the country (and resulted in lawsuits filed against CBS) for its supposed misrepresentation of their sport. We cannot even begin to gauge the veracity of the hunter's claims without making reference to the actual characteristics of hunting in relation to what "The Guns of Autumn" showed and implied. Nonfictions point to more than mere discourse, are *about* something, and make *claims* and *assertions* about extrafilmic reality.

Many would not dispute my claim here. However, strong theoretical currents in critical and film studies – both postmodernist and poststructuralist – not only deny the importance of filmic reference, but deny reference altogether. The best-known postmodern analysis of the image comes to us from Jean Baudrillard, who claims that we have become a society of the "simulacrum," or *simulation*. Baudrillard says that we have lost contact with reality, and have access only to simulacra, of which photographic images are an important class. For Baudrillard, the generation of simulacra is no longer a function of referentiality, but of "the generation by models of a real without origin or reality: the hyperreal."[5] On Baudrillard's model, writes Allen Weiss, postmodernist "epistemology . . . entails precisely the conflation of representation and reality, resulting in the inherent loss of (political) pathos and the failure of the modernist utopian project." The tragedy or pathos of the photograph is the recognition of the "hermeneutic incommensurability of signifier and signified, surface and depth, image and referent."[6] For Baudrillard, then, this is not merely an inability to reach beyond appearances to reality, but a fundamental, irrecoverable loss of access to reality. The human condition is to be mired in a world of mere simulation.[7]

Despite what Baudrillard writes, the common sense perspective is that images have referents. The George Holliday video of the Rodney King beating, most of us believe, makes reference to actual historical events, and specifically to the beating of Rodney King. Of course, common sense is often mistaken. But it is difficult to see what Baudrillard might mean if he were to deny referentiality in this case. If the Holliday video is a mere simulacrum, does that entail that it refers to nothing beyond itself, or that it holds no information about an extradiscursive event?[8]

Fortunately, Baudrillard does use a particular example to illustrate his theory – Craig Gilbert's observational film *An American Family* (1973). This film initiated much discussion about the legitimacy and ethics of the direct cinema approach. It was intended as an extensive observation of the workings of an American family. Through its twelve one-hour episodes, we see something quite shocking, as the Loud family disintegrates before our eyes. *An American Family* raises questions about the influence of the camera crew on the family. Philip Rosen notes that Baudrillard cites the influence of the camera and crew to contradict claims that a film can ever simply record a preexisting reality. Instead, the actual making of the film becomes a part of the reality being recorded, just as, for Baudrillard, the production of any discourse is incorporated into the discourse itself. For Baudrillard, *An American Family* makes reference to the hyperreal, and not to a preexisting reality.

In response, one might note that Baudrillard's example is carefully chosen to fit his claims; the Holliday video of Rodney King's beating, for example, or footage of natural disasters, would be more challenging examples – there the cameras had no effect on what was recorded. (One could argue that the value of the Holliday video stems precisely from its invisibility to the offending policemen, and thus its utter lack of influence on the profilmic event.) More important are the criticisms leveled by Rosen. Rosen argues that whether or not the cameras influenced the Loud family in *An American Family*, ". . . the status of the shot as document of a real that preexists the spectator's viewing remains in force."[9] For Rosen, the question is not whether the camera influences the profilmic events; if so, those influenced events are the reality to which the photograph refers. Nonfiction *representation* does not depend on an "Ideal Chronicler," or on the *re-presentation* of pristine reality. From its very beginnings, the *documentary* has always admitted to being more than a mere *document*. Its style and sequencing do not diminish its ability to make reference to an extrafilmic real.

The denial of referentiality isn't confined to Baudrillard and post-modernism, however. The suspicion of images reaches back at least to Plato, and more recently has been forcefully described by Susan Sontag. In her well-known essay, "In Plato's Cave," Sontag accepts Plato's metaphor of humans in a cave, facing the interior cave wall, who see only images and shadows of the reality beyond the cave, mere appearances and insufficient approximations of Truth. The camera, she claims, has effected "a tremendous promotion of the value of appearances," such that "photographs have become the norm for the way things appear to us, thereby changing the very idea of reality, and of realism."[10]

Similar ideas about the effects of the image have been central to poststructuralist film theory. As representative of such theory, consider Colin MacCabe's claims in his well-known essay, "Theory and Film: Principles of Realism and Pleasure."[11] MacCabe argues that film does not reveal reality, but "is constituted by a set of discourses which (in the positions allowed to subject and object) produces a certain reality" (82). He doesn't claim that filmic discourse *invents* reality; neither does he claim that filmic discourse uses "a transparent discourse to render the real." His claim, in the Marxist vein, is that film discourse is productive work, in its transformation of reality.[12]

If MacCabe's claim is that specific instances of film discourse do not have separable extrafilmic references, then we should question him as we did Baudrillard. Clearly, the Rodney King video did not "produce" the beating of Rodney King; it recorded it. However, one can take MacCabe's claims at an abstract level, and in so doing render them more plausible. At a global level, film discourse does not passively represent a reality from which it is totally separate. As discourse, it not only itself becomes an element of the actual world, but it has the potential to *transform* that reality in certain cases, as a part of the cultural discourses which carry on the process of transformation.

At this general level, it is not a question of the strict separation of discourse and the real, but of their mutual interaction and influence. Thus the Rodney King beating became a catalyst for important events – including the generation of additional discourse – as a result of the video representation that advertised it throughout the world. Notice that to believe this about filmic discourse is wholly compatible with separating a film from its referent *in specific cases*. Film discourses all have separable references; in general, however, film discourse mutually interacts with the profilmic real in a mediated relationship. Film discourse has effects both on other discourses and on extrafilmic reality; it can transform them, or perform "work" on them. To put this in the terms of a pragmatic theory, nonfictions are instruments of action, not mere passive reflections of the real.

Referentiality must be preserved in our theoretical discourse about film. Even granting the largely conventional and rhetorical nature of nonfiction film communication, the relationship between discourse and referent is still of central concern. With regard to the nonfiction film, at least, denying referentiality becomes perversely insular. However, Mac-Cabe's claims are a worthwhile corrective, with their emphasis on the transformative potential of discourse. He reminds us that it is possible to overestimate referentiality, forgetting that it is but one of the functions of nonfiction films within the constellation of their possible uses and purposes.

The Iconic Image

The most convincing argument for referentiality is to describe the processes by which it occurs. The respect in which photographic images are thought to be unique among communications media is in their iconic resemblance to the photographed scene together with the indexical, mechanical means by which they are produced. Suppose we begin by considering whether and how photographs (moving or still) can function as icons. Does the photograph "look like" its referent in some respect, or is it linked to it by arbitrary convention, as the name "Grand Canyon," in the English language, is conventionally used to refer to that mammoth chasm in Arizona? Is the relationship one of *both* convention *and* resemblance? One of the difficulties of this issue is that picture theorists have tended to posit a false dichotomy, as though the photographic image were *either* a "conventional" *or* a "natural" representation of the profilmic scene, but not both. For many, it seems, either the photograph is, on the one hand, a natural, transparent, unmediated icon, or, on the other, a conventional, purely arbitrary construction on the order of sign language or verbal language.

Bazin and subsequent realists hold that the image bears a special relationship to reality due to the mechanical nature of its production, which to some extent neutralizes the human, subjective element of photography. For Bazin, the photograph becomes more than a representation of reality; it shares the very "being of the model of which it is the reproduction." In other words, the photograph is no mere "sub-

stitute"; it "actually contributes something to the order of natural creation. . . ."[13] Bazin writes of the film *Kon Tiki* (1951) as an historical
artifact analogous to moss-covered ruins, ruins that allow us to imagine buildings and statues which have long since deteriorated. Like
those ruins, the photograph is not merely evidence of a "having been
there," but actually shares the "being" of the original bit of reality of
which it is evidence.

Philosophy has produced similar realist views of the image. Kendall
Walton, for example, claims that "the invention of the camera gave us
not just a new method of making pictures and not just pictures of a
new kind; it gave us a new way of seeing."[14] Walton notes that the
camera is an optical instrument like a telescope, binoculars, or micro-
scope. When we look at stars or at distant vistas through a telescope or
binoculars, we actually see the stars or distant vistas. In the same way,
Walton claims, we *see through* photographs. For Walton, when we
look at photographs of our dead relatives, we *quite literally see them*,
and not merely their representation. For both philosophers, photography and film are the ultimate realistic media; they literally show us the
world.

Most contemporary film theorists take a position opposed to realism, and hold that photography, in its use of Renaissance perspective
and in other respects, bears a purely conventional and symbolic relationship with the profilmic scene. How, they might ask, could a two-dimensional image "look like" or "resemble" the three-dimensional
world? Many film theorists also foreground the historical origins of
photography (rather than its ties to human perception), finding in those
origins a specific political agenda that the development of photography
fostered and out of which it emerged. Jean-Louis Baudry, as I write
above, claims that bourgeois ideology is an inherent aspect of cinematic representation because the cinematic apparatus makes use of the
codes of Renaissance perspective, a system of representation developed
by the bourgeoisie at a particular moment in history as a tool to serve
class interests.[15]

Outside the field of film studies, philosophers have also argued for
the conventional nature of photography. Nelson Goodman is perhaps
the best-known champion of such a view, contending that all depictions, whether photographic or not, are descriptions, and hence, like
natural language, are conventional. A depiction of a person – a photographic portrait, for example – is just one possible description; other
descriptions are possible. Far from *seeing through* photographs, Good-

man argues that we must learn to *read* pictures just as we must learn to understand the conventions involved in the understanding of any description.[16]

How shall we clear our way through these conflicting accounts? We can begin by rejecting the false dichotomy between "natural" and "conventional." These terms are often used loosely and ambiguously; more important, they impose a false antinomy on the nature of photographic representation. On one hand, if by "natural" one means that photography makes use of the laws of physics and chemistry, then photography is natural. On the other hand, when "natural" is taken to mean "that which is untouched by human culture," then photography is manifestly unnatural, since it is firmly embedded in human affairs. Similarly, if by "conventional" one merely means that which is a part of human culture, then photography is conventional. But when we think of "conventional" as that which is established by arbitrary decision alone, then photography is not conventional, since it makes use of natural laws governing the optic array. Depending on how we define our terms, then, photography can be both natural and conventional, one or the other, or neither of the two.[17]

Both still and motion photography are cultural practices making use of technological instruments that – to a degree – could have been designed differently in another culture. In other words, both the practice of photography and its technology are culture-bound. However, this does not imply that cameras could be designed just any way, and photographs taken in any arbitrarily chosen fashion. Like many cultural artifacts, the camera was designed to satisfy particular human needs. Although the means of fulfilling those needs vary, the variations must come within parameters determined by the intended use of the camera in relation to requirements of the physical world.

As Noël Carroll argues, most cultural products must have some properties determined by nature, physical characteristics necessary for the fulfillment of their function. Take the case of the plow, for example. Carroll writes:

They [plows] are cultural productions. . . . Is the design of a plow a matter of convention? . . . the adoption of the design of the plow could not have been reached by fiat. The plow had a purpose – digging furrows – and its effectiveness had to be accommodated to the structure of nature. It would have to be heavy enough and sharp enough to cut into the earth, and it had to be adapted to the capabilities of its human users – it had to be steerable and pullable by creatures like us with two arms and limited strength. A device like the plow had to be discovered; it could not be brought into existence by consensus.[18]

In part, then, a cultural instrument designed to fulfill a particular function must meet certain physical standards in order to perform its task.

On the other hand, we should not underestimate the variations possible in the types of plows capable of digging furrows. Plows may be pulled by tractors or by oxen; they may dig one furrow at a time, or as many as sixteen at once; they may be decorated and ornamented in various ways. The point is that a cultural product designed to meet specific needs consists of characteristics both conventionally determined and dependent on the considerations of nature.

In the same way, photography and the camera were developed to capture and record the look of a scene. With this function in mind, the camera could not have been developed along purely arbitrary lines. The invention of the camera and photographic process proceeded in deference to the physical laws that make photography possible. Like the plow, however, the technology of the camera, film, and processing can be altered in various ways and still fulfill the function for which it was designed. Thus the photographic process is both culture-bound *and* dependent on physical laws. Any analysis of the photographic process that does not recognize the mix of the natural and conventional is bound to be misleading.

Let us begin with those aspects of photography that might be termed "natural." What some film theory has denied (or repressed), is the ability of the camera to provide the same kind of visual information about the profilmic scene that would have been available to an observer at that scene. In order to understand this, we must consider the photograph in relation to "natural" perception. Objects in the environment structure light in particular ways. As an observer moves through the environment, she receives and processes an optical flow pattern, and through this has access to information about the sources of that pattern. This information is exhibited in families of abstract invariant ratios, contrasts, and proportions of structured light, which give information, for example, about surfaces, edges, corners, and the spatial layout of a scene.

The psychologist J. J. Gibson claims that the three-dimensional environment provides generous visual information to an observer.[19] A photograph *records a sample of ambient light* from a particular environment, and the picture surface, under specified conditions, is treated in such a way that it contains the same kind of information as that available at the profilmic scene. In the case of video, the visual information is projected onto the surface of the video screen; in the motion picture, the visual information is recorded on strips of film and projected onto a flat surface in front of the audience. In either case, this process accounts for our ability to receive accurate visual information about an extrafilmic referent from photographs. This, together with the mechanical nature of its production, is why we see the Rodney King video as evidence for an extrafilmic event. The video gives us the same type of visual information we would receive were we an actual observer.

As Gibson notes, the quality and quantity of the visual information available from the photograph will typically be inferior to the visual data that could be gleaned from the actual scene. A picture can never preserve all of the information available to a perceiver of the natural environment; it can only preserve *selected and degraded* information. Looking at a photograph, then, is analogous to looking at a natural scene (under certain conditions), though the photograph is often inferior in the quality and quantity of the visual information available. (On the other hand, photography can sometimes reveal visual information unavailable to the naked eye, with telescopic or macro lenses, or with extreme slow motion, for example.)

However, despite perceptual homologies between looking at photographs and natural perception, those who think of representational photographs as illusions ignore important differences between the two kinds of perception. Differences such as the photograph's visual inferiority to the actual scene, the presence of a frame or border to the image, and the "artificial" situation in which the viewer finds herself (for example, museum, movie theater, looking at a book of photographs) prohibits her from mistaking what she sees for the actual scene. The perception of pictures, Gibson claims, is always a *dual perception*. Photographs yield dual optical information, and require two kinds of apprehension which occur simultaneously: seeing what is "in" a photograph and seeing the surface on which the things are depicted. When we see *Nanook of the North*, we are simultaneously aware both of Nanook patiently waiting to spear a seal, for example, and of the fact that we are seeing a two-dimensional representation (e.g., light on a screen in a theatre). We do not see what is "in" the film as actually occurring; neither do we see what is depicted in a representational film as the mere play of light and shadows. This is in part what is unique about the perception of representational pictures – the dual perception of two and three dimensions.[20]

What I've claimed about still photographs applies to the moving images as well, and to a greater degree. The moving photograph can provide more information about a scene than a still image. Motion pictures consist of a series of still photographs; small displacements from one picture to the next are perceived not as a series of static views, but as movement, either the movement of entities in the scene or movement of the camera through space. The still photograph can give us some of the same visual information a stationary observer would have while looking at the scene; the moving camera, under certain conditions, is like a stand-in for the human body as it moves through the scene, at least with regard to the types of visual information it makes available to the viewer.[21]

This illusion of movement has consequences for the informative power of the image. First, the static picture cannot provide movement cues to help the spectator gauge distances and proportions. In contrast, camera movements such as tracking and dolly shots provide the viewer with much of the visual information she would get were she to traverse the path followed by the camera. In other words, movement gives us more information about depth. Second, movement often gives us visual information from different spatial perspectives, often allowing us to observe the scene from various heights, distances, and lateral vantage points. The still photograph *fixes* the point from which the visual information is apprehended, whereas the moving image provides additional information by changing spatial vantage points through camera movement and editing.

Let me be clear exactly what of J. J. Gibson's perceptual theory I am using here. David Bordwell locates three broad views in the recent psychology of visual representation: the perspectivist, Gestaltist, and constructivist positions.[22] Bordwell associates Gibson's position with perspectivism, since Gibson claims that a perceiver's understanding of the visual environment depends essentially on the way light is structured according to the laws of geometrical optics. Gibson allows little room for the cognitive activity of the perceiver, arguing that the information necessary to discover the meaning inherent in an environment is present in that environment. We do need to act to perceive; we must turn our heads and direct our attention. However, we need not posit inferences through which the perceiver adds to the data picked up through the senses. Another term for Gibson's perceptual theory is "ecological." His basic contention is that the organs of living creatures have evolved in such a way as to receive the information required to survive and flourish. We need posit only an environment giving up information and a goal-oriented perceiver who *discovers* meaning within that environment.

The Gestaltist perceptual psychology, on the other hand, attributes much more power to the mental operations of the perceiver. According to Gestalt theory, certain mental tendencies, such as laws of simplicity and good continuation, are much more important in visual perception than the visual stimulus itself. Gestalt theory is Kantian in its giving heavy emphasis – almost constitutive powers – to the mind in the perception of reality.

The third position is constructivism. Unlike the perspectivist, the constructivist claims that the consideration of the visual stimulus alone cannot adequately account for the intricacies of visual perception. For the constructivist, Bordwell writes, "perception is an inferential process which reworks stimuli." Constructivism also differs from Gestalt theories in that the inferential process it finds as central to perception is "a temporal process of building the percept in a probabilistic fashion," rather than Gestalt theory's "imposition of a mental order upon the world."[23] As Bordwell describes it, constructivism occupies a middle ground between perspectivism and Gestalt theory, taking into consideration the cognitive activity of the mind in addition to the requirements of objective visual stimuli.

Note that accepting J. J. Gibson's account of the nature of photographic perception does not require adherence to his entire perceptual theory. In fact, it doesn't imply either a perspectivist, Gestaltist, or constructivist account of visual perception in general. Accepting Gibson's account of the nature of two-dimensional photographs need not entail embracing his "ecological" program as a whole. A Gestaltist, for example, could accept the view that the photograph captures some visual information, and still hold that the mind must order the information to make sense of it. A constructivist can accept Gibson's account of photography and nonetheless recognize the important perceptual and cognitive activities of the spectator in comprehending the photograph. Even if photographs retain the same type of information as that available at the profilmic scene, as Gibson suggests, the means by which the mind perceives the visual information in the photograph remains open to question.

If we accept Gibson's account of photography and visual information, we can see in what respect still and moving photographs may be icons, that is, likenesses or resemblances of their referent. *The photograph, whether still or moving, functions as an icon when it presents visual information similar to that available to an observer at the profilmic scene.* It is important to note that photographs do not necessarily bear likeness to the scene they picture; not all photographs are icons. We can always devise strategies by which the cinematographer may short-circuit the photograph's usual iconic tendencies. Photographs that are out of focus, under or overexposed, scratched, charred, or boiled in oil will likely not function as icons. The iconic function is one function of the photographic image, not automatic and not the only function. Only when established procedures are followed will the photograph resemble the profilmic scene in certain respects, and yield veridical information.

My claim is not that an observer on the scene would get *identical* visual information from a photograph of the scene. Joel Snyder and Neil Walsh Allen argue that the assertion that a photograph shows us what we would have seen had we been there ourselves "has to be qualified to the point of absurdity." For the photograph to give us *exactly the same* visual impression, we would need to look at the scene from the same vantage point as the camera, with head immobile (except in the case of the moving camera shot), and with one eye closed. Moreover, they ask, do we see with a 150 mm or a 35 mm lens, in Agfacolor or Tri-X? Our seeing what the camera "saw" also depends on the particular developing process and the choice of photographic paper. As Snyder and Allen write, "By the time all the conditions are added up, the original position has been reversed: instead of saying that the camera shows us what our eyes would see, we are now positing the rather unilluminating proposition that, if our vision worked like photography, then we would see things the way a camera does."[24]

However, we do not see *exactly* what the camera "sees," but rather the camera gives us the *same kind* of visual information that we would get, were we looking at the scene in place of the camera. We don't get all of the possible information. Moreover, though the cinematographer must satisfy conditions to fashion a photograph that gives such information, this in no way makes such a claim absurd. Just as your auto will function properly only if driven in a certain manner, a photograph yields information only if taken in a certain manner. If you want to drive your car to the post office, you follow certain procedures – not the same procedures, incidentally, that you would follow to walk to the post office. If you want to take an informative photograph of a giraffe, you must load an appropriate film stock into the camera, point the camera at the giraffe (and not a hippopotamus), adjust your zoom lens to an acceptable focal length, gauge the exposure, focus the lens, and so forth. The point is not that photographs are exactly like human vision, or that they give veridical information under any conditions whatsoever. The point is that one important function and capability of photography is to give visual information that would have been available to an observer at the scene.

Perceiving Pictures: Empirical Evidence

The iconic nature of photographs is not merely a topic for philosophical discourse, but also an empirical claim. Much evidence suggests that photographs can provide visual information without converting that information into a mode different than natural perception. But can this really be true? Anyone familiar with debates about photography has heard the following oft-repeated anecdote: a Western anthropologist shows photographs to "primitive" people unfamiliar with photography. The people stare blankly at the little pieces of paper, unable to see the photograph as a representation of the three-dimensional world. This anecdote is meant to show that even for simple object recognition, humans must learn to "read" photographs, because photographs consist of arbitrary marks on paper and represent the photographed scene by convention alone, not by any likeness between image and referent.[25]

Indeed, cross-cultural research in picture perception *has* shown that cultures have different conventions for the two-dimensional representation of three-dimensional scenes, and that members of some cultures may need to learn to respond to two-dimensional pictures as representations of three-dimensional scenes. However, what such people learn is not how to "read" photographs, but rather that a three-dimensional scene can be represented on an unfamiliar two-dimensional surface.[26] Once such an epistemic "jump" has been achieved, persons typically can recognize any object in a photograph with which they have a real-world familiarity. In fact, a convincing argument can be made not only that recognizing objects in nondegraded photographs makes use of real-world perceptual skills and requires no special learning, but that, as Stephen Prince writes, "the use of specifically cinematic devices . . . such as montage, camera movement, or subjective shots, does not pose substantial interpretational obstacles for naive viewers."[27]

The most telling evidence that photographs do not convert fundamental visual information into a mode different from real-world perception, however, comes from research on nonhuman subjects. Some of these studies show that this universality of picture comprehension extends to animals, including some species of spiders, chickens, monkeys, pigeons, and dolphins.[28] In one fascinating case, pigeons were able to identify human figures in color slides. The experimenters selected over 1,000 slides of urban and rural landscapes, half of the slides showing one or more persons and half showing no persons. The slides with persons featured them "in foreground or background, standing or sitting, clothed or unclothed, and often partly obscured."[29] Each day the pigeons were shown eighty slides, one minute for each slide, half with people and half not, mixed randomly. The bird could activate a food hopper by pecking a switch to the side of the slides, but the switch would only function when accompanied by a slide showing one or more persons. After one week the birds pecked more vigorously when shown slides with people. After two more weeks the birds made clear distinctions between slides with and without people, pecking the switch about 50 pecks per minute during people slides, and 0–10 pecks per minute during "no-people" slides. Each day a random selection of slides was made from the overall collection of 1,000, ensuring that the pigeons could not memorize the slides according to graphic characteristics instead of responding to what the slides represented.

The experiment shows that pigeons can identify persons in photographs, and in addition, can do so in photographs taken from various angles, camera distances, heights, and perspectives. Other experiments have shown that pigeons can distinguish between photographs of pigeons and other birds, oak leaves versus leaves from other species of tree, landscapes with or without trees, and can even recognize particular human beings. On the other hand, pigeons are poor at detecting the presence of object categories such as bottles and vehicles, suggesting that their natural unfamiliarity with such objects prevents them from identifying them consistently in photographs. Like humans, then, pigeons can identify familiar objects in photographs without the type of learning necessary to use verbal language.

A second case involves the bottlenosed dolphin. In this experiment, dolphins already familiar with a sign language were shown videotapes of familiar gestures previously presented only by live trainers at tankside. The dolphins had no prior experience with any kind of photography, but were immediately able to understand the gestures on video, even on intentionally degraded video displays. The experimenters claimed that their experiment showed that with no prior learning, dolphins were able to interpret a television scene as a "representation" of a real-world event.[30]

The conclusions drawn here were imprecise, however. Like the previous experiments, this one provides evidence for the ability of photography to present the same type of visual information that would be available at the profilmic scene. If pigeons, dolphins, and other animals can glean basic visual information with no prior learning, it is likely that humans can as well. However, to say that the dolphins and pigeons see the slides and videotapes as "representations" of a real-world event would be hasty. To see the videotape as a representation would be to see it as a human artifact with a conventional function. This presumes that dolphins have an understanding that a two-dimensional display can represent a three-dimensional scene. Alternatively, it is possible that the animals suffer the illusion that when they view their slides and videotapes, they are actually viewing a three-dimensional scene. In other words, gleaning visual information from a video or slide does not necessarily imply an understanding of the source of visual information.

The ability to see photography *as representation* may be a unique human capability that depends on the dual perception J. J. Gibson describes. We see what the photograph is of, and simultaneously understand that it is a two-dimensional piece of paper, or a video monitor, or light on a screen. To see photographs as representations requires not only that we see them as veridical displays that carry potentially useful information, but that we recognize some of the contextual factors that make the photograph a means of communication rather than (what the dolphin might mistake for) a hand gesturing from within a box. Though education plays an essential role in the sophistication with which we approach visual communication, most humans are aware that the images they see are not three-dimensional reality, but a purposive human communication.

Icons and Veridical Information

The most important conclusion to be drawn is the following: we do not need to learn to recognize objects in typical photographs; for sighted persons, that comes naturally, because photographic images can display the same type of information as that available at the profilmic scene, and make use of many of the same perceptual skills we develop to perceive the natural environment. The alternative view – the conventionalist theory of photography – contends that photographs communicate much like a verbal language, via symbols that have conventionally come to represent objects and concepts, and bear an arbitrary relationship with their referents. Thus we must learn to "read" photographs just as we learn to read printed language. Although many complex aspects of photographic communication must be learned, the conventionalist theory cannot be wholly correct, unless it can somehow account for the ability of animals to learn this "language" of photography, given their lack of formal schooling.

Using photography as a tool for the communication of information has some disadvantages. It may be that spectators are too hasty to draw conclusions from what they see in moving pictures. Moreover, visual information often misses subtle, unseen elements of an event, and cannot account for human motivation or causal relationships. This became especially apparent in the case of the Rodney King video because, though the video clearly showed the man's beating, it remained mute about his or the policemen's intentions and motivations. In addition, the camera witnesses events from one angle, and rarely gives its information with such clarity that multiple interpretations are not possible.

Nonetheless, the positive consequences of this iconic bond between image and referent are many. Although visual data is but one type of information about the world, nonfiction films are particularly well suited to communicate that data. Any visual element of the world can be more efficiently communicated through the nonfiction film than through verbal language. For example, verbal language may describe the social behavior of the leopard, but the nature documentary *shows* us their sleek coats and nimble movements. We may read about Adolph Hitler's speaking style, and of his rapport with audiences, but seeing film clips of Hitler speaking at Nazi Party rallies in Leni Riefenstahl's *Triumph of the Will* (*Triumph des Willens*, 1935) is a frightening experience that can communicate that information more fully and powerfully. Viewing Michael Wadleigh's *Woodstock* (1970) gives a good sense of the performances at the Woodstock festival and the dress and behavior of the crowds. The 8 mm Zapruder footage of John Kennedy's assassination provides a stark and almost unbearable record of that horrific event. The iconic moving photograph has become an essential means of historical record-keeping and the dissemination of information. While recognizing its limitations, we can also celebrate its unprecedented ability to convey visual information of unlimited variety and rich detail.

Nevertheless, iconic resemblance is not always required of nonfiction cinematography. Though iconic images can give reliable information, it may actually benefit the photographer to distort or alter the photograph to reveal some aspect of the profilmic scene. The photographer might want to photograph a scene or event in a manner foreign to natural perception in important respects. The inventor Eadweard Muybridge, for example, wondered whether when a horse gallops, its feet all leave the ground simultaneously. To discover this he took a series of still pictures (of a horse galloping) at intervals along the horse track. One of these photographs clearly shows all of the horse's feet simultaneously airborne. Thus he used the photograph to prove something difficult to perceive through natural perception. The camera can also use slow motion, telephoto and wide angle lenses, various film stocks, and other devices to provide veridical information about the scene in front of it. The image at times bears an iconic resemblance to the profilmic scene. However, maximizing iconic resemblance does not necessarily yield pertinent veridical information. As we shall see in the next chapter, what makes photographic communication unique and powerful is not only its iconicity, but also its use as an indexical sign of its referent.

CHAPTER 4

Indices and the Uses of Images

Paintings can function as iconic signs just as photographs can, for like photographs, paintings can provide accurate visual information with a marked perceptual realism. Photographic realists, for example, produce paintings that resemble photographs in their intricate visual detail. However, the painter's image is wholly the product of the painter's art, whereas the photographer's image is her product only in part. The camera, which gathers and records patterns of light on the film stock, is the co-producer of the photographic image. Unlike the painting, the photograph is in part the product of a series of mechanical cause-and-effect operations performed in and through a camera. Insofar as those causal relations are governed by physical laws, are discoverable, and can be specified, they allow us to impart a veracity to photographs that we do not to a painting. When we watch the Holliday video of Rodney King's beating, for example, the veracity of its record is independent of questions about the videomaker's biography and intentions. The relevant factor is that a normally-functioning video camera recorded those events according to the protocols by which the machine was designed.

In special circumstances we might want to know about the person who made the recording. For example, we would want to know if she or he had access to digital image processing equipment, or had intentionally used the camera in a misleading way. But in the absence of those special circumstances, it is the mechanical recording function of the camera that lends veracity and emotional power to the images produced. As Barry Keith Grant notes, when we see nonfiction images of the space shuttle Challenger exploding, or of a Vietnamese bonze's self-immolation, the horror is stronger because we understand the events recorded to be actual rather than fictional.[1] This veracity of the image stems from the fact that under specifiable conditions, the mechanical recording function of the camera makes human intentions less important than the automatic mechanisms which produced the picture.

This is the photograph in what C. S. Peirce calls its *indexical* aspect.[2]

Though André Bazin did not use the term "index," the causal relationship between photograph and profilmic scene is precisely what he emphasizes when he compares the photograph to moss-covered ruins or to a fingerprint.[3] This enables us, as Stanley Cavell notes, to ask questions of photographs that would be peculiar in reference to paintings.[4] For example, we can ask about what is behind a subject, or what is adjacent to it off-screen.

Images and Evidence

The photograph's status as an index is also a matter of controversy. Joel Snyder and Neil Walsh Allen, for example, say that the mechanical nature of photography never *guarantees* that it will provide clear evidence. They note several examples of types of photography, such as infrared photography, where the visual evidence is difficult to apprehend, and other examples of photographs that provide only ambiguous evidence about their referents. They write:

In all these cases, the picture is valuable as an index of the truth only to the extent that the process by which it is made is stated explicitly, and the pictures can be interpreted accurately only by people who have learned how to interpret them. . . . Needless to say, the explicitness that provides guarantees to the scientist is rarely demanded of most photographs we see, and if demanded couldn't be provided, and if provided wouldn't explain much anyway.[5]

Furthermore, the authors claim, the mechanical workings of photography become submerged under the numerous "requirements" for making "acceptable" pictures, and "simple mechanical procedures must be augmented by additional processes [such as pointing the camera at the relevant subject] to produce a number of different degrees and kinds of acceptability."[6]

Those who wish to defend the photograph's indexicality might respond that Snyder and Allen set up a straw man, then knock him down. To claim indexicality for photography, we need not assert that photography *guarantees* evidence, or that *every* photograph has evidential force. Of course, to yield useful information or evidence, a film or video shot must meet certain requirements. One can easily find counterexamples to the claim that photographs yield veridical information; one example would be J. J. Murphy's *Print Generation* (1974), in which shots have been reprinted to the extent that they have become almost abstract. However, such counterexamples would have force only to the claim that *all* photographs yield veridical information. I do not say that photographs *necessarily* give the evidence we want or need, but that under certain conditions, photographs are able to yield such information. Snyder and Allen say that the mechanical nature of photography is submerged under the subjective requirements of the photographer or filmmaker. Of course, we must account for subjectivity in interpreting any photography. Nonetheless, as I suggested with regard to the Rodney King video, some photography escapes and transcends the intentions of the videographer or photographer.

The most interesting point made by Snyder and Allen is that photographs have no value as indices because to have such value, the spectator would need to be aware of the physical processes involved in producing the photographs. This is true, if we are to require that indexical photography meet the same standards as scientific or legal evidence. In U.S. federal court, photographs must generally satisfy three conditions to be admitted as evidence: 1) they must depict information relevant to the issues in dispute, 2) they must be shown to be "true and accurate" representations, and 3) their value in establishing matters of fact should not be outweighed by their gruesomeness or inflammatory character (which may unduly influence a jury).

How can a photograph be shown to be "true" and "accurate," according to the practices of criminal law? Three factors are vital here. First, it must be shown that the photograph has not been retouched, enhanced, subject to digital image processing, or tampered with in any way. Second, a photograph or videotape is only admitted in tandem with a "testimonial sponsor," normally the person who operated the camera, but in some cases extending to a witness who can testify that the film or videotape provides an accurate representation of the event it records. Any photograph or film without such a testimonial sponsor will be considered hearsay. Third, a photograph is considered "true and accurate" only within a specific context. The records police photographers are advised to keep illustrate the contextual factors that the courts require:

... details concerning date, time, other officers present, location described with particularity, type of film [stock], camera, and lens used, exposure, lens opening, and any other relevant information. After development and printing, the photographer will be able to complement the photographic record with information about the types of chemicals, papers, and equipment used in the darkroom.[7]

The point is not that scientific or legal evidence meets some perfect standard of objectivity. Rather, it is that photographs, as they function in nonfiction films, rarely meet even these requirements. No "testimonial sponsor" appears to vouch for the accuracy of the photography or the absence of retouching or image enhancement. We can only rely on the producer(s)' reputation, and must admit that we have no final assurance that all of the film's images accurately portray the filmed events. Moreover, we typically have little information about the contextual factors important in treating images as legal evidence. We know little of the film stock or camera type, shooting ratio and editing decisions, or the time or date the various shots were taken.

If indexicality depends on the kind of evidence required in the criminal courts, then clearly it is in trouble. The typical nonfiction film offers no photographic evidence that would by itself satisfy the courts. However, in a nonfiction film, our criteria for what counts as evidence need not be so strict. Were we to demand such evidence before we assented to any discourse, we could believe nothing we see and hear. The type of evidence a nonfiction film offers is rhetorical, and its proof "artistic" rather than legal, scientific, or logical.

We may further qualify the nature of photographic evidence by recognizing Roland Barthes' distinction between the photograph's *denotations* and *connotations*. On the one hand, Barthes claims that the photographic image is a message "without a code." On the purely denotative level, it is an analog of the profilmic scene. Barthes says that photography produced a new sort of consciousness, of the *having-been-there* of the thing represented. The image provides evidence because it denotes that certain events occurred, and occurred in a certain way. On the other hand, no photograph used for communication exists purely as denotation; all carry heavy connotational meaning. This "photographic paradox" makes images a rhetorically powerful means of communication, because, for Barthes, the "denotated image naturalizes the symbolic message, it innocents the semantic artifice of connotation, which is extremely dense."[8]

Consider *The Thin Blue Line*, in which director Errol Morris films interviews with Randall Adams and David Harris. The film effectively shows that David Harris is guilty of the policeman's murder, for which Adams has been wrongly sentenced to death. The interviews denote the men speaking (together with their facial expressions, gestures, clothing, etc.), and the recorded sound denotes what they say.[9] However, the staging of the interviews is remarkable for its connotations. David Harris wears red, and the space behind him is bathed in reddish-orange light, whereas Randall Adams wears a bright and clean white, and the background light is relatively colorless. Although in this case the use of color marks the correct men as guilty and innocent, it may still be too easy, as Barthes would say, to allow the denotative force of the image to mask the artificiality, or connotative use, of staging and light.

We must also recognize the kind of evidence moving images provide, together with their dependence on contextual information and the perceived reliability of their source. Consider the scene in Frederick Wiseman's *High School*, in which an adult hall monitor speaks abruptly and rudely to a student who talks on a public telephone in the school corridor. The hall monitor acts as though the student is cutting class, while the student claims that the call is an emergency call. If we assume that Wiseman's editing is not misleading (and this determination depends on our opinion of Wiseman, among other factors), this scene is evidence that such an event occurred. (A drawing or verbal description could not provide the same evidential force.) However, the scene provides insufficient evidence to show that the hall monitor is a "rude man," for the scene by itself gives us no context for the event, and little understanding of the motivations of the monitor or the student. Has the monitor had an especially bad day, causing him to be rude when he normally is courteous? Is the student a repeat offender, often skipping class to talk to a friend on the telephone, or is he merely conducting some emergency business, as he says? None of this is disclosed by the photographed scene itself. Fuller information about the events depicted in this scene requires contextual information absent from the moving photographs. To meet the requirements for rhetorical (as well as legal) evidence, the image must be given a context, and the discourse should be presented by an individual or institutional source considered credible.

Photographic evidence is often ambiguous because *seeing itself* is ambiguous and subject to interpretation. Consider the famous Vietnam War photograph of terrified Vietnamese children running toward the camera after a napalm attack on their village. Prominent in the frame is a crying naked girl, whose burned flesh hangs from her arms. General William Westmoreland cynically proposed that her burns may have been caused by "a hibachi accident."[10] Though the political motivations for Westmoreland's perverse interpretation of the photograph are apparent, they in no way challenge the iconicity or indexicality of the image. For iconicity and indexicality, as also in the case of the Rodney King video, hardly determine how the image can be interpreted as evidence. As Frank Tomasulo suggests in a recent paper, the phrase "I'll believe it when I see it" rings no more true than its converse: "I'll see it when I believe it."[11]

Photographic evidence in nonfiction films cannot be wholly discounted, but it is problematic. When we ask for evidence for a claim or implication, we would ideally like indisputable proof. Images used in nonfiction films rarely, if ever, provide such proof in themselves, apart from our independent knowledge of contextual and historical factors. It is a rhetorical "proof" that images indexical allow, perhaps a bit stronger than verbal evidence or an artist's rendition of a scene, but nonetheless subject to the same confusions, misrepresentations, and multiple interpretations that complicate any evidence. Although an indexical bond may exist between moving image and profilmic scene, we must approach that bond with a healthy skepticism about what it "shows" or "proves." Our assent to a film's claims or implications must depend on the image in relation to its context, the credibility of its source, and our independent evaluation of the film's rhetorical project and aims.

Digital Imaging and Photographic Evidence

The evidentiary status of still and moving photographs has met a new challenge in the rise of digital image processing. Digital imaging technology allows for the sometimes undetectable creation and/or manipulation of highly realistic visual images by computer technology, thus calling into question the causal nature of the photograph, and its status as indexical sign and visual evidence.

The typical contemporary camera, whether film or video, records information analogically; the newer digital systems either record information digitally in terms of configurations of binary numbers called digital bits, or translate analog photographs into digital information. The visual (and aural) information in a digital system is represented by some combination of 1s and 0s. Visual or aural information can be recorded, stored, altered, and transmitted digitally, providing a more powerful, flexible, and efficient means of information creation and transmission than the previous analog equipment. For example, a still photographer can take a photograph with a digital camera (that makes use of a silicon chip) and, via satellite, instantaneously transmit the digital information to a home base on the other side of the world. There the image can be altered and reproduced with none of the degradation that occurs with the copying of successive generations of analog media. However, for our purposes, the essential difference between analog and digital recording is the ease with which digital images can be manipulated and even fabricated wholesale.

Digital imaging technology makes it possible to significantly alter photographs via computer software; because the visual information is stored in the form of digital bits, simply changing their configuration alters the photograph. Although currently the available consumer-grade technology is complex, relatively expensive, and lacking adequate image resolution, in the future it may become possible to design and artificially fabricate (seemingly) veridical moving photographs at home. In addition – and this is an essential point – unless the digitally-produced photograph presents something absurd or patently impossible (such as Paula Abdul dancing with Fred Astaire), alterations may be undetectable; it may be very difficult, if not impossible, to distinguish between fabricated photographs and unmanipulated photographs of actual scenes.

Digital imaging technology is already commonly used for still photography by major magazines and journals, and this use has sparked widespread debate about the ethics of the technology. In 1982, for example, *National Geographic* moved one of Great Pyramids of Giza on a photograph to better fit its magazine cover. For its photo coverage of the 1984 Olympics, *The Orange County Register* regularly changed the color of the sky to a smog-free shade of blue.[12] *Time* recently apologized to readers for digitally darkening a mug shot of O.J. Simpson for its cover, initiating an amusing exchange of charges and counter-charges between *Time* and *Newsweek* spokespersons.[13] How long will it be before such seemingly innocent manipulations become fabrications of television documentaries for political purposes? Although at the time of this writing, only primitive and expensive forms of digital technology exist for television journalism, and the computer manipulation of moving pictures (as in colorization) is a slow and expensive process, it may soon be possible to manipulate digital moving images swiftly and inexpensively at the office and at home.

Digital imaging has significant implications for nonfiction film and video. Fears about the uses of digital imaging fall along three general lines. First, some claim that in light of this new technology, the indexical status of the photograph is forever banished. If so, digital imaging will revolutionize the uses of photography, just as the invention of photography changed the nature of painting. Second, digital techniques will encourage deceptive practices through the undetectable manipulation and wholesale fabrication of photograph-like images. Third, some argue that digital technologies will cause a loss of faith in the veridicality of all still and moving images, resulting in a loss of credibility for photojournalism and the documentary. An MIT Press advertisement for William J. Mitchell's *The Reconfigured Eye: Visual Truth in the Post-Photographic Era*, quotes Mitchell on the rise of digital imaging technology: "From this moment on, photography is dead – or, more precisely, radically and permanently redefined as was painting one hundred and fifty years before."[14] Brian Winston, similarly, claims that digital image processing "calls into radical question the entire mimetic status of the photographic image."[15]

Although the new technologies will have wide-ranging effects, we should nonetheless take hyperbolic pronouncements about the death of photography with a grain of salt. Remember that we've heard similar arguments in the past; pundits forecasted the death of film and movie-going after the introduction of videotape. We know now that rumors of the death of film were premature and greatly exaggerated. Inasmuch as the iconic nature of the photograph remains essential to its mimetic status, digital processing cannot threaten that; even paintings can function as icons. Only the indexical status of the photographic sign is threatened by digital image processing. Moreover, some talk as though the digital future had already arrived, but at least for most nonfiction filmmakers, present-day image recording and manipulation is still performed the old-fashioned way – with analog equipment. Although this may change (and quickly), current digital imaging technology holds little temptation for nonfiction filmmakers due to its expense, inefficiency, and inability to provide the resolution film affords. The digital manipulation of moving images is still prohibitively expensive; even for big-budget Hollywood features, digital manipulation is reserved for short segments of film. To preserve any acceptable resolution, digital manipulation requires massive amounts of computer memory; a single digital still image with photographic resolution carries 16 MB of information. At 24 frames per second, the amount of computer memory required for moving images becomes astronomical. Digital cameras improve every year, yet even for still cameras, cost is still a problem. Whereas top-range analog cameras cost roughly $2000, professional quality digital still cameras range upwards from $9000.[16] Moreover, whereas a frame of Kodachrome offers over 18 million pixels of information (and can be processed at about $10 per roll), the best current digital photography offers about 2 million pixels per frame. So long as nonfiction moving images are still recorded and manipulated on analog equipment, we need not worry about the potential manipulations of digital image processing.

In addition, the problems of the future can easily be exaggerated. In the case of deception, it is important to note that one *can* distinguish between analog and digital images; an image stored on film or videotape is analog, whereas one stored on a computer hard drive is digital. It *is* possible to record an image analogically on film or video, transfer the image to a digital medium, alter it, then transfer it back to analogical film or video. However, the process is time consuming and very expensive. For nonfiction filmmaking, the significance of digital image processing will become most apparent in the future, when (and if) all or most images are recorded digitally, digital equipment is readily available, and the presence of manipulation becomes virtually undetectable.

Some observers also assume that with the ascendancy of digital technology, analog technology will automatically become obsolete. If predictions about the new technology are correct, digital imaging will become an inexpensive, quick, and infinitely flexible means of manipulating visual information, antiquating the analog equipment and rendering it virtually useless. André Bazin argued that photography forever changed the nature of Western painting by freeing it, "once and for all, from its obsession with realism" and allowing it "to recover its aesthetic autonomy."[17] One might argue that digital image technology "freed" photography from its obsession with indexicality in much the same way.

However, the comparison is faulty. If Bazin is right, photography freed painting from its obsession with realism because photography can produce realistic images more efficiently and with more detail. In other words, photography performs that realist function better than painting. But digital technology doesn't enhance photographic indexicality; it threatens to destroy it. If we do value photography in part for its indexicality, that indexicality is precisely what digital imaging calls into question. If it *is* important that we be able to verify the veridicality of an image – if indexicality is one of the functions we value in documentary photography – then analog technology still has value. The mere presence of digital imaging technology does not imply that everyone must use it in every circumstance, especially if for some uses analog equipment is superior.

Critics are nonetheless right that digital image manipulation introduces new means of possible deception. It has *not* introduced manipulation and deception themselves, however. Cropping, retouching, arranging scenes, and other forms of manipulation have long existed in nonfiction photography. The fabrication of scenes for nonfiction films, for example, occurred in the earliest American newsreels, when Albert E. Smith and J. Stuart Blackton energized their lackluster footage of Teddy Roosevelt's charge up San Juan Hill with the staging of a table-top Battle of Santiago Bay. It has often been difficult to tell whether a documentary scene was arranged or manipulated by the filmmaker. Deception occurs more subtly as well. A carefully chosen angle, or in still photography, the right moment caught and preserved on film, can imply much that isn't actually true. Digital image processing does not *introduce* the possibility of manipulative uses of photography; it merely *extends* it.

Deception in digital imaging may be more problematic because in some cases it is undetectable. Yet the possibility of deception in no way implies that the viewer will believe anything, or that photography will lose its special status. Some claim that the supposed "scientific" status of the photograph causes us to unproblematically believe everything we see, or that with the invention of digital images, an "interlude of false innocence has passed."[18] Yet it is too easy to emphasize the sophistication of our postdigital epistemic condition by exaggerating the naiveté of past viewers. William Mitchell writes that for "a century and a half photographic evidence seemed unassailably probative."[19] I would speculate, however, that most spectators are more sophisticated than such arguments allow, and recognize at some level that no image tells its own story. We are all familiar enough with fantastical images in pulp magazines to know that photographs are not and have never been automatically veridical (though one can always find some poor soul who accepts them as truth). If the image is patently absurd or impossible, the typical viewer will be skeptical. Viewers rely on assessments of the context and source of the photography before automatically accepting what they see as the unproblematic truth. For example, think of conservative critics of the "liberal media." The photographic images Dan Rather shows them on the evening news will typically not alter their prior convictions.

Audiences often consider the source of the visual information before they make judgments about its reliability. For example, I have no proof that Frederick Wiseman didn't hire actors and arrange scenes in his film *Hospital* (1970), or that he didn't coach various doctors or patients to behave in certain ways. My belief that Wiseman remained as unobtrusive as possible in filming *Hospital* stems from his reputation and from my confidence that he followed certain protocols while making the film. Whatever one thinks of Wiseman, his methods will have the same force (or lack thereof) after the ascendance of digital image processing. If he forswears the use of digital equipment, we will have just as much trust in his images as we do presently. Digital imaging will require the future spectator to be even more cognizant of the integrity of a film's source. Increased vigilance in this case will be a welcome development.

Nonfiction-producing institutions and individual filmmakers must develop policies regarding the use of digital image processing, to distinguish between "cleaning up" images and using the technology to deceive. In print and magazine journalism, this has already begun. Many publications forbid the retouching or manipulation of news photographs; at some institutions an employee who ignores such prohibitions may be fired.[20] In television journalism, such policies will also be necessary. The Radio Television News Directors Association (RTNDA) passed a resolution in 1989 advising all "reality-based" programs "not [to] mislead the public by presenting as spontaneous news any material which is staged or rehearsed." The RTNDA also advised that any simulations or re-creations should be announced as such. We can expect that if and when digitally created images become common, such policies will be directed towards their use as well.[21]

My skepticism regarding the effects of the digital revolution is not to belittle the changes digital image processing may bring. When the technology becomes readily available, there will be ample opportunity to create manipulative and distorting visual images, and no doubt the propagandists, advertisers, zealots, practical jokers, and congresspersons will use all available means to achieve their purposes. Although institutional constraints may help to minimize the effects of digital manipulation of news and journalistic images, unscrupulous individuals and institutions will find ways to circumvent those constraints. Yet the changes digital processing brings are matters of degree, not of kind. As I have argued, the indexicality of image, problematic as it is (and always has been), will still be functional and available if a discursive community finds it useful.

Doing Things with Photographs

Indexical evidence becomes central when a film makes an explicit argument using images and sounds as evidence. *CBS Reports'* "Harvest of

Shame" (1960), for example, documents the degrading plight the nations' migrant farm workers, placing the blame squarely on the landowner/farmers, and advocating specific legislation to alleviate the problem. Filmed testimonials come from twenty-six persons, including migrant children and adults, men and women, blacks and whites, a crew chief, employers, police, government officials, journalists, lobbyists, students, and teachers. A filmed interview has several advantages over the merely verbal report. It offers evidence that the person before the camera said what she said (although questions of context must always inform our evaluation). The filmed interview allows us to *see* and *hear* the interviewee, giving us information about spatial context, gesture, facial expression, tone of voice, and inflection that could not come across in a written interview. The cameras of "Harvest of Shame" also provide direct photographic evidence; having recorded images of the homes and neighborhoods of the migrants, their poverty and poor living conditions are established.

In other nonfictions, however, the moving photograph provides uncontentious information, evidence only in a weak sense of the word. For his *35 Up*, Michael Apted filmed various English nationals at ages 7, 14, 21, 28, and 35, presenting a cross-section of English society and a complex view of differences in human development. One of the marvels of the moving image is its ability to transmit visual information in great detail. In the case of *35 Up*, we learn much about the subjects of the film, not only from what they say, but from how they look and their gestures, actions, voices, and vocal inflections. Here, as in nature films and instructional videos, for example, the use of recorded images and sounds is more *illustrative* than evidential, because the film makes no contentious argument.

Visual images in nonfictions function as icons and indices, but that is not all; they do more than give information, illustrate, and provide rhetorical evidence. The uses of images are diverse and limited only by the imagination of the filmmaker (and what her/his sponsors will allow). To discuss images only as icons and indices implies that their only importance is backward-directed, or in other words, that their function is to refer *back* to the profilmic event either in a relationship of resemblance or causality.

I mentioned in the introduction a pragmatics of nonfiction, in which one recognizes the multiplicity of uses to which nonfiction texts are put in the realm of human action. The same multiplicity of uses applies to individual images within specific texts. A picture can quickly reveal what could be described only with difficulty, even by the most talented writer. But any given picture (in conjunction with other factors) can be used in an indefinite number of ways to perform any number of illocutionary acts – to amuse or entertain, to inform, explain and identify, to arouse sexual passion, anger, or compassion, to energize to action, to criticize and analyze, to forecast the future, to account for the past, express a wish, give a warning, snub and ridicule, or lavish praise.

Consider again *The Thin Blue Line*. The film is structured as a series of edited interview segments, featuring several people, most prominently Adams and David Harris. Supplementing these interviews is a rhythmic, hypnotic musical score by Phillip Glass, and a wealth of visual images that perform varied functions. Images in *The Thin Blue Line* are often evocative or expressive, rather than informative. They do not primarily refer to the profilmic event, but contribute to the rhetorical purpose of the film. The first image features an odd ball of lights atop an enormous building, followed by long shots of other Dallas high-rises at night. The camera distance and angle make the images function not so much to establish the Dallas setting, but as a means of "making strange" that urban environment. The shot compositions suggest less the urban skyline than the gothic horror of the hulking forms and the rhythmic blinking of their night lights. Dallas becomes an alien environment, and the buildings representations of monolithic institutions that might kill an innocent man. This corresponds with the eerie Glass music, and with Adams and Harris talking about their fateful meeting on the night of the murder in Dallas. The scene establishes a sense of the uncanny that Morris sustains throughout.

Morris also uses images to evoke ironic humor. On the night of the murder, Adams and Harris attended a drive-in movie together, an R-rated "cheerleader" film. To illustrate Adams' testimony, Morris re-creates the scene, alternating shots of "Adams" and "Harris" sitting in their car – guzzling beer and smoking cigarettes – with scenes from the actual movie. This isn't an especially important element of Randall Adams' testimony, but Morris draws it out to linger on a particularly inept scene from the film, featuring dismal acting and laughable dialogue.

Morris's images also contribute to the theme. The film provides typical illustrative shots of newspaper headlines, police photographs, maps, and court diagrams. However, Morris's use of illustrative cut-ins usually serves an expressive rather than informational function. For example, authorities hypnotize the murdered policeman's partner in an attempt to obtain more complete information from her. To illustrate the hypnotism, the film shows a close up of a pocket watch on a chain, as it swings rhythmically from side to side. As we hear testimony about a pistol, we see a drawing of a pistol, rotating slightly as we watch. We see extreme close-ups of clock hands that mark the slow passage of time, the rotating light atop a police car, newspaper reports, and a typewriter typing, all filmed in extreme close-up. In each case, the shots give no information unavailable in the testimony, but establish a feel of contextless detail; they support Morris's thematic points about flawed memory and the veil with which time covers past events. Again, these visual images do not function as information, but as the expression of style and as a contribution to the themes developed by the film.

Morris also presents staged recreations of both the murder and the interrogation of Randall Adams. Staged scenes show the murder of the policeman, Randall Adams' interrogation, and other events of the evening of the murder. The recreations in *The Thin Blue Line* are illustrations of the testimonies of various persons interviewed, and the recreated accounts of the murder sometimes conflict in their details, depending on who tells the story. They do not function as information so much as the illustration of testimony, from which the film often withholds assent or support.

For *The Thin Blue Line* to succeed in establishing Randall Adams' innocence, we would expect at least *some* visual evidence, and we do get it. The evidential strength of Morris's film stems from the quality and force of the interviews he presents in *The Thin Blue Line*. Of course, here the evidence comes from the recorded voice as much as from the visual image. In fact, Morris was able to get his most important interview – one in which Harris more or less admits his guilt – only on audio tape. Although these interviews constitute powerful evidence, the case for Adams' innocence that Morris presents depends on his *organization of materials* as much as on any single interview. A documentary is more than the sum of its documents.

Although the image can function as a form of visual evidence, that is but one of its many functions, and one that has often been exaggerated. Although the image may refer back to the profilmic scene as an icon and index, it may also serve diverse other functions.

Making Claims with Photographs

The film medium excels at the cinematographic equivalent of description – *observation*. It can represent the visual and sonic qualities of the world to our senses as could no medium before it. But can the image alone – or sequences of images – communicate abstract propositions and make conceptual arguments without words? The Soviet filmmaker Sergei Eisenstein thought that it could, and devised a form of editing – "intellectual montage" – to communicate or argue for abstract propositions. As he put it, intellectual montage consists of the "conflict-juxta-position of . . . intellectual affects" that accompany any film shot.[22] Eisenstein hoped to develop an intellectual cinema that would unite the physiological and intellectual effects of montage; he hoped eventually to film Karl Marx's *Das Capital*, but never realized that dream.

As an example of intellectual montage, consider the "God and Coun-try" sequence in Eisenstein's *October* (1928). There we first see icons of Mary and Jesus, then Russian Orthodox icons, then gradually the grotesque artifacts and figurines of earlier, more "primitive" religions. Among other things, the sequence implies claims about the origins of re-ligion by tracing contemporary religious icons back to earlier and earli-er religious idols; the point, Eisenstein suggests, is that religion has its roots in pantheistic beliefs about a universe inhabited by spirits and monsters. The implication is that this "opiate of the people" must be dis-carded for the state atheism of Soviet Communism. Here the proposi-tional content is communicated through images alone. However, it relies on the spectator to make the explicit inferences it implies, and to draw the appropriate comparisons between the various images shown.

Although few spectators would miss the point of the sequence, the same conceptual argument could be communicated more efficiently, if perhaps less powerfully, through words. And words could make *explic-it* the connections and conclusions that remain *implicit* in the sequence; film images alone may imply or suggest propositions, but cannot assert them with the directness of verbal language. Film without words can communicate conceptual information, but cannot match the efficiency, intricacy, directness, nuance, and complexity of argument that words allow.

The image by itself is rather indeterminate and ambiguous, and makes no particular claims. Photographs by themselves cannot be translated into specific sentences. A picture of a dog, for example, might be thought to mean at least, "Here is a dog." But it could also mean, "This dog is sitting," or "Mangy dogs sit a lot," or "This is what an adult Boxer looks like in profile." Moreover, how can we be sure that the photograph is meant to depict a particular dog, or a particular breed, or the general class, "dog," or even "a furry beast"?[23]

A photograph's intended function and meaning is interpretable only in relation to three factors: its (1) conventional use, (2) linguistic accompaniment, and (3) context.[24] In the case of nonfictions, the conventional *use*, when recognized by the audience, in part determines their prior expectations and how they approach the image. For example, the meaning of an image depends on whether the images and text have been indexed as fiction or nonfiction. Consider the famous scene in Hitchcock's *North by Northwest* (1960), where Roger O. Thornhill (played by Cary Grant) is pursued by a crop-dusting plane. Within the context of the film, the images do not refer to Cary Grant running from a plane, but to Thornhill, a fictional character. However, one could also edit this scene into a filmed biography about Cary Grant's acting career. In this hypothetical film, as the crop dusting sequence unfolds, the voice-over narrator describes Grant's acting technique. In this case, the audience sees the images differently, according to the assertive stance taken toward the states of affairs presented. We see Cary Grant *playing* Thornhill running from a plane, and the image is used to illustrate information about Cary Grant, not to refer to the imaginary character Thornhill. The recognition of conventional use also helps audiences to determine whether the image portrays a particular or a class, or is meant to function as accurate portrayal or whimsical fantasy (as in the Pepsi commercial where Paula Abdul appears with Cary Grant through digital imaging).

Linguistic accompaniment also determines meaning; in nonfiction films, this occurs primarily through voice-over narration, interviews, recorded speech of other kinds, or printed titles. Perhaps the best illustration of linguistic accompaniment occurs in Chris Marker's *Letter from Siberia*. There we see three times the same visual sequence showing a group of men building a road, each time with an alternative voice-over narration. The first narrator takes the Soviet "party line," boasting of the modern city of Yakutsk and describing the "happy Soviet workers," whereas the second, like a capitalist propagandist, speaks of Yakutsk as a "dark city with an evil reputation," and the workers as "miserable" and "slaves." The third narrator feigns objectivity, asserting the "courage and tenacity" of the workers who "apply themselves to improving the appearance of their city, which could certainly use it."[25]

Roland Barthes goes some way toward describing the functions of linguistic accompaniment in his discussion of *anchorage* and *relay*. Barthes notes that Western culture is sometimes thought of as an image culture, but that in truth images are rarely presented in isolation from verbal discourse. Barthes claims that the verbal text accompanying press photographs never simply duplicates the image, but adds to or narrows the meanings already present. He terms two major functions of the linguistic message in relation to the iconic, photographic message as *anchorage* and *relay*.

If I see a photograph depicting a man on a park bench, I can attend to any of the almost limitless aspects of the image – the man's posture, hairstyle, age, the size of his ears, his clothing, the parrot on his shoulder, the figure lurking in the nearby bushes, etc. One function of the linguistic message is to anchor or fix the photograph's meaning: "the text *directs* the reader through the signifieds of the image, causing him to avoid some and receive others; by means of an often subtle *dispatching*, it remote-controls him toward a meaning chosen in advance."[26] Anchorage directs the viewer's attention toward those meanings of the image favored by the text's producer. The second broad function of the linguistic text is *relay*. Here the verbal text sets out meanings not found in the image itself, and relates these to a higher level of meaning. Thus the unity of the message is realized at that higher level. Although Barthes means these observations to apply to print journalism and still photography, they apply equally well to the nonfiction film in relation to voice-over narration and informational titles. Linguistic text often accompanies nonfiction photographs, and explicitly makes the claims of the text.

The third element that determines photographic meaning is *context*. The intended meaning of a moving image depends on its placement within a textual whole, in relation to the other images and sounds that make up the text. Through conventional use, linguistic accompaniment, and context, images can be used to convey clear-cut messages that could (roughly) be translated into words. They can be used to express propositions, or in other words, to indicate a subject and attribute certain properties to it. Pictures do not mean or function by virtue of their internal characteristics alone, but always in relation to their conventional use in a particular context.[27]

Despite this, the real value of moving photographs may be their capacity to provide information unavailable by any other means, and with a force unique to photography. Whereas the context of the image directs the spectator toward preferred meanings (via diverse discursive strategies), the image often exceeds that, providing details that are extraneous to the text's purposes. This complexity may account for some of the fascination we have with images, because they offer a plenitude that escapes the intentions of their users.

The Soundtrack and Sonic Information

So far I have ignored that second discrete element of nonfiction films, the soundtrack.[28] By discussing sound here, at the end of the chapter, I do not mean to minimize its importance. It is rather that a discussion of the use of images remains more clear when conducted separately. For now, in relation to what I have said about the photographic image, we might ask the following question: Is it possible for sounds to function as icons and indices, as I have argued it is for photographic images?

Sounds in films can be characterized across two dimensions – whether they are diegetic or nondiegetic, and according to the type of sound. The diegesis, of course, is the "world" of the film, inhabited by its characters, furnished with its settings, and in which events unfold through time. Diegetic sounds are those portrayed as emanating from the profilmic scene, such as *voices*, *birds singing*, or the *sounds* of heavy machinery. A nondiegetic sound is purely discursive, not motivated by realism but "added on" as discursive commentary or accompaniment. Examples of nondiegetic sound include voice-over narration and music not emanating from a source in the profilmic scene.

Kinds of sounds include sound effects, spoken words, and music. All three can be either diegetic or nondiegetic. For example, spoken words can emanate from an on-screen narrator (such as the *See It Now* broadcasts with Edward R. Murrow) or from a voice-over narrator (as in the newsreel *The March of Time* or many *Frontline* documentaries). Music can be recorded at the scene of the profilmic event, as in music recorded at concerts in *Gimme Shelter* (1970) or *The Last Waltz* (1978), or added as narrational accompaniment, as is Benjamin Britten's music for *Night Mail* or Philip Glass's in *The Thin Blue Line*. Sound effects, including all ambient sounds except narrating voices, are typically diegetic, although in principle sound effects could be used as discursive comment on a scene as well, without being taken as emanating from the profilmic scene.

My first question is whether sounds in nonfiction films can resemble the sounds they represent, and function as icons. Thus I am here interested in diegetic sounds of any of the three types listed. Can the recorded voice *sound like* the actual voice? Does recorded music *sound like* the original music? Do sound effects in nonfiction films *sound like* the sounds they represent, or can they under certain conditions? Or, conversely, are film sounds related to the sounds they represent only by arbitrary convention, determined by sound recording and reproduction practices?

Before deciding whether a recorded (and played back) sound can resemble the original sound, we must first decide what a sound is, or at least, how to think about sounds. Some theorists, Alan Williams points out, think of the image as a *representation*, whereas the soundtrack is thought to be a *reproduction* of the original sound recorded: "From this point of view, sound recording would seem to be capable of providing a literal replica of the 'real' events that served as the 'original' raw material; it would not reduce them or change in any way their nature. . . ."[29] Williams claims that since sound recording is a conventional signifying practice, the soundtrack represents, rather than reproduces, the aural event it signifies.

We can agree that the use of sound in the nonfiction film is a signifying practice, but at the same time hold that many recorded sounds resemble the original in significant respects, as images can resemble the profilmic scene. Williams argues against the iconicity of recorded sounds by defining sound in such a way that it incorporates its entire three-dimensional environment. For Williams, a sound is "the entire volume of air that vibrates during a sonic event; the volume and its vibration, and nothing less, must be termed the 'sound' in question."[30] This implies that a sound can never be thought of as independent of the environment from which it comes; it is a three-dimensional, material event, in principle unreproduceable. According to Williams, one can never record the sound as a whole, but only a sample of it. Thus, a recording can never reproduce a sound, because recordings are not *of* three-dimensional environments.

This account of the ontology of sound has a serious drawback, however. For if we define sound as a three-dimensional event, not only is it impossible to record a sound as a whole, but no human can *hear* such a sound either. If the sound recorder records only a sampling and not the sound itself, that is also what the human ear hears. To define a sound in such a way that the human ear cannot hear it is unhelpful.

Better would be a definition of sound as a sampling of vibrations – with all their complex and minute variations – within a three dimensional environment; then a sound becomes, logically enough, a physical event that the human ear samples, or a machine records and plays back. A recorded sound, then, can function as an icon in much the same way that an image can. Both are recordings of physical events in an environment, and may bear a relationship of resemblance with some aspect(s) of that environment.[31] Yet both *represent* the original scene and/or sound and should not be confused with it.

The relationship between the original and recorded sound may be one of resemblance if the sounds share physical characteristics. Sounds have physical qualities such as pitch, loudness, and duration. In addition, as J.J. Gibson notes, the characteristics of a sound can be described in more complex ways:

Instead of simple duration, [sounds] vary in abruptness of beginning and ending, in repetitiveness, in rate, in regularity of rate, or rhythm, and in other subtleties of sequence. Instead of simple pitch, they vary in timbre and tone quality, in combinations of tone quality, in vowel quality, in approximation to noise, in noise quality, and in changes of all these in time. Instead of simple loudness, they vary in the direction of change of loudness, the rate of change of loudness, and the rate of *change* of change of loudness.[32]

Gibson notes that the human auditory system is capable of distinguishing among these variables, and that these variables are found in the source of the sound:

... it is just these variables that are specific to the source of the sound – the variables that identify the wind in the trees or the rushing of water, the cry of the young or the call of the mother. The sounds of *rubbing, scraping, rolling,* and *brushing*, for example, are distinctive acoustically and are distinguished phenomenally.[33]

Although Gibson has written at length about photographs and other visual images, he neglected to write about sound recordings. However, certain similarities between images and sound recordings are apparent. Just as the photograph can record the look of a scene (parts of its ambient array of light), the sound recording may preserve some of the physical characteristics of the original sound. In order for a recorded sound to sound like a typical American car horn, for example, it must preserve, enhance, or imitate some of its distinguishing characteristics, for example, its abruptness, its timbre, and its rate of change of loudness at the beginning and end of the sound. A recorded sound, barring extreme manipulation, will sound like the original in some, but probably not all, respects, just as a photograph cannot preserve all of the visual information available at the profilmic scene.

Yet, as Williams points out, sound recording is still a signifying practice because nearly all of the sorts of manipulations possible in image recording have counterparts in sound.[34] The sound recorder can manipulate volume, sound perspective (analogous to camera distance and angle), and with an equalizer can change various of its physical aspects. In addition, sounds are not only recorded (or manufactured), but placed within a textual system for certain rhetorical purposes. Although recorded sounds may sound like the original sound, there is no *guarantee* that they will. Even if they do, that in itself cannot fully account for their meaning within the text. It is in these senses that sound recording is expressive rather than simply imitative, and for this reason we need detailed analyses of different strategies of sound use.

For example, the sounds of some nonfiction films are wholly constructed by sound technicians, and do not originate from a source in the profilmic scene. For his World War II documentary *The Battle of Midway* (1944), John Ford procured the services of Hollywood technician Phil Scott. The sound track of the battle scene, for example, consists solely of diegetic sound effects. We hear the droning of airplane engines, machine guns firing, fires roaring, and explosions. At one point we hear the high-pitched sound of metal breaking as some anti-aircraft fire hits a plane, and splashing as the plane plummets into the ocean. The sound effects are believable, adding excitement to some otherwise uninteresting footage. Yet all of the sound in the film, including that for the battle scene, was constructed by Scott in postproduction.[35]

Such sounds, although constructed, may resemble in some respects similar sounds in an actual environment. A sound may be iconic without indexicality, as a photorealist painting may be. A constructed sound sometimes resembles that which it represents in sharing certain of the original's physical characteristics. It is true that a distorted or enhanced sound may sound more "realistic" to a listener due to conventions of sound reproduction (a clear example is the sound of the gunshot). Nonetheless, even after years of sound practice, we cannot substitute the physical characteristics of a cat's meow for the sound of a nuclear explosion, nor the characteristics of a baby crying for the sound of an internal combustion engine, because they do not sound alike. Even in conventional signifying practice, certain of a sound's physical characteristics must be preserved for an audience to recognize what the sound signifies.

For certain nonfiction films, the indexical aspects of the recorded sounds have special importance. *From Mao to Mozart*, for example, shows violinist Isaac Stern's travels to China. Stern notes that while many young Chinese musicians are superior technically, they lack an understanding of the "emotion" behind Western music. Scenes of Chinese musicians playing illustrate Stern's contentions and underscore the indexical importance of sound here (and the importance of veridical, informative images). In a film such as this, we want to know that the music functions as an indexical sign for the original music recorded, just as we require indexicality of the interviews so important in *The Thin Blue Line*. In these cases, the indexical link gives us more confidence that the films' claims and implications are accurate.

In many films, however, the strands of sound and image denotation tend to disappear within the dense fabric of the discourse. As with the image, considerations of iconicity and indexicality are sometimes beside the point, for the denotative aspects of the image and sounds may carry little weight in comparison with the work of conventional use and context. When the particular image or sound becomes situated within the broader context of the textual whole, overarching communicative and rhetorical functions may submerge the informational qualities of the shot or sound.

Images and Sounds in Context

As this chapter concludes, it is important to specify what I am *not* claiming. I am not making the vague claim that photographs or sounds show us reality, or the past, "as it really is." Individual shots or sounds may give us the same type of information that the spectator could have received, were she a stand-in for the camera or sound recorder. But the information is incomplete and often inferior in several respects, as I noted above. In addition, all visual and sonic information taken from the nonfiction film must be interpreted (1) in relation to its source and (2) in relation to its conventional use and context. For example, the photographic images in *Triumph of the Will* are veridical in the sense that they reveal some of the visual information that would have been available to an observer standing in for the camera. Without a knowledge of the production history and the context of the film, however, one would have an inadequate understanding of that visual information. We would have no knowledge of the purposes of Nazi party rallies, or of the extent to which the events photographed were arranged for the benefit of the camera. The rhetorical *use* of the shot in nonfiction films often overrides considerations of the shot as pure visual information.

Furthermore, as should be clear by now, I am not claiming that photography and sound recording are transparent and unmediated. Although we do not need to learn to recognize objects in photographs, we *do* need to learn the uses of photographs within the context of visual communication, as representations with diverse functions and purposes. That which is "natural" about the photograph and sound recording has various "conventional" uses, and we must recognize the play between them. What *is* conventional must be foundational for a rhetoric of visual and sonic communication. We must investigate when photographs and sound recordings, by their veridical nature, can be considered evidence within the context of a film, and when the indexical "artistic proof" they theoretically provide breaks down. We must explore the diverse *other* uses of photographs and sounds within the context of the nonfiction film.

Last, I do not claim that photography and sound recording escape ideology. On the contrary, it is that bond between the image, sound, and the profilmic event that can mislead audiences into too easily assenting to a film's claims. For example, a presidential candidate may use a still or moving photograph of an opponent in a political advertisement on television. The photograph may be veridical, in that it gives some accurate visual information about how the opponent looks. Yet that in no way lessens the importance of noticing that the photograph is from a high angle (making her look small), happens to capture an uncharacteristic grimace on her face (making her seem unpleasant), and that the candidate fails to stand out from a confusing, jumbled background (giving the viewer an uncomfortable sensation). Thus the photograph is veridical in some respects, yet rhetorical (and deceptive) in others.

Conventionalists often assume that to claim a physical resemblance between image, sound, and profilmic scene diminishes the function of ideology. I argue that to the contrary, it is precisely that possible veridical bond between image, sound, and referent that can foster an easy assent on the part of the viewer, can cause us to overlook the rhetorical strategies of a film, and in general makes photography and sound recording in the nonfiction film more potentially misleading, not less. There is no single ideological function or effect of photography and sound recording in the nonfiction film; both can be superficial or informative, veridical or misleading, depending on their specific use and context. Theory cannot predict in advance, independent of historical context, the ideological effect of images.

If film is a language, the language of film lies in those aspects of visual and aural communication that are conventional, in the means by which despite their possible veridical ties to the actual scene, shots and sounds can be manipulated for various purposes. In choosing a film stock, for example, the producer weighs varying degrees of graininess and sharpness, different responses to color, various exposure latitudes, and sensitivities to light. Filters influence color and contrast, whereas lenses of varied focal lengths change the apparent spatial relationships between elements of the image. Focus may be deep or shallow, exposure manipulated, and camera height and angle varied. The camera operator must choose a camera distance between camera and subject. The filmmaker may arrange the spatial layout or look of the profilmic scene by moving objects or persons or using artificial light. In short, although photography may present visual information similar to that available at the profilmic scene, there are ample opportunities to manipulate not only the scene itself but the way it is photographed. This has not yet touched on the importance of the textual context in which the photographed shot is used. Similar claims could be made for sound recording.

Though we may "see through" photographs (or "hear through" recorded sounds), this is at best a partial description of the use of photography and sound in nonfictional communication. A critical consideration of the uses of photography and sound never blithely accepts photographs and recorded sounds as neutral representations, but subjects them, in context, to scrutiny and interpretation. Photographs and sounds may present veridical visual and aural information, but they may also be highly misleading. There is nothing automatic about photographic communication or sound recording, nothing preordained or independent of specific context. Equipped with a general knowledge of the potential of images and sounds, we must nonetheless examine their particular uses, in particular contexts.

CHAPTER 5

Nonfiction Discourse

Despite their importance, it is easy to overestimate the significance of iconic and indexical representation. As many compilation films have shown, the same image – say of goose-stepping Nazi soldiers – can be used for diverse purposes. The fact that the image gives iconic visual information and has indexical force never exhausts the connotative and symbolic uses to which it can be put. Both images and sounds operate within a global textual system that often overrides denotational aspects, or even gives contrary significance to meanings the elements might have in isolation.

The surface features of the nonfiction film – particular moving images or sounds – gain meaning in relation to deeper strands of textual organization. Images are surrounded by that which come before and after, and are accompanied by voice-over narration, music, and/or ambient sound. The nonfiction film enables understanding only to the degree that it puts images and sounds into a meaningful sequence. As Susan Sontag writes:

Photography implies that we know about the world if we accept it as the camera records it. But this is the opposite of understanding, which starts from *not* accepting the world as it looks. . . . In contrast to the amorous relation, which is based on how something looks, understanding is based on how it functions. And functioning takes place in time, and must be explained in time. Only that which narrates can make us understand.[1]

To investigate nonfiction film rhetoric is in part to explore the complex web of signification of which images and sounds are a part; this is nonfiction film discourse.

Discourse and Projected World

A film's discourse is its formal *presentation*, in narrative, rhetorical, associational, categorical, or abstract form – or a mixture of forms.[2] Although actual content is never devoid of form, the form/content distinction is theoretically useful because it allows us to distinguish between *what* is represented and *how* it is represented. It also shows how similar subjects can be represented in different ways. Narrative theory nearly always distinguishes between a *what* and a *how*. Any work of narrative fiction gives us a story and the telling of the story, a distinction borne out in the narratology of Seymour Chatman, Roland Barthes, Tzvetan Toderov, Gerard Genette, Shlomith Rimmon-Kenan, and David Bordwell, to name a few.[3] The names given the "what" and the "how" are several. Chatman distinguishes between story (what is told) and discourse (the telling).[4] Following Gerard Genette's *histoire, recit*, and *narration*, Rimmon-Kenan distinguishes among story, text, and narration.[5] David Bordwell makes use of the Russian formalist distinction between *fabula*, the story events as constructed by the viewer, and *syuzet*, the plot or actual textual order of events.[6] I use the term *discourse* to refer to abstract organization of filmic materials – the *how*. The *projected world* of a film is the *what*; in the case of nonfiction, the projected world is a *model of the actual world*.

The narratological accounts cited above assume narrative discourse in a fictional text. How might such principles apply to nonfiction? Bill Nichols writes that although the spectator enters a fiction film and a fictional world through *narration*, she enters the documentary world through *representation* or *exposition*. In making this claim, Nichols rightly points out that documentaries differ from fictions not in their "constructedness as texts," but rather in "the representations they make." But Nichols goes on to present a false dichotomy. "At the heart of the documentary," Nichols writes, "is less a story and its imaginary world than an *argument* about the historical world"[7] (Nichols' emphasis).

However, both nonfiction and fiction films make use of story and narrative. As Edward Branigan writes, narrative principles have been found in diverse types of discourses, including law, history, biography, psychiatry, and journalism, demonstrating that "narrative should not be seen as exclusively *fictional* but instead should merely be contrasted to *other (nonnarrative) ways of assembling and understanding data*."[8] Nichols understands this, and elsewhere he explicitly acknowledges that narrative is at work in many nonfiction films. Still, his means of distinguishing between fiction and nonfiction as story versus argument is misleading on this point. "Argument" does not well characterize the nonfiction film, and "story" is common to nonfiction as well as fiction. As I have argued, it isn't the form of the discourse that distinguishes nonfiction from fiction, but the stance taken toward the world it projects.

In addition to categorical, rhetorical, and associational form, nonfiction films also tell stories, as in historical narratives like *The Battle of San Pietro* and *Harlan County, U.S.A*. Whatever their form of textual organization, the nonfiction film also demands a distinction between a what and a how. For any possible topic, one can imagine diverse treatments. Consider Frederick Wiseman's *High School*, for example. This marvelous film about a public high school of the late 1960s could have concentrated on relationships between the students rather than solely on the interaction of teachers and students (a matter of selection and emphasis). It could have ordered its scenes differently, since the scenes correspond to no historical or narrative chronology. Wiseman uses only a fraction of the footage he shoots, and could have selected scenes other than those he included for the finished work. *High School* makes consistent use of extreme close-ups of teacher's hands, parts of faces, and other minute details. Alternatively, it could have represented the high school mainly in long shots. Though *High School* constitutes a narrative only in a weak sense, it still employs all of the strategies available to narrative fictions, and we must distinguish between *what* and *how* it represents.[9]

A film's discourse is its purposive organization of sounds and images, the mechanism by which it projects its model of the world and through that performs diverse other actions. Whereas the nonfiction film text is a physical entity – a string of projected images and amplified sounds, discourse is abstract – a formal arrangement. The discourse is the means by which the projected world or story events are communicated; its principle strategies, at the most abstract level, are selection, order, emphasis, and voice.

The projected world is broader than Seymour Chatman's "story." Like a story, it consists of the events, settings, and characters of the presented "world," plus their various attributes granted or implied by the film's discourse. Since we cannot limit nonfiction discourse to the presentation of stories, *projected world* is here the appropriate term. According to Chatman, the "story" is both a logical extrapolation based on what the work shows and asserts, and a construction of the spectator or reader: ". . . *story* in one sense is the continuum of events presupposing the total set of all conceivable details, that is, those that can be projected by the normal laws of the physical universe. In practice, of course, it is only that continuum and that set actually inferred by a reader, and there is room for difference in interpretation."[10]

Discourse is fundamentally communicative, for when we say that the discourse selects elements, orders their presentation, emphasizes certain representations at the expense of others, and manifests a "voice," we speak only metaphorically. What has actually occurred is that the film's producers constructed the physical text, and in so doing fashioned its discourse. The selection, ordering, emphasis, and voice of the discourse have been completed by the time the film or video is released, and become a more or less inert characteristic of the text (though subject to various interpretations).

A nonfiction film asserts or implies that the states of affairs it presents occur in the actual world as portrayed. Why then do we require the concept of the projected world as a kind of mediation between discourse and actual world? The concept of the projected world as a model is necessary to preserve the notion that *nonfiction films can be mistaken in their assertions and misleading in their portrayals.* Although a nonfiction purports accuracy for the scenes it presents, the accuracy of its projected world cannot be guaranteed. Although it makes assertions or truth claims, they may not necessarily be true. If we think of the projected world as a model, this helps account for the ways in which films may be inaccurate or accurate, misleading or illuminating, truthful or deceptive – either in full or in part.

It is therefore important to study the relationship between discourse and projected world, of the means by which films construct models to make claims about reality. The discourse represents its world-model along four broad parameters: (1) it selects, by controlling the amount and nature of the information about the projected world, (2) it orders, through a formal correspondence between discursive presentation and projected world information, (3) it emphasizes, by assigning weight and importance to the information, and (4) it takes a "point of view" toward what it presents, which here I call its "voice."

Selection

To analyze a nonfiction, we may first ask what is selected and omitted, of the possible or relevant features of any given topic. We don't necessarily need to know the production history of a film to ask why certain subjects or topics were omitted and others included. For any given representation, we can imagine the discursive choice of features other than those present, and that is often enough to tell us something about the rhetorical effects of selection for that film. Knowing a film's production history helps, however, because discourse is a construct of the producer(s), and selections and omissions may stem from practical considerations as well as rhetorical purposes. If we are fortunate enough to know the production history of a particular film or the methods of a filmmaker, that knowledge is useful to understand the motivations for a film's selections.

An excellent example of the powers of selection comes from the production history of *Common Threads: Stories from the Quilt*. This film, directed by Jeffrey Friedman and Robert Epstein (who previously made *The Times of Harvey Milk* [1986]), won the 1989 Academy Award for Best Feature Documentary, and was funded in part by Home Box Office. Its primary aim is to overcome prejudice against homosexuals, to enable audiences to see AIDS victims as flesh-and-blood people who deserve our care and attention, and to encourage efforts to find a cure for the disease through research funded by the government. Although the film deals with tragic loss, it ends on a hopeful note, with an account of the Names Project and a memorial ceremony near the White House, where an enormous quilt is unfolded, each panel of which represents one of the victims of AIDS.

The film employs many tools to meet its ends, including news and archival footage accompanied by the voice-over narration of Dustin Hoffman and a memorable musical score by Bobby McFerrin and Voicestra. The most important strategy of *Common Threads*, however, is its use of interviews with five individuals or families who were touched by death caused by AIDS. Each of these people tells an articulate and moving story about the discovery of AIDS, the process leading to the deaths of their loved ones, and their adjustment to those deaths. Each of the five stories is interconnected so that the narration can present similar points in the personal narratives simultaneously, from discovery of the syndrome to death to adjustment and healing for those who survive.

Directors Epstein and Friedman selected the interviewees very carefully, as each of their stories is meant to illustrate but one among the thousands of painful stories that could be told, one of the common threads of both humanity and the Names Project quilt.[11] After compiling a list of persons who had lost a loved one to AIDS, Epstein and Friedman contacted at least 500 of them and conducted telephone interviews. One of their objectives was to find articulate and compelling storytellers. From the initial list of 500, they decided to videotape interviews with 50 persons. From those videotaped interviews, Epstein and Friedman eventually chose five individuals or families for the filmed interviews.

The selection of persons for the interviews reveals much about the rhetorical project of the film. The persons interviewed include (1) a heterosexual couple who had lost a hemophiliac son, (2) a gay writer who had lost his partner, (3) a gay military officer whose partner had died, (4) a lesbian woman who lost the father of her child, and (5) an African-American woman whose husband, a former intravenous drug user, had contracted the disease and died. The selection of interviewees is intended to shatter stereotypes and to represent a real cross-section of American life. Stereotypes about the "typical" victim of AIDS fall away when we see the diversity of people afflicted – a military officer, a witty and articulate writer, a suburban middle class family, a devoted gay father who is a physician, a deeply-religious African-American woman who helped her husband quit using drugs. In this case, selection plays a major role in making the rhetorical point of the film, that AIDS is a common human problem, and that victims of AIDS deserve our compassion and our action to combat the disease.

Selection is often tied to questions of objectivity, balance, fairness, and bias. Although absolute balance and objectivity are elusive goals, the choices filmmakers make about who to interview and what to show inevitably alter the perceived reliability and bias of the work. The PBS *Frontline* program on the recent Los Angeles riots, "L.A. is Burning: Five Stories from a Divided City" (1993), is a case in point. The documentary consists of intercut interviews with five persons from diverse ethnic backgrounds and radically different ways of viewing the Rodney King incident, policemen's trial, and riots. Had the filmmakers chosen to interview only Korean-Americans, for example, our perception of its assumed objectivity would be radically different. Selective choices also reveal point of view or voice; Kevin Rafferty's *Atomic Cafe* (1982) uses archival material to question and make fun of 1950s and 60s attitudes toward atomic bombs and nuclear destruction. The very choice of "naive" archival material (from Government information films and promotional material) and dated songs such as "Duck and Cover," "Atomic Cocktail," and "Atomic Love," makes the satirical perspective of the film clear.

Order

One of the most important relationships between discourse and projected world is temporal. The discourse presents projected world information in temporal succession, and the formal order of that succession – the order of information – is formulated in accord with a rhetorical strategy, according to the communicative functions and purposes of the film. We may call this formal ordering a *structure of information*. Here I initiate a discussion of the ordering of information, and explore the issue in more depth in following chapters.

A film's discourse can take many broad forms. It may be reflexive or observational, narrative or associational. Whatever form it takes, however, it must give an order to the information it presents. If projected world events occurred in an A, B, C order, the discourse can present them, for example, as C, then A and B in flashback, or as C, B, A in reverse causal order (C was a result of B, which was caused by A, etc.) One can likewise order topical information in various ways, according to desired emphasis. Through the ordering of categorical, rhetorical, and/or narrative information, the discourse gives primacy to particular data, less importance to some, and ignores other data altogether.

The spectator's mental activity in viewing a film or video is itself a kind of narrative. The viewer grasps information successively, and at times this can be a central factor in determining textual meaning. We must always consider what comes first and last in a film, because both the initial and final stages of viewing have an important effect on the comprehension and interpretation of the entire film. Comprehending a text, Menackem Perry writes, is a "process of constructing a system of hypotheses and frames which can create a maximal relevancy among the various data of the text."[12] Much of the information a viewer gets from a text she supplies by choosing mental frames, or schemas, by which gaps in the text are filled with pertinent data.

Ross McElwee's *Sherman's March*, for example, might initially seem to be rather odd; its subtitle is "A Meditation on the Possibility of Romantic Love in the South During an Era of Nuclear Weapons Proliferation." Part of the playfulness and reflexivity of the film lies in the proliferation of nonfiction genres it mixes, and the means by which it keeps the spectator guessing about the "appropriate" schemas for processing the film's information. *Sherman's March* looks conventional at its beginning, as we see an animated map of General Sherman's Civil War march of destruction through the South. An "omnipotent" voice-over narrator (the voice of Richard Leacock) introduces the subject: "Union General William T. Sherman began his famous march to the sea. With an army of sixty thousand men he swept into the South, destroying Atlanta, Georgia; Columbia, South Carolina; and dozens of smaller towns. . . ." As the voice-over speaks, stills of destroyed buildings, cities, and finally of General Sherman himself dissolve into each other. As the image fades to black, however, we hear an off-screen voice – McElwee's – as the narrator clears his throat: "Great. Do you want to do it once more?" With this "intrusion," the discourse at once subverts conventional schemas of understanding, and signals the reflexive nature of the film.

In the early stages of a film's viewing, all possibilities are open. Nothing from earlier stages suggests what frames and hypotheses the spectator should make reference to. When processing a text, we do not first determine the meaning of textual elements and then seek an appropriate schema from which to view the text. The operation is simultaneous; we guess at schemas and select the one we think fits the material. This is why the most intensive closing of options occurs at or near the beginning. Once spectators make hypothesis, furthermore, they are stubborn in their tendency to retain them through the duration of the text, and to resist alternative frames. Perry calls this the *primacy effect*, implying that the prologue – the first stages of a text – are important in cueing the spectator about how to interpret and comprehend.

The discourse must also chose which data to present last. The viewing process involves retrospective action or backward-directed activity on the part of the spectator. The viewer continually refers back to the schemas she used to make sense of earlier textual information. New material in the text can encourage the spectator to develop or modify the schema previously constructed, or to substitute a new frame for the old one. The epilogue of a text, then, assists the viewer in this backward-looking process by filling in gaps, summing up, and suggesting a frame by which the previous data can be interpreted. Any analysis of temporal ordering must pay particular attention to the beginning and ending of a film, since this is often where the discourse suggests overarching schema to direct and assist interpretation and comprehension.

Exposition in a film or other discourse introduces the viewer to the projected world, providing the background information indispensable for an understanding of the narrative events or argument. It is helpful to understand the ways in which exposition and narrative (or argument) interweave throughout a text. Meir Sternberg has explored the interactions of narrative and exposition in fiction, but his discoveries have just as much relevance for the nonfiction film.[13] In drawing on the relationship between exposition and narrative, Sternberg implies that for fiction, exposition is necessary to set up schemas that allow for the suspense, anticipation, and spectatorial hypotheses that make narratives interesting.

Sternberg parcels the sorts of expositional strategies in narrative into several categories, each with unique rhetorical implications. First, Sternberg writes that exposition may be *preliminary* or *delayed*, depending on its position in the narrative. A preliminary exposition is positioned prior to a recounting of narrative events, in the initial stages of a film. But a film might alternatively begin by recounting narrative events, then pause later to give the necessary background information; this is delayed exposition. Second, exposition may be *concentrated* or *distributed*, depending on the degree of unity of the exposition. A concentrated exposition, at one extreme, is given in one block in the text, whereas distributed exposition is interspersed intermittently. Concentrated exposition may be either preliminary or delayed, whereas distributed exposition must be at least partially delayed. Sternberg's third opposition depends on the textual location of exposition in relation to the narration's presentation of projected world events. Exposition *in media res* occurs after the film has plunged the viewer into the narrative action; such exposition is at least partially delayed. Exposition *ab ovo* occurs in the prologue or introduction of the film, prior to important narrative events.

Sternberg gives an account of the reasons for using these ordering strategies. The formation of what Sternberg calls the *fabula* (and what I call the projected world) is wide open to the fiction writer or filmmaker, who owes no allegiance to "scientific standards" that may fetter the historian. One of the primary aims of fiction, Sternberg writes, is the creation and manipulation of narrative interest. The orientation of the fiction writer is primarily rhetorical; techniques are manipulated to that end. Because most writers and readers tend to think of preliminary exposition as a necessary evil, as the "dull" part of the fiction, the writer experiments with variations on preliminary exposition that pique the reader's interest through the opening and manipulation of what Sternberg calls *expositional gaps*. Gaps in reader knowledge, whether temporary or permanent, evoke suspense and surprise, and encourage inferential activity. Are the ghosts in James' *The Turn of the Screw* merely the hallucinations of the governess? In *A Passage to India*, what really happened in the Marabar Caves? Gaps serve what Sternberg calls "the dynamics of expectation."[14] They keep the spectator interested by encouraging mental activity.

Do these strategies have a place in the nonfiction film? Sternberg writes that the historian, unlike the fiction writer, is bent on reconstructing the truth, and thus often resorts to a strict chronological ordering. The need to portray events accurately "determines the historian's principles of combination and ordering as well as selection." "Qua historian," Sternberg continues, ". . . his prime aim cannot be to interest, let alone to amuse, his reader; and he certainly cannot afford to do so at the expense of historical truth or scientific methodology. He will usually adhere, therefore, to the 'natural' order, however dull this may prove."[15]

Sternberg's claims too neatly separate the realms of fiction (as creation) and history (as science). This is true for both history proper, that is, the written history of professional historians, and for the less "rigorous" nonfiction film. Many scholars, and most notably Hayden White, have written extensively on the literary roots of written histories and on how they use what are mistakenly thought to be fictional techniques.[16] The same is true of nonfiction films and filmmakers, only more so. Most nonfiction filmmakers are by no means professional historians; many have economic, political, and commercial obligations that manifest themselves in the films; many have no wish to present an impartial account of history. As we shall see, even those films aspiring to historical accuracy make use of the techniques Sternberg describes. We often find a serious tension between the nonfiction requirement to "tell the truth," the need to entertain the audience, and the rhetorical aims of the filmmaker(s).

Here an example succinctly illustrates the problem. The 1989 feature documentary *Roger and Me* aroused considerable controversy not only for its spirited attacks on the employment policies of General Motors, but for its manipulation of the chronology of the historical events it recounts. Of course, all films must give order to their presentation of data. Many structuring choices clearly fall within the bounds of creative license or "artistic proof," and are unavoidable for the nonfiction filmmaker. First, consider what Hayden White would call the chronicle of events from which Michael Moore draws for his film. Included in this chronicle are the General Motors factory closings in Flint, and the Flint visit of several celebrities: future Miss America Kaye Loni Rae Rafko, evangelist Robert Schuler, presidential candidate Ronald Reagan, and the pathetically vulgar host of the *Newlywed Game*, Bob Eubanks. We might also consider the planning, construction, and failure of the hapless schemes Flint authorities devised to revitalize the Flint economy: the Auto World theme park, the Water Street Pavilion enclosed shopping mall, and the downtown Hyatt Regency Hotel.

Such a chronicle is not yet a narrative, however. At the second level of conceptualization, as Hayden White argues, the historian must fashion the chronicle into a *story*, with a discernible beginning, middle, and end; motifs of inauguration, termination, and transition; and the determination of a hierarchy of significance to the recounted events. The inaugural motifs used in *Roger and Me* are, in part, derived from those of the classical fiction film. *Roger and Me* begins by positing a "steady state," a romantic past in which Flint is the thriving home of the prosperous General Motors, and Michael Moore an innocent, somewhat goofy boy from a family of happily employed auto workers. As screenwriting manuals suggest, some type of catalyst must spark events in the classical narrative. The catalyst consists of a violation of the steady state, a disruption that sets the narrative in motion. In *Roger and Me*, the catalyst occurs when in 1986/87, General Motors closes eleven of its older plants in Flint, which the film represents as an unprecedented, catastrophic event.[17] The classical script consists of well-placed "turning points" or "reversals," which route the story in a new direction and keep it fresh and interesting. Together with the inauguration of Moore's quest to take Roger Smith to Flint to force him to see the damage he has done, the 1986/87 plant closings represent the first major turning point of *Roger and Me*.

In *Metahistory*, Hayden White also notes that histories must make use of what he calls *terminating motifs*. A common terminating motif in the nonfiction film (and in fiction) is to end the narrative with a celebration, often centered around a ritual occasion such as a holiday or a birthday. *Roger and Me* ends during a celebration of Christmas, although Moore inverts the celebration with a blunt and savage irony. Here the narration cross-cuts between Roger Smith reading a spectacularly dull "wonders of Christmas" homily while a family of unemployed autoworkers is evicted from its home.

White points out that for any given set of events, one can represent them via any of the modes he describes (myth, romance, comedy, tragedy, irony). Although it might be difficult to represent the demise of Flint through the narrative structure of romance, one could easily imagine the events in a tragic dramatic structure. General Motors might be fitting as the tragic hero (of the corporate kind), which through its moral flaw – lack of long-range planning, perhaps – suffers a mighty fall, a kind of death. To treat the story of the relationship of General Motors to the city of Flint as tragedy rather than irony would imply a radically different interpretation of the historical data, but not one truer to those events or more realistic. We can perhaps agree on much of the data; whether the events are best represented as tragedy or irony, on the other hand, is relative to one's perspective.

Roger and Me gives the Flint story an ironic narrative structure, ending with the apparent disintegration of Flint, the failure of Moore's quest to bring Roger Smith to the community, and little hope for the future. Whereas to represent these Flint events in an ironic narrative structure is certainly legitimate (and perhaps even fitting), using such a structure certainly has implications. Hayden White implies that ironic history – as a narrative structure – is disabling and impotent, that it engenders belief in the "madness" of civilization and dissolves optimism about the possibility of positive political action. In addition, the political inertia of ironic history is masked by what passes for sophistication. White claims that ". . . characterizations of the world cast in the Ironic mode are often regarded as *intrinsically* sophisticated and realistic. They appear to signal the ascent of thought in a given area of inquiry to a level of self-consciousness on which a genuinely 'enlightened' – that is to say, self-critical – conceptualization of the world and its processes has become possible."[18]

So far I have dealt with what I would call normative structure in *Roger and Me*. By normative structure I mean ordering decisions of a type common to nonfiction films, and certainly closed to suggestions of manipulation or deception. What I will discuss now are the more questionable ordering devices of the film. According to Harlan Jacobson in his interview with Moore in *Film Comment*, *Roger and Me* manipulates the actual chronology of events in Flint. Jacobson claims that Moore "has created the impression of a direct sequence of events that didn't happen in Flint in the one-to-one causal fashion his documentary implies."[19]

To illustrate, I give two central examples. First, *Roger and Me* implies that the massive layoffs in Flint occurred 1986 and 1987, and that 30,000 workers were laid off. In actuality, the layoffs began in 1974 and continue to the time of this writing, and in 1986–87 about 10,000 workers were laid off. *Roger and Me* represents an extended process as a single catastrophic event. Second, *Roger and Me* suggests that in response to the massive 1986–87 General Motors layoffs in Flint, the city devised three hair-brained schemes to revive itself: a downtown Hyatt Regency hotel and conference center, a theme park called AutoWorld, and the Water Street Pavilion, a mall designed to draw shoppers and tourists to the area. According to Jacobson, *Roger and Me* is deceptive because *all three* projects had opened, run their course, and in two cases failed before the 1986–87 layoffs. Several other chronological "problems" exist in the film, but these are the most central to the film's argument.

Although controversy ensued when these chronological discrepancies came to light, many defended Moore on the following grounds. From an ethical standpoint, they argued, the chronological manipulations of *Roger and Me* are unimportant because all documentaries must select and structure their materials. Gary Crowdus, for example, writes that Jacobson's charges against Moore "actually betray the interviewer's surprising naiveté, an artistically and even journalistically prudish notion of the actual nature of documentary filmmaking, especially in terms of the amount of rearrangement and editing – manipulation, if you will – that goes on in the making of almost any documentary."[20]

Moore defends himself in the Jacobson interview by claiming that everything the film shows as happening actually occurred, and that the skewed chronology is less important than the fact that the film captures the essential relationship between the city of Flint, General Motors, and their thousands of unemployed workers. Several sympathetic critics cite Moore's explanation that "everything that took place in the 1980s was a 'single blow' to Flint," and that small divergences in sequence matter little in the larger scheme of "artistic truth." All nonfiction filmmakers must struggle to structure their materials both honestly and engagingly. Why quibble with the distorted chronology of a few events?

In the case of *Roger and Me* we have a clear instance of a discourse that implies a false chronology, and does so knowingly. Michael Moore had full knowledge of the discrepancies between representation and fact in his film. His 1987 essay in *The Nation* gives a more accurate representation of the chronology of events in Flint, noting, for example, that Auto World had closed by 1985, after seven months of operation, and was not built in response to the 1986–87 layoffs.[21] If deception is saying or implying something that one knows is not true, then Moore deceived us. This is a different matter than the normative structuring of events into a narrative, which is not necessarily deceptive.

Even if Moore is deceptive, however, we may ask about the weight of these deceptions. Perhaps these "white lies" are forgivable in light of the political benefits the film brings. Unfortunately, discussion of the film's chronological deceptions tends to fall along party lines. Those who agree with the film's politics forgive them, whereas those unsympathetic to Moore tend to exaggerate their importance. Along the way a larger and arguably more important issue falls by the wayside – that of the quality of public discourse.

The quality of public discourse depends in part on a voluntary willingness not to deceive the public, or if you will, on standards of truthtelling. The extent to which we can trust public discourse to tell the truth, whether it be the network news, independent documentaries, or the advertising of corporations, depends on the standards to which society holds its communicants. It isn't that our public discourse is perfect as it is. Whatever credibility it *has*, however, is in part a function of a willingness to abide by strict ethical standards. The discrepancies of *Roger and Me* may not be of importance in themselves. In light of the prominence of the film, its deceptive practices may contribute to the demise of public standards of discourse, as members of the discursive community accept such practices as normative and acceptable. Many of those who *minimize* the deceptions of *Roger and Me* would *emphasize* the dishonesty of similar deceptions in a film advocating a morally reprehensible cause – neo-Nazi groups, for example. We should instead apply standards of discourse equally, to maintain and improve the overall quality of public discourse, in all of its political manifestations.[22]

So far I have discussed some of the complex means by which the discourse manipulates the *order* of projected world data. The other two means of temporal manipulation are *frequency* and *duration*.[23] As a technique of manipulation, frequency is used least, though it is not uncommon. An event in the projected world of a film occurs once. For various rhetorical purposes, however, the narration may portray the event more than once. Consider the aforementioned *Letter from Siberia*, where the same shot of Siberian workers constructing a road is repeated three times, each with a different voice-over narration. The first voice-over mimics anti-Communist propaganda, the second pro-Soviet propaganda, and the third an ostensible "objective" account. Here the manipulation of frequency defamiliarizes the phenomenon of voice-over narration and foregrounds the precariousness of its interpretive function. Another example occurs in *The Thin Blue Line*, in which Errol Morris repeats a reenactment of the murder of a policeman several times, each illustrating (and subtly undermining) the testimony of one of the witnesses.

Duration in the projected world is the actual time an event is assumed to endure, whereas discursive duration consists of the screen time allotted to the event. The relationship between projected world and discursive duration may be one of equivalence, reduction, and expansion.[24] In an equivalent relationship, discursive duration approximates projected world duration. Reduction condenses the projected world time of an event, whereas expansion augments the projected world time and stretches it in discursive presentation.

Most common in the nonfiction film is reduction. Barbara Kopple's *Harlan County, U.S.A.*, for example, could not possibly portray every event of the mine worker's movement in that Kentucky county in real time. Neither could *The War Room* possibly have shown every feature of Bill Clinton's campaign for the U.S. presidency. The discourse must necessarily pick and choose, representing only the most salient events, and must often compress the projected world time of events (usually) into a span of under two hours. Thus temporal omissions involve the *selection* and *omission* of events as well as their condensation. When examining a particular film, it is often useful to explore the motivations for strategies of compression, for they inevitably require that certain events be condensed, and others elided altogether. What choices were made, and why?

Expansion is most often achieved through slow-motion. *The Thin Blue Line* again provides an example. There the reenactments of the policeman's murder often appear in slow motion. As in temporal condensation, expansion *emphasizes*, because when discourse time of an event is extended, it focuses spectator attention on its textual importance, and makes its visual details more comprehensible. One might initially think that slow-motion photography would be rare in nonfiction films, as slow-motion distorts a sense of realistic time. Remember, however, that it is not realism that distinguishes the nonfiction film, but the assertion or implication that the represented states of affairs occur in the actual world. The prevalence of slow-motion and time lapse photography in nature films, for example, shows that the use of "distorting" cinematography might actually be more revelatory than "normal" speed cinematography, and thus a perfectly appropriate nonfiction film technique.

Emphasis

An element may be selected and put into a textual order, yet either emphasized or deemphasized depending on a host of structural and stylistic variables. Emphasis or its lack may come through structural arrangement, in which the mere placing of an element at the right moment, say at the beginning or at a climactic point, draws our attention to or away from it. An example comes from John Huston's *The Battle of San Pietro* (1945), the history of a famous battle in the Italian campaign during World War II. Although one might expect such a film to glamorize victory, Huston instead emphasizes the harsh conditions endured by the foot soldiers and the war's high cost in human life. When the Allies, after heavy casualties, finally do take the tiny village of San Pietro, one might expect the filmmaker to revel in the glorious victory. Huston instead briefly skims over the results, as though they were merely incidental. As Huston claims (in his voice-over narration), a thousand more San Pietros await the soldiers who survived this horrendous battle.

Emphasis or its lack can also be achieved through a thousand stylistic devices, from a carefully-chosen angle, to editing patterns, to lighting, to the duration that a shot is shown. The latter is the case in Ross McElwee's *Time Indefinite* (1994), which in part takes as its theme the transcience of life. At one point, McElwee holds for a very uncomfortable time on the gut-wrenching photograph of a horrendous skin tumor. Bonnie Klein's *Not a Love Story*, to take another example, makes the point that pornography confuses love, sex, and aggression. Throughout Klein emphasizes the color red, and in a series of montages, juxtaposes pictures of the heart, a conventional symbol for love, with images of female degradation. Some argue that various styles carry an emphasis in themselves, before any footage is shot. For example, direct cinema, with its use of portable cameras and sound recorders, attempts to record the spontaneous and the accidental. Could such a style have the effect of making its subjects look silly or disorganized, since it concentrates on mistakes, unplanned encounters, and common people who say common things? Emphasis clearly holds a central place in nonfiction film analysis; some of the following chapters describe how emphasis is achieved through structure and style.

Voice

A fourth discursive manipulation of projected world information is *voice*. Voice is related to "point of view," but the terms are not coextensive. Few terms in film and literary theory have so many varied meanings as "point of view." In relation to film, the term may imply (1) the visual vantage point of the spectator or character, (2) the attitude of a character or a narrator toward projected world events, or (3) the attitude of the film's discourse overall. Shlomith Rimmon-Kenan dispenses with the term altogether, arguing that it encourages a confusion between the perspective of a character or narrator (either visual or attitudinal) and the perspective of the discourse (or as he terms it, "who speaks or presents the text"). Following Genette, Rimmon-Kenan substitutes the word "focalization" to describe the process by which the "story is presented in the text through the mediation of some 'prism,' 'perspective,' or 'angle of vision.'"[25] To help dispel that same confusion, Seymour Chatman posits a difference between *point of view* and *voice*. For Chatman, point of view "is the physical place or ideological situation or practical life-orientation to which the narrative events stand in relation," whereas voice "refers to the speech or other overt means through which events and existents are communicated to the audience."[26]

Both Rimmon-Kenan's use of the term "focalization" and Chatman's distinction between point of view and voice help distinguish between the origin of narration and its perspective, but they leave one ambiguity untouched. Point of view can also refer to the physical point from which a character or spectator can view a scene; this can easily be confused with the attitude of the character or spectator. A shot taken from the presumed position of a character is called a point-of-view shot, because it is literally from her physical point of view.

My main concern is with point of view as "focalization," in the sense used by Rimmon-Kenan. Every nonfiction film presents its projected world from a perspective (or perspectives), in relation to a tone and attitude.[27] The word I use to describe this is *voice*. My use of the term is broader than Chatman's, and is closer to the "voice" described by Bill Nichols:

. . . that which conveys to us a sense of a text's social point of view, of how it is speaking to us and how it is organizing the materials it is presenting to us. In this sense 'voice' is not restricted to any one code or feature such as dialogue or spoken commentary. Voice is perhaps akin to that intangible, moiré-like pattern formed by the unique interaction of all a film's codes, and it applies to all modes of documentary.[28]

In *Representing Reality*, Nichols substitutes "argument" for "voice," an unfortunate choice in its implication that all documentaries make arguments. I think that "voice" is the better term, for although "argument" applies only poorly to many nonfiction films, every nonfiction film has a voice or perspective. When we say that someone has "found her voice," we mean that she has matured and developed as an artist and/or communicator. In one sense, a voice is not simply a perspective, but an instrument that must be developed. As I use the term voice, however, it implies no evaluation and no significant achievement. Even a banal or confounded nonfiction film has a voice, however confused, ambiguous, or superficial it may be.

To say that all nonfiction films have a voice is not to anthropomorphize. Not every nonfiction film has a voice-over narrator, but every nonfiction film has a discourse that takes an implicit stance or attitude toward what it presents. Every film is constructed by humans for some communicative function or functions, and the use of *voice* to denote the perspective of the narration pays homage to nonfiction filmmaking as a human form of communication. The nonfiction film is a physical text used for communication, including an abstract discourse that presents projected world information, and a "voice" that expresses that information from a certain perspective.

The voice of the nonfiction film can be described in countless ways, and no set of terms can delimit the types of perspectives and tones the discourse can take. The position or attitudes the discourse takes toward the events depicted are richly varied, as varied as the possible stances humans can take toward anything we come into contact with. Like a person reporting an event to an audience, the discourse of a nonfiction film may manifest voice as ostensibly objective as in television news, angry and hostile as in the *Why We Fight* series, blatantly or subtly ironic as in Michael Moore's *TV Nation*, sympathetic and praising as in *Say Amen, Somebody*, subtle and understated as in Humphrey Jennings' *Listen to Britain*, and, as I discuss in the following chapter, confident or hesitant with respect to the truth claims the film or video makes.

CHAPTER 6
Voice and Authority

Modes of Documentary

One of the best known and most useful typologies of nonfiction films comes from Bill Nichols.[1] Nichols' four forms or modes of documentary – expository, observational, interactive, and reflexive – have been of value because they offer a framework at once historically descriptive and heuristically useful. The modes are historical because they follow a rough order of chronological development, from the Griersonian documentary with its "Voice-of-God" commentary (expository), to direct cinema (observational), to films incorporating interviews and/or the filmmaker's presence (interactive), to works acknowledging their constructedness and foregrounding the process of representation itself (reflexive). On the other hand, the four modes are of heuristic value because they represent four alternative styles of nonfiction filmmaking, and four different assumptions about the proper functions of the nonfiction film in relation to the historical world and the audience.

However valuable, Nichols' typology raises problematic issues. The typology features a built-in teleology that favors the last mode, reflexive films, and assumes that the expository mode is the most naive or politically retrograde, since it constitutes the most primitive stage of development. To his credit, Nichols does not present these modes as strictly-defined categories with clear boundaries, and reminds us that any of the four modes was available to filmmakers from early in the history of nonfiction film, and that specific nonfiction films can and often do mix modes. Still, the move from expository to reflexive, as Nichols admits, "gives the impression of . . . an evolution toward greater complexity and self-awareness."[2]

The expository documentary, with its "Voice-of-God" commentary, is sometimes thought to be problematic because it presumes to forward truths from a position of authority. It is also considered illusionistic because it presents a "transparent" discourse that fails to foreground its processes of representation and constructedness. The reflexive film, on the other hand, challenges spectator assumptions by making plain its representational functions, or by upsetting spectator assumptions through its political content. Within this account of the move from primitive expository to postmodern reflexive film lurks the implicit assumption that the latter type of filmmaking is ethically superior, because reflexive films acknowledge the complexities, or "magnitudes," of the historical world. Nichols makes his stand clear when he calls for reflexive documentaries, and writes that in the "act of radical defamiliarization lie magnitudes that conventional discourses of sobriety can only deny or disavow."[3]

There is a danger here. It remains to be seen how historians of the future will see reflexive and expository nonfiction films. If expository films are patronizing in their "teaching" from a position of authority, can't we say the same of reflexive films, with their assumption of a homogeneous audience that is ignorant and unreflective? Expository filmmaking is sometimes thought to be illusionistic in its failure to foreground its means of representation. Could it be that those who favor reflexive films are underestimating the intelligence of audiences in assuming their need for continual reminders that they view a constructed representation? The answers to these questions are by no means clear, but one should be suspicious of the tendency to favor our present (which is some future scholar's past) as the apex of sophistication.

The four-mode typology, as I have said, is valuable in part for its historicity. But as a description of the historical development of the nonfiction film, it may oversimplify history. The expository documentary, Nichols writes, "addresses the viewer directly, with titles or voices that advance an argument about the historical world," and the viewer expects it to take shape "around the solution to a problem or puzzle: presenting the news of the day, exploring the working of the atom or the universe."[4] One could get the impression that before the development of the observational film in the late fifties, all nonfictions were expository, made use of authoritative "Voice-of-God" commentary, and so forth.

On the contrary, nonfictions made before the rise of the observational film are enormously diverse. The expository documentary is sometimes called the "Griersonian" documentary. But when one looks closely even at the films made under Grierson's aegis, many do not fit the expository category neatly. Edgar Anstey's *Granton Trawler* (1934), for example, is almost observational with its lack of voice-over commentary and its attention to the sights and sounds of the fisherman's trawlers. Or consider the lack of voice-over in the films of Humphrey Jennings. His *Listen to Britain* (1942) uses no commentary in constructing its subtle portrait of wartime Britain, although due to its staging of action it can hardly be called observational. Even Griersonian films such as *Night Mail* (1936) and *Song of Ceylon* (1937) fit the "Voice-of-God" model poorly, since their voice-over commentaries are highly poetic, and not limited to the authoritative transmission of information. To my mind, the best example of "Voice-of-God" commentary is in the newsreel series *The March of Time* (parodied by Orson Welles in the "News on the March" segment of *Citizen Kane* [1941]). Although early filmmakers used bulky, primitive equipment by today's standards, they nonetheless managed to create some remarkable films that cannot be easily lumped together under a single rubric such as "expository documentary." It isn't that Nichols wishes to do this, but rather that his typology may encourage false impressions in those unfamiliar with early documentary history.

My last observation about the division of nonfiction films into expository, observational, interactive, and reflexive categories is that it cannot deal well with poetic or experimental nonfiction films (unless they are reflexive) – the films of Robert Flaherty, Humphrey Jennings, Bruce Baillie, Joris Ivens' *The Bridge* and *Rain*, Bert Haanstra's *Glass*, Walter Ruttman's *Berlin: Symphony of the City*, and so forth. Because many of these films were produced in the twenties and thirties, Nichols thus wants to put them into the expository category, because that is where they fit according to historical periodization. He calls the films "poetic exposition": "The emphasis shifts from a direct argument or statement, to which illustrations attach, to an indirect evocation of a way of being in the world that derives from the formal structure of the film as a whole."[5]

However, although these films fit with the expository documentary by historical periodization, they do not fit conceptually or stylistically, because their primary function is *poetic* rather than expository, observational, interactive, or reflexive. We need a category of the *poetic nonfiction film* to recognize the fact that some nonfiction films are concerned not primarily with argument, or with the assertion of propositions about the world, but have an aesthetic function that serves as their primary organizational principle. Again, my concern is that Nichols' typology will implicitly marginalize poetic nonfiction films, just as John Grierson explicitly criticized the films of Robert Flaherty for their lack of what he thought to be "hard-headed" social analysis.

Narrative, Argument, and Categorical Form

We can also distinguish between narrative, rhetorical, and categorical structures.[6] A narrative nonfiction film is usually historical, representing historical events as they occurred in time. Ray Boulting's *Desert Victory* (1943), for example, presents the history of the Allied defeat of German forces in North Africa during World War II. Similarly, Fu Ya and Huang Bao-shan pieced together an account of the history of the People's Republic of China with their *A Spark Can Start a Prairie Fire* (*Hsing Hsing Chih Huo Keyi Liao Yuan*, 1961). Narrative nonfiction may also deal with the more recent past, as in news reports or journalistic documentaries. Where the fiction filmmaker freely creates imaginative events, the nonfiction filmmaker portrays and/or makes explicit claims about actual historical events. Imagination nonetheless plays a role for the nonfiction filmmaker, because she must decide *how* to represent historical events, and in this choice exercises considerable freedom. Narrative remains the most pervasive method of organization in the nonfiction film largely because history is a prevalent topic, even if it is simply the history of the day's events, as in a news broadcast. Narrative is a fundamental mode of explanation with roots in the human need to represent events and history to others. Narrative history may employ many of the techniques common to fictional narratives to maintain interest, arouse suspense, or create, delay the fulfillment of, or fulfill expectations. Nonetheless, narrative *itself* is neither inherently fictional or nonfictional.

Categorical and rhetorical form, although less pervasive, still are common. Categorical discourse normally presents subjects of a topical nature. Its representation is synchronic – of entities existing simultaneously, rather than diachronic – of entities and events as they unfold in time. A categorical nonfiction film, for example, Les Blank's *Garlic is as Good as Ten Mothers*, shows American social practices involving garlic. It features various ways to cook the "stinking rose," responses to its taste and smell, and shows a California festival devoted to the plant. Although it incorporates what might be called micro-narratives, or "small" stories, within the overarching structure of the film, its fundamental organization is topical rather than narrative.

The third common formal organization, rhetorical form, makes recourse to reasoning and persuasion to call for some course of action or to simply persuade the spectator about some issue. In a broad sense, every discourse has a rhetorical dimension, as it implies a perspective on the world. However, rhetorical discourse as I conceive of it here makes explicit use of strategies of argument and persuasion, asserting premises, presenting evidence, employing various persuasive devices, and generating a conclusion. Connie Fields' *Rosie the Riveter* (1980), for example, strongly implies that the women who worked in American heavy industry during World War II were done an injustice when they lost their jobs to returning male veterans. The *CBS Reports* documentary "Harvest of Shame" (1960) argues that the treatment of migrant workers on U.S. farms is shameful and recommends legislation to correct the problem. Again, this documentary incorporates micro-stories in its description of the plight of the migrants. However, the overall structure is that of an argument or a persuasion, and its aim is "artistic proof."

It is rare that particular nonfiction films make use of one of these categories to the exclusion of the others. For example, Werner Herzog's *The Dark Glow of the Mountains* (1984) mixes narrative and expositional techniques in its study of German mountaineer Reinhold Messner. The film's chief concern, Herzog tells us in voice-over, is to discover the psychological processes that drive Messner and those of his ilk to subject themselves to the dangers of the incredible mountains they climb. Herzog thus conducts several fascinating interviews with Messner and his climbing partner. Herzog frames these topical interviews within a broad narrative that gives structure to the film at the highest level. The interviews are thus interspersed within the overall structure of a narrative, at various stages of Messner's expedition to the peaks of Gasherbrum I and II in Pakistan. This narrative cover envelops the interview segments – which are topical in nature – and gives the film suspense and atmosphere.

Textual Authority and Voice

Bill Nichols' modes of documentary – expository, observational, interactive, and reflexive – are similar in some ways to the modes David Bordwell describes for the fiction film: the classical, art cinema, parametric, and historical materialist modes of narration. A mode of narration, Bordwell writes, "is a historically distinct set of norms of narrational construction and comprehension."[7] Genres are more malleable than modes, as they change more rapidly across time and with cultural differentiation. Modes, for Bordwell, transcend genres, subgenres, schools, movements, and national cinemas, and tend to be "more fundamental, less transient, and more pervasive."

I do not see the existence of nonfiction modes in the Bordwellian sense. Bordwell ties the modes he finds to historical developments during specific time periods. With few exceptions, the history of the nonfiction film has not seen the same powerful and relatively stable institutions that shaped modes of the fictional cinema. Unlike the classical fiction film, nonfiction has never had the homogenizing force of the Hollywood motion picture industry to enforce consistent narrative patterning and stylistic conventions. Historical forces have obviously contributed to the development of movements such as direct cinema or the Griersonian documentary, but these movements are smaller, less cohesive, and less enduring. In addition, some of the most interesting nonfiction filmmakers have been resolutely individualist in their work. One would be hard-pressed to fit Dziga Vertov, Robert Flaherty, or Chris Marker into an historical mode of nonfiction filmmaking. Although industrial films, PBS documentaries, network newsmagazines, independent productions, and promotional videos doubtless have their conventions, none is so pervasive a phenomena to constitute a mode in the sense Bordwell uses the term.

Suppose that we step back from specific historical movements and historically-grounded genres to consider nonfiction films in relation to broad purposes or functions, functions that become more or less prevalent at certain historical junctures, but that ultimately cannot be confined to single movements or eras. I propose that, as an heuristic device, we consider a difference between what I call the *formal, open,* and *poetic* voices of the nonfiction film. This typology is based on the degree of narrational authority assumed by the film (in the case of the formal and open voices), and on the absence of authority in favor of (broadly) aesthetic concerns in the case of the poetic voice. I propose this as a heuristic typology because although we could sometimes call nonfiction films formal, open, or poetic films, the purpose of the typology is not so much to categorize as to draw attention to some of the major functions of nonfictions and the textual means by which films perform those functions. These three "voices" are not meant to exhaust what we mean when we speak of a film's distinctive voice. The formative, open, and poetic voices refer to a film's broad epistemic and aesthetic concerns; the films may have other functions and qualities in addition to those.

The formal voice of the nonfiction film (hereafter referred to simply as the "formal voice") is so named for three reasons. It functions epistemically to explain some portion of the world to the viewer; this I take to be a central function of many nonfiction films. It not only asserts that the states of affairs it presents actually occur as portrayed; all nonfiction films do that. It goes on to give significant form to its representata, a form which together with other textual elements constitutes an *explanation* of some element of the actual world. It is in this sense that the formal voice reserves for itself a high degree of *epistemic authority*.

Second, films of the formal voice tend to be "classical" in form and style, having the classical aesthetic characteristics of harmony, unity, and restraint. This is evident not only in the structure of the films, which tends to be symmetrical, unified, and "closed," but in technique as well, which usually serves a communicative function. Third, films of the formal voice bear significant similarities to the classical fiction film. Noël Carroll writes that the classical fiction film features what he calls an erotetic narrative. The erotetic narrative reflects the processes of practical reasoning by generating questions that ensuing scenes answer: "A successful erotetic narrative tells you, literally, everything you want to know about the action being depicted, i.e., it answers every question, or virtually every question, that it has chosen to pose saliently."[8] David Bordwell notes that the classical narrative elicits "a series of questions which the text impells us to ask," and then offers "unequivocal" answers; it opens gaps in our knowledge, then fills them.[9] The classical narrative elicits macro-questions, large questions that fuel the narrative movement as a whole, and micro-questions, questions at a more local level within or between scenes.

Nonfiction films of the formal voice – although they may be rhetorical or categorical more than narrative – have affinities with the classical fiction film and its erotetic narrative. They perform two significant operations: (1) they pose a clear question or a relevant and coherent set of questions (or they elicit such questions on the part of the spectator), and (2) they answer every salient question they pose. This is not meant to suggest that such films are simplistic or inane; the formal voice is capable of subtlety and complexity within the bounds of this conventional structure. Neither do I pose this characterization as a rule so much as a convention. Thus it is open to exceptions.

An alternative to the formative is the *open* voice. Nonfiction films of the open voice differ radically from their formal counterparts; instead of asserting a high degree of epistemic authority, we may characterize this voice as *epistemically hesitant*. Where the formal voice asks clear questions and answers every salient question it asks, the open voice is more reticent in the impartation of presumed knowledge. It often formulates no clear, overarching question, or if such a question *is* generated, it offers no answer, or a tentative and ambiguous answer. It is reluctant to give explanations or to make high-level, abstract claims about the world. In short, the open voice refuses to assert explicit epistemic authority over the viewer, and does not impart a clear, high-level explanation of the phenomena it presents.

The open voice *observes* or *explores* rather than explains. Narration in such films is sometimes implicit rather than explicit, avoiding the overt narrational marks and knowledge claims of the formal nonfiction film. To a degree, the open voice can be associated with direct cinema and cinéma vérité – or what can be called observational film for short. However, the open voice is not limited to these two types of filmmaking. Discourse in the open voice need not be implicit or hidden, as it often is in direct cinema. The withdrawal of strong knowledge claims is not necessarily coextensive with "invisible style." Highly reflexive films may also have the open voice, as I shall show below.

Nonfiction films with an open voice have many affinities with the art cinema. In the classical fiction cinema, reality is assumed to be fixable and knowable. Characters have clear goals and work toward attaining them. The narration works toward a state of complete knowledge and the resolution of narrative events. Art cinema narration and that of the open voice in nonfiction, on the other hand, propose a different conception of the world, one in which reality may be unknowable, character ineffable, and events follow one another without resolution.[10] The strict causal structure of classical narration is often replaced by chance and the vagaries of existence. The salient detail and the urgent moment are exchanged for meanderings and digressions, explorations that may or may not contribute to an answer to overarching spectatorial questions. It is often pointed out that art cinema narration is "character-centered" where classical narration is "plot-centered." Furthermore, the art cinema protagonist differs from that of the classical cinema. In the classical cinema she or he is goal-directed, whereas in the art cinema she may lack clear goals and is caught up in episodic events beyond her control. Narration in the art cinema focuses on the limitations of character knowledge. Similarly, the narration of the open voice abdicates some of its epistemic authority to explain the world.

The third sort of voice in the nonfiction film, examined more completely in Chapter Nine, is the poetic voice. The poetic voice is less concerned with observation, exploration, or explanation – traditional epistemological concerns – and more with the nonfiction film as art and/or as a means of exploring representation itself. In this sense, we can say that narration in these films maintains a sort of *epistemic aestheticism*. "Aestheticism" is sometimes used disparagingly to describe an affected or excessive attention to "beauty" or to the sensual qualities of things. A Griersonian puritanism with regard to the purpose of the documentary would denigrate many films of the poetic voice, but I understand these films as important examples of the nonfiction film.

The poetic voice is a broad designation, encompassing not only what are generically termed poetic documentaries, but also many avant-garde films, metadocumentaries, and documentary parodies. Emerging from the experiments of the cultural avant-garde in the 1920s and 30s, the poetic film – for example, Joris Ivens' films *The Bridge* (1928), *Pile Driving* (1929), and *Rain* (1929) – employ classical form and style to represent the sensual, aesthetic qualities of their subjects. The avant-garde nonfiction film shares affinities with what Bordwell calls "parametric cinema," a type of discourse that is style-centered. Bordwell's conception of the "parametric" stems from Noël Burch's conception of "parameters," a term for the formal possibilities inherent in various film techniques.[11] Parametric discourse, as conceived by Bordwell, blocks interpretation or thematization in favor of a concern with film form, as is the case with certain avant-garde films by Bruce Baillie, for example. Metadocumentary invokes style and form to examine the documentary itself, usually explicitly through reflexive strategies and a high degree of self-consciousness. Finally, documentary parody takes on the forms and conventions of the nonfiction film, usually of the formal voice, and parodies them.

Two theoretical issues must be distinguished here. All nonfiction films, I have argued, are defined as such in part due to the assertive stance taken toward the projected world of the film. The states of affairs presented in the nonfiction film are asserted to occur as portrayed in the actual world. However, I do not distinguish between the three voices based on a "degree of assertiveness." The formal, open, and poetic films all are equally nonfiction. The discourse of all three voices equally asserts that the states of affairs presented occur in the actual world. The differences between the formal, open, and poetic voice lie not in the assertive stance taken toward the world projected, but in the discursive voice of epistemic authority, hesitance, or aestheticism. The formal voice is more likely to make broad claims about its subject matter. The open voice usually confines itself to the representation of appearances, and lets the spectator infer generalizations. The poetic voice foregrounds the aesthetic qualities of what it presents. The differences in epistemic authority and function manifest themselves in the types of states of affairs selected and in the formal means of their expression. All equally assert that what is depicted occurs in the actual world, and thus all are equally nonfiction.

Think of the formal, open, and poetic voices as possibilities, or poles, of the nonfiction film, rather than as genres. Certain films, for example, may exemplify the formal voice almost completely, to the exclusion of the other two. More commonly, films will mix the voices described below, although one or the other may be clearly dominant. In other cases, it may be difficult to say if a film "speaks" with one voice, and many films do straddle the fuzzy boundaries between these heuristic categories. What I call the formal, open, and poetic voices of the nonfiction film are not meant as strictly defined categories with clear boundaries, but as descriptions of broad tendencies within the nonfiction film, tendencies that in actual films may be mixed and matched. A film may speak with heterogeneous voices, or a single voice.

The Formal Voice

The formal voice takes a position of epistemic authority toward the film's projected world, and thus also toward the actual world. The erotetic narrative is well-suited to films of the formal voice, because it (1) poses a clear question or a relevant and coherent set of questions, and (2) answers every salient question it poses. The formal voice possesses ostensible knowledge and imparts it to the viewer. It asserts that certain states of affairs hold true, and explains them. It envelops those assertions in a structure of information that implies that knowledge of the subject is not only possible, but is communicated by the film.

The authoritative voice of Robert Gardner's ethnographic film *Dead Birds* (1962), for example, manifests itself in many ways. Titles in the prologue announce that the film is a "true story," and the voice-over narrator confidently makes assertions concerning the remote Dani tribe of New Guinea: "These people's wars and raids yield neither territory, prisoners, nor plunder. They fulfill the obligations of the living toward the slain, toward in fact the ghosts of the slain. Unavenged ghosts bring sickness, unhappiness, and possibly disaster. It is for this reason they go to war, and for the reason that they like to." The film explicitly imparts what it considers knowledge to the spectator, a knowledge of the Dani people and their cultural practices. It partakes of a central function of documentary – to teach, to explain, to show the ostensible truth.

The use of the formal voice implies a position about the possibility of knowledge. I say a "position," rather than a well-developed philosophical theory, because the epistemological position of the formal voice is an attitude. As opposed to skepticism, which questions our ability to understand the world, the formal voice is optimistic in this regard, forging ahead in its categorizations, definitions, and generalized proclamations, structuring the discourse in such a way as to make grounded claims about the world.

One way to understand the issue is to distinguish between various levels of states of affairs, the "first-level" (or low-level) and the "second-level" (or high-level).[12] The basic properties of the physical world – of human anatomy, of the height of a tree, of the nutritional value of a cucumber – can be called first-level states of affairs. Second-level states of affairs consist of more abstract propositions, having to do, for example, with standards of morality, religion, the origins of the universe, political systems, and the extent and effects of racism. If we would apply such a distinction to our interaction with film texts, comprehension apprehends first-order properties, whereas interpretation finds second-order properties. It is obvious that the assertion of the latter will be more controversial than the assertion of the former. Discourse in the open voice confines itself for the most part to representing first-level states of affairs and usually refrains from explanations; this is why the term "observation" fits the open voice well. Discourse in the formative voice, on the other hand, *explains*, and thus routinely asserts second-level propositions about the projected world; it is thus more likely to use voice-over narration. When the narrator of *Dead Birds* claims that the Dani enjoy warfare, that is a second-level assertion, because it is offered as a partial explanation of why the Dani engage in it.

It is in this sense that the formal voice offers an explanation, where the open voice confines itself to observation or exploration. *The Times of Harvey Milk* not only recounts the story of Harvey Milk's life and brief political career, but invests them with significance for the gay rights movement in America. *The Wilmar 8* (1979) does not merely recount the details of the struggle of women workers at a bank, but implies the importance of their struggle for the general fight for women's equality in the workplace. *Why Vietnam* (1965) is a U.S. Department of Defense film that recounts a history of communism as an explanation for the presumed need for American forces in Vietnam.

As one might expect, the formal voice is relatively omniscient, assuming complete knowledge of relevant high-level aspects of its subject; it knows more than the people represented in that world. Ralph Steiner and Willard Van Dyke's *The City* (1939) represents the growing squalor of large urban areas and proposes solutions which, it claims, would result in superior cities. *Dead Birds*, in its representation of a foreign culture, implies that the Dani love of war grows out of the universal human condition of inevitably facing death. "Prelude to War," of the *Why We Fight* series, presumes to give the necessary information for the American soldier to understand what it is he fights for. In all of these cases, the discourse assumes an authoritative knowledge of the subjects it depicts. The teaching function, in these cases, is not first to explore or observe, but to impart prior knowledge. Not satisfied with mere observation, the formal voice goes beyond to explanation.

Since its function is one of teaching, the formal voice tends to be highly communicative and reliable. Discursive reliability is a textual construct, and does not refer to the accuracy or truthfulness of the discourse. Reliable discourse can be trusted by the spectator, not necessarily to "get it right" or "tell the truth" (although that is its aim in the nonfiction film), but at least not to intentionally mislead. Unreliable discourse, on the other hand, is intentionally misleading and is revealed as such within the text (usually after a period during which the spectator *has* been temporarily misled). The discourse of the classical fiction film is most often characterized as reliable by the end, since any discrepant previous discourse is shown to be unreliable and its falseness corrected. The formal voice rarely goes even this far; it usually maintains a resolute reliability throughout.

For the same reasons, the formal voice is highly communicative, rarely withholding pertinent information. As David Bordwell writes, in the classical fiction film communicativeness can be gauged with respect to the way the discourse handles gaps in information: "If time is skipped over, a montage sequence or a bit of character dialogue informs us; if a cause is missing, we will typically be informed that something isn't there. And gaps will seldom be permanent."[13] Usually the narration withholds only what will happen next, and any delays in the impartation of knowledge are brief and serve only to create suspense. This is true especially of the narrative documentary, in which some of the techniques of fiction are borrowed. In *On the Bowery* (1956), director Lionel Rogosin concentrates on two alcoholics in the Bowery area of New York. One of these men, Gomer, secretly steals Ray's suitcase, raising several questions concerning whether he will be caught, what he will do with his loot, etc. These questions are finally answered when Gomer gives Ray half of Ray's stolen money in a self-aggrandizing gesture of "goodwill." To a certain extent, narrational communicativeness depends on the type of documentary. As a rule, however, the formal voice is highly communicative; gaps in information are filled by the film's end.

The classical fiction film is moderately reflexive, seldom acknowledging its address to the audience except for the overt reflexivity of the titles and credits at the beginning and end of a film. The temporal progression of the discourse brings fluctuations in reflexivity; typically the beginning and ending of a film are the most reflexive, whereas the dramatic action in between is presented "invisibly," as though it were playing itself out unnarrated. The overt discursive marks of the type offered in expository titles and end credits are apparent in the body of the film only in certain conventional instances, such as the beginning and ending of scenes, certain camera movements, and so forth. These techniques of reflexivity are also apparent in documentaries making use of reenactment and staging, the documentaries closest to the classical narrative fictional form such as *Fires Were Started* (1943), *A Diary for Timothy,* or *Farrebique* (1946).

Many nonfictions are blatantly reflexive, making questionable all claims that nonfiction films typically present themselves as unmediated truth or "reality" (whatever that would entail). For example, *The Bridge* (1944), Willard Van Dyke's film about the economic problems of South America, maintains relatively overt narration throughout. The beginning presents the typical credits and titles, one reading "The people in this film are not actors. They are the men and women of South America" (which some may interpret as paradoxically encouraging the viewer to see the film as unmediated reality). Obvious marks of discourse appear consistently, however. First, voice-over narration constantly reminds the spectator that she is being spoken to, that she is the audience of a discourse. Second, the film constantly makes use of animated maps to illustrate the various geographical characteristics of the continent. The maps take the spectator out of the projected world – so to speak – and again are reminders of a discourse at work. Furthermore, sudden shifts in tone or subject matter occasionally wrench the spectator from involvement in the projected world of the film, reminding her again of the discursive function of the text. The focus of the film changes radically from the concentration on one family making pack saddles for mules, to the problems of a small town, to the characteristics of an entire country, to the South American continent as a whole, and finally, to the effects of world events (World War II, in this case) on trade between South America and other continents. Many nonfictions of the formal voice exhibit significant reflexivity in formal technique. Although it does not typically disrupt the continuity of the projected world, the formal voice, in its use of maps, voice-over, and shifts in focus, tone, and subject matter often make its status as discourse quite apparent to the spectator.

The last element of voice – tone – raises interesting questions with respect to the characterization of modes of documentary. Describing the tone of a discourse is a subtle task, akin to describing a person's character or the ambience of a room. Could there be one discursive tone associated with the formal voice, and others for the open, poetic, or parodic documentary? Here again one is forced to speak of broad tendencies rather than immutable laws. A central characteristic of the formal voice is its dissemination of full and adequate knowledge of its subject. What tone might accompany such an epistemological function? In broad terms, we could describe such a tone as "serious" and "forthright." This is unsurprising, since for the most part, formal documentaries are born of a need to inform the public about some issue. *Harlan County, U.S.A.*, takes a solemn pro-union stance; a flippant or jovial tone would scarcely do justice to the resolve with which the miners fight for their cause. The American World War II documentaries of the *Why We Fight* series are more strident and warlike in tone, encouraging a contempt for the enemy and an energetic and simple patriotism on the part of their audiences. Again, such is to be expected in times of war, and the tone fits the seriousness of purpose.

But to call the formal documentary earnest is not to proclaim dullness in the same breath. Within this tendency, and at times bordering it, are a diffusion of tones that point to a marvelous diversity of films. The tone of *Dead Birds* is highly poetic, sympathizing with the magical world of the Dani people, and at times very literary in describing the inner psychology of the two major characters, Wayak and Poo-ah. Like *Harlan County, U.S.A., The Wobblies* (1979) is overtly pro-union. It is more energetic and celebratory, however, with its jovial pro-union songs and interviews with lively old activists. The war documentaries of Humphrey Jennings stand in sharp contrast to the American *Why*

We Fight series. Their subdued artfulness emphasizes the quiet resolve of the British to get the job done, and rarely breaks into angry tirades against the enemy. Michael Moore's *Roger and Me*, although formal in its epistemic authority, also uses humor and irony to express its points.

The Open Voice

The formal voice disseminates ostensible knowledge of the actual world, and teaches from a position of superior knowledge. Other films have been produced in alternative voices and with different epistemological aims. Fred Wiseman's *High School, Law and Order* (1969), and *Basic Training*, Robert Drew's *Primary* (1960) and *Crisis: Behind a Presidential Commitment* (1963), Rouch and Morin's *Chronicle of a Summer* (*Chronique d'un Été*, 1961), Ricky Leacock's *Happy Mother's Day* (1963), the Maysles Brothers' *Salesman* (1969) and *Christo's Valley Curtain* (1974), Ross McElwee's *Sherman's March* and *Time Indefinite* (1994), Les Blank's *God Respects Us When We Work, But Loves Us When We Dance* (1968) and *Sprout Wings and Fly* (1983), D. A. Pennebaker's *Don't Look Back* (1966), George Nierenburg's *Say Amen, Somebody* (1984), and Kevin Rafferty's *The Atomic Cafe* (1982), all "speak" with what I call the "open voice."[14]

The formal voice explains; it teaches and directs. It maintains a hierarchical relationship with the viewer, such that the viewer is taught by a discursive presence that assumes a position of knowledge. The organizational and stylistic forces coalesce to present a unified representation of a subject, marked by clear contextualization of knowledge within a relatively conventional structure – be it narrative, categorical, or rhetorical. It argues about, categorizes, and gives canonical narrative structure to events and topics. The formal voice *makes sense of* its subject and passes on that sense to the spectator.

The open voice, although it can never completely divest itself of this formative teaching function, is more hesitant in its epistemological position, and at times opposes the dissemination of knowledge within a clear-cut conventional framework. In the case of direct cinema, Paul Arthur argues, this epistemic hesitance expressed itself in "an abiding mistrust of top-down solutions . . . expressed in cinema as a complete abandonment of extratextual appeals to authority, the refusal of history as causal explanation, and the disavowal of preconceived agendas and concrete social prescriptions."[15] Where the formal voice may be said to *explain*, the open voice *shows, provokes,* and *explores*. It may also *imply* propositions about the projected world, but these implications differ from the explicit, high-level assertions of the formal voice. The open voice is always *implicitly* rhetorical, but it does not take the overt rhetorical positions of the formal voice. This epistemological position, basically an unwillingness to claim full knowledge on its part, results in representational strategies markedly different than those of the formal voice. One sees a meandering, open, unpredictable structure rather than the conventional patterns of its formal counterpart. The open voice implies an attitude different from that of the formal voice; it is hesitant to make broad claims about its subject, and provides neither neat contextualizations nor a strong sense of closure. It is content to observe or to explore; it lets the viewer draw her own conclusions.

Some may assume that films of the open voice are coextensive with the observational film. However, observational film is indebted to specific historical movements, and the open voice to functions not as an historical category but as an heuristic – a description of the voice of any nonfiction film in which the discourse takes the appropriate epistemic position toward the projected world. For example, some of the films of Les Blank fit the open category, although they are not thought to be "observational" films.

But in addition to this, observational film is in fact two methods of filmmaking, not one. It is useful to distinguish (within observational film) between the American school of direct cinema and the primarily French school of cinéma vérité. Cinéma vérité often takes an active role in provoking events it films, whereas direct cinema aims to remain as unobtrusive as possible in recording a subject.[16] Although the films of direct cinema – Fred Wiseman's films about institutions, for example – exemplify the open voice, many other types of films do as well. Among these are the films of cinéma vérité, which openly flaunt their constructedness, are highly reflexive, exhibit obtrusive techniques, and openly influence the profilmic event. Although Rouch and Morin's *Chronicle of a Summer* comes to mind as a prototype of cinéma vérité, Ross McElwee's *Sherman's March* and *Time Indefinite*, with their consistent reflexivity, exemplify an American approach to that method.

Still, the influence of direct cinema in encouraging films of the open voice cannot easily be overestimated. Direct cinema has been the most discussed subgenre of documentary since the middle sixties, and for good reason. The sixties in North America brought a virtual renaissance to documentary filmmaking, both for the screen and for video. Not only were the alarming events of that period inherently the stuff of documentary, but also nonfiction film technique itself underwent something of a revolution, a technical and stylistic revolution that has left a strong mark on today's documentary practice. Several more recent documentaries, for example, *California Reich* (1976), *American Dream, Say Amen, Somebody,* and *The War Room* (1993) have been made in the direct cinema style, and many others incorporate important elements of it, combining commentary and interviews with direct cinema footage (shot with available light and with synchronized sound recording).

Direct cinema practitioners remain unobtrusive in filming a scene. The purpose is to represent a subject, as much as possible, apart from the mediating subjectivity of the filmmaker. The direct cinema filmmaker refuses to arrange the profilmic event, and in postproductions avoids use of the omniscient voice-over narrator or nondiegetic music. The intended effect varies from filmmaker to filmmaker; it is often to give the spectator an experience similar to that which the filmmaker had while making the film, to represent reality free of preconceptions, or merely to allow the spectator more freedom to interpret events. Direct cinema implies a method of filmmaking, a stance toward representing reality, and an attitude toward the spectator.

The open voice does not necessarily attempt to mirror reality or to attain "absolute objectivity," although these have probably been among its varied aims from time to time. Films of the open voice, and especially cinéma vérité, may be highly reflexive and may take an idiosyncratic or ironic perspective toward their subject. But even those open documentaries falling within the realm of direct cinema should not be thought of as objective imitations in the absolute sense. Of all types of documentary, direct cinema is most prone to the mistaken notion that documentary films imitate or copy reality. This notion is more often attributed to direct cinema by its critics than actually held by its practitioners. Direct cinema is often criticized for its ostensible objective stance, for posing as transparent reality or as an objective representation of its subject. Although the films of direct cinema may encourage viewers to *see them* as objective representations, absolute objectivity and the mirroring of reality are not the goals of most of the filmmakers themselves, and the subjective traces in the films are not difficult to uncover.

Perhaps fearing the appearance of naiveté, direct cinema filmmakers go to great pains to reject the notion that what they are doing is representing reality "just as it is," or "objectively." David Maysles talks of the impossibility of "being strictly objective in anything that is at all artistic." He goes on: "I don't think we ever strive for that kind of reality. There is no worth in 'this is the way it was – exactly.'"[17] Wiseman, who is careful to distance himself from the "school" of direct cinema, dissociates himself from any claims of objectivity: "I think this subjective-objective stuff is a lot of bullshit. I don't see how a film can be anything but subjective. . . . They are not objective, because someone else might make the film differently."[18]

If the films are not objective, or imitations or reality, why make films in this style at all? That is, if we must reject the notion of the direct cinema documentary as a copy of reality, then why make direct cinema films? To explore the motivations for direct cinema or cinéma vérité is to explore the motivations for the open voice, because these subgenres are the central exemplifications of the open voice. Films of the open voice can be justified not simply for some presumed copying function, but for their epistemological hesitation. The open voice recognizes that we must approach some subjects with the humility of one who does not claim to know. The open voice may withhold high-level generalizations about its subject not in the name of imitation, but in an unwillingness to offer neat explanations and contextualizations. Withholding such high-level explanations also may facilitate a democracy of interpretation, allowing the spectator to come to her own conclusions. The open voice self-consciously reacts against the epistemic authority implicit in films of the formal voice.

Moreover, the open voice often fully exploits the capabilities of camera and sound recording equipment, and emphasizes the iconic and indexical functions of the image rather than their symbolic function. It is possible to represent the looks and sounds of profilmic scenes without claiming for a film either absolute objectivity or a pure imitating or copying. I'm convinced that Michael Wadleigh's *Woodstock* (1970) offers a wealth of information about the famous music festival at Yasgur's Farm, despite its clear romanticization. Likewise, *Say Amen, Somebody* offers an invaluable introduction to the sights and sounds of African-American gospel music, although again one could hardly call this celebratory film objective, balanced, or complete.

The open voice shows rather than tells. It presents images and sounds not only as mere symbolic pieces in a chain of signification, but for their qualities as icons and indices with revelatory potential. Whereas the formal voice uses images and sounds to generate explicit, high-level explanations, the open voice exploits the ability of cameras and microphones to observe and show, record and play back. And whereas the open voice cannot avoid the implications of perspective through structure and style, we can nonetheless appreciate its ability to *show* and *inform* through images and sounds.

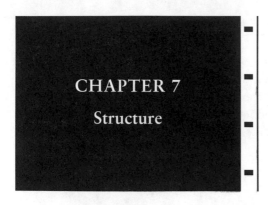

CHAPTER 7

Structure

It is sometimes thought that the structure of a nonfiction film arises naturally from its subject matter, just as a road follows the contours of the terrain on which it lies. However, we can also build the road high above the ground on pylons, run it through tunnels beneath the earth, and dig and blast the terrain to suit the road builders. I have claimed that the nonfiction film, similarly, may legitimately represent a subject in a variety of ways, and in diverse *structures*.

It is true that in a historical documentary, the order of projected world events must correspond to the chronological order of actual events. If I make a documentary about the beating of Rodney King (event A), the criminal trial of the policeman who beat him (event B), and the ensuing riots in Los Angeles (event C), the projected world of my documentary should represent the events as having occurred in the order: A, then B, then C. However, the *discursive presentation* need not follow such an order. I may first recount event C, then examine events B and A as causes. Or in a film about the policemen's trial, I may first briefly cover A and C to provide context, then go on to examine the trial (B) in greater detail. As I argued in Chapter Five, the discursive order of presentation may differ from the order of events as they are thought to have occurred. Form does not naturally follow content, and the structure of a nonfiction film depends as much on the rhetorical choices of the filmmaker as it does on subject matter.

Rhetorical and Other Structures

Narrative is but one means of structuring the projected world of the documentary. Nonfictions also use associational, categorical, and rhetorical forms. Associational structure emphasizes likenesses or relationships between entities, as *The Bridge* juxtaposes various elements of a bridge, *Chronicle of a Summer* features interviews about "happiness," and *In Heaven There is No Beer* chronicles Polka music by showing a sequence of dances and clubs, culminating in the annual "Polkabration." Associational structure well fits the open voice, as it requires only the loosest of structures, and can be based on likenesses or similarities of any sort, including the contiguities of a single location, event, or institution. Thus Wiseman's explorations of institutions follow a loose associational form, as do numerous other observational films.

Although, at its simplest, categorical form may consist of a mere list of entities, it is often conventionally structured, featuring definition, classification, and comparison and contrast. It may consist of a catalogue of parts or elements, together with an explanation or analysis. An analysis distinguishes between the parts of the thing described. *Functional* analysis goes a step further, determining the function of the parts in relation to the whole. *Causal* analysis determines the function of the parts as they cause and effect one another.

Alain Resnais' *Night and Fog* (1955), in its formal voice, analyzes the horrifying phenomenon of the Nazi concentration camps by giving a catalogue of the various elements that ensured their "efficient" operation. We see the transportation of people to the camps in trains, the social designations and hierarchies in the camp, living conditions, medical facilities and cruel medical experiments, camp prisons, gas chambers, and ovens for the disposal of bodies. We also see the Allied arrival at the camps after the defeat of the Nazis. At each point, the voice-over offers explanations of what we see, or statements that describe what we are not shown. "Many are too weak to defend their rations against thieves." "They take the dying to the hospital." The film's music, although muted, gives a clear context of sorrow to the subject. The end of the film offers a firm conclusion, and an explicit context in which to put the prior information. The Nazis ensured that nothing would be wasted in their drive to exterminate millions of people. We see piles of eyeglasses, women's hair to be used to make cloth, human bones for fertilizer, bodies for soap, and skin for paper. The appalling cruelty and destruction of life is apparent, and the voice-over intones: "There is nothing left to say." But in the conclusion of the film, and in its alternating black and white footage of the past with color footage of the present, the discourse does make explicit claims that sum up the warning central to the film. The explicit point is that we must be ever vigilant to prevent similar occurrences in the future. "War nods, but has one eye open," the voice-over says. The scourge of the death camps is still among us.

Lee Grant's Academy Award-winning *Down and Out in America* (1986) stands at the shading between the formal and open voices, and between categorical and associational form. Its use of voice-over narration is a technique associated with the formal voice, since it carries much of the information of the film, clearly identifying the images and illustrating their pertinence for the broader issue – unemployment and poverty in America. The film begins to analyze the situation by partitioning it into several categories: farmers having financial difficulty and losing their farms, workers facing unemployment due to industrial plant closings, a parking lot in Los Angeles – Justiceville – turned into a living space for the homeless, and Hispanic families in New York renovating abandoned apartment houses. In the last segment, the film focuses on a particular family of six who lack the resources to escape their dismal life in a welfare hotel.

The film straddles the boundaries between the open and formal voices because explicit analysis occurs only *within,* and never *between,* each of these partitioned scenes; the relationship between scenes is one of association but never explicit analysis. The voice-over describes each situation, but draws no comparisons between them. *Down and Out in America* stops short of coming to any generalized conclusions about what the several scenes add up to, refraining from linking the various situations with generalized comments on the state of poverty in America. The film remains open in this respect, because it leaves the viewer to come to her own conclusions.

Other films feature a rhetorical structure. In the realm of rhetoric, some make a distinction between persuasion and argument. Argument is typically thought of as a formal, logical process. To settle a matter by formal argument is to appeal to reason. To make an argument is to claim that a conclusion, usually in the form of a proposition, merits belief on the basis of salient evidence, true premises, and valid reasoning. Persuasion, on the other hand, is a much less formal process – the art of getting someone to do or believe what you want them to do or believe. We might describe such a process not as argument, but as "artistic proof."[1] Following Aristotle's *Rhetoric,* successful persuasion wins assent to the will of the persuader, and depends on *dispositio,* or structure, *elocutio,* or style, and *inventio,* argument or proof. Three types of "proof" equip the persuader: (1) ethical proof – the presumed character and credibility of the persuader, (2) emotional proof – the persuader's ability to stir the emotions, and (3) demonstrative proof – the appeal to evidence (testimony, statistics, examples). In the case of demonstrative truth, the aim is to present evidence in the best possible light, so that it is persuasive (although not necessarily accurate or authentic). Whereas the aim of formal argument is to establish a reasonable conclusion, the end of persuasion, or artistic proof, is to win the assent of the listener or spectator.

All films are rhetorical in the sense that they imply an ideological position toward their subject. One could say that all films of the formal voice are persuasions, since they proselytize – implicitly or explicitly – for their ideological position, and since their function is to teach and explain. But not all films employ overt artistic proofs as their overall organizational principle. Explicit argument and artistic proof are often antithetical to the whole project of the open voice, because they eschew the teaching function (and thus presume to persuade the spectator of very little). Nonetheless, the discourse in such films often smuggles in rhetorical material, and no nonfiction film can escape rhetoric entirely. The formal voice, on the other hand, often makes use of explicit strategies of persuasion to win the spectator's assent.

With few exceptions, a persuasive case in a formal film is stated verbally by a voice-over narrator or interviewee. To structure a film as an artistic proof usually requires the use of language. Only verbal or other symbolic discourse, perhaps in tandem with images, can explicitly make complex arguments and persuasive cases. Willard Van Dyke's *Valley Town*, for example, makes its position verbally explicit. Over shots of men working on an airplane engine, the voice-over sums up the film's argument: "Let's keep the workers up to date. Let's keep their skills as modern as the new machines." In addition, films of the formal voice do not simply include local rhetorical moments (as in open films), but are often globally structured according to an artistic proof that becomes the motivating principle of the work.

A clear example of rhetorical structure is *CBS Reports'* 1960 "Harvest of Shame," an hour-long episode featuring Edward R. Murrow as voice-over narrator. "Harvest of Shame" is structured as an artistic proof, bringing evidence and emotional appeals to bear on a set of propositions to which the film wishes to gain assent. (This is a rare example of a network documentary that sharply criticized American society, placed blame for a social problem squarely on a particular group, and advocated specific legislation to alleviate the problem.) The propositions can be condensed into two general theses. The first is that migrant workers suffer under inhumane living and working conditions. The second is that federal legislation is needed to alleviate the problem.

The overall rhetorical structure is very simple, as the film (1) presents visual evidence and oral testimony in making its case, (2) makes an emotional appeal for action, and (3) suggests a plan of action, in that order. It also couches its rhetorical structure within an overarching narrative movement, a cyclical journey as we follow the migrants from job to job and from location to location.

Formal Narrative Structure

Any film that recounts a chronology of events makes use of a narrative structure. In their narrative structure, nonfiction films of the formal voice share important structural similarities with classical fiction films. One of the means by which David Bordwell, Janet Staiger, and Kristin Thompson characterize the classical Hollywood style of filmmaking is through Hollywood's discourse about itself in trade manuals, memos, production and screenwriting books, etc.[2] To characterize what is "classical" about nonfiction films of the formal voice by similar means, however, would be impossible.

Trade manuals for nonfiction film are not only less common than those for fiction, but with few exceptions, they do not treat the structure of the films.[3] For example, an early handbook of documentary film production, W. Hugh Baddeley's *The Technique of Documentary Film Production,* wholly ignores the structuring and composition of documentary discourse.[4] Baddeley's book is highly technical, covering such topics as budgets, equipment, editing, and distribution. This neglect of narrative structure has stemmed in part from the widespread idea that the documentary, as a representation of reality, should be formed "in sympathy" with its subject. What is usually meant by such a claim is that the documentary must somehow copy, trace, or imitate reality not simply in its model of the real (the projected world), but in its discursive presentation. In his book, *Directing the Documentary,* Michael Rabiger writes that the documentary "owes its credibility to acts, words, and images quite literally plucked from life and *lacking central authorship.*" In fiction, Rabiger writes, the artist "has control over the form in which content is expressed," whereas in the documentary, "freedom of expression is severely curtailed by the idiosyncratic nature of the given materials, even circumscribed by them."[5] Once again, the correspondence theory of nonfiction film raises its head.

The projected world of a nonfiction film is a model of the actual world. The subject matter of the nonfiction film may circumscribe that model. Responsibility requires that the filmmaker give up an element of freedom in the name of accuracy, for to preserve truth in discourse, one's assertions, to the best of one's knowledge, must be accurate. But this does not require that the *discourse* not manipulate projected world data in myriad ways, both structurally and stylistically. For any given subject, one can devise numerous and diverse means for its presentation. A highly structured, stylized discourse may still assert true propositions and function as nonfiction. The ethical filmmaker strives for accuracy in representation; yet to claim that each subject naturally *requires* a particular documentary form goes too far. The assertion of truth claims, and even what might be called "accurate portrayal," can come in many varied packages.

When one examines the structure of many narrative nonfiction films, one sees repeated patterns – conventional structures. The constant repetition of these structures leads to one of two conclusions. Either the world is naturally structured according to the dictates of conventional structures, or the schemas with which documentarists work impose a conventional structure onto their subject. I suspect the latter. If nonfiction filmmakers take structure for granted, the result is that many implicitly embrace canonical structures inherited from prior documentary practice, from the classical fiction film, and from time-honored conceptions of narrative, rhetoric, and composition.

Whether employed intentionally or not, these structures are derived from centuries of discursive and artistic practice, having classical formal qualities such as unity, coherence, emphasis, harmony, and restraint. Such a discourse defines its dominant topic, distinguishes the relevant from the irrelevant, and subordinates minor to major topics. Since it explains phenomena, the formal voice selects, unifies, orders, and gives emphasis to appropriate elements of the projected world. These are features so ingrained in the Western viewer's mind that they qualify as schemas, extrinsic norms we expect to find in many documentaries.

Beginnings

Temporal ordering principles, along with voice and style, are primary means by which the discourse develops the projected world as a model, and thus makes assertions and implications about the actual world. The beginning of a formal nonfiction film – the titles and credit sequence, prologue, and preliminary exposition – carries as much weight as does the beginning of a classical fiction film. This "classical" beginning serves both a formal and an epistemological function.

Formal narrative structure follows canonical story formats in positing an initial "steady" state that is violated and must be set right. In both fiction and nonfiction film, the violation of the steady state is a catalyst for further textual movement, whether it be narrative or argument. Robert Flaherty's *The Land* (1942), for example, begins by showing idyllic scenes of American farming, while the voice-over urges that this is good land and these are good people. But these harmonies are soon interrupted when the discourse introduces a significant, threatening problem – widespread erosion. Because the steady state – good farmers farming profitably on good farms – must be restored, the discourse now is driven forward by the need to find a solution to the problem. The steady state has been made unstable, and according to the conventions of the canonical story format, must be set aright.

Humphrey Jennings' *The Silent Village* (1943) reenacts the Nazis' brutal treatment of the people of a small mining town in Czechoslovakia during World War II. The opening sequence is a poetic celebration of life before the Nazi occupation. We see church sanctuaries filled with singing parishioners, busy workers and the sounds of heavy machinery, children watching a Donald Duck cartoon, miners drinking at a pub, a mother combing a child's hair. The sequence is comprised solely of these sorts of atmospheric images accompanied by diegetic sound. The voice-over then announces that such was village life before the Fascists. We then see the first signs of the Nazi occupation – a black car with a loudspeaker, blaring propaganda. Again, the steady state has been violated, and the movement of the narrative typically works to reinstate such a state.

The violation of the steady state is the *formal* function of such a beginning; its *epistemological* function is to raise the question or questions that the narrative will gradually answer. Whether or not a steady state has been violated, the epistemological function of the beginning is always present. It initiates the cognitive processes of the spectator, encouraging hypothesis- and inference-making about the narrative and the knowledge it (ostensibly) imparts. The beginning of the film suggests frames of reference that the viewer may employ in comprehending the text. These frames enable the spectator to fill in narrative or expositional gaps with appropriate data. The formal narrative film is an erotetic narrative of the sort I described in Chapter Five; it encourages the spectator's attention by posing questions and answers, or problems and solutions, by the end of the film having answered most of the salient questions posed, and having offered solutions to problems it identifies.

No clearly identifiable steady state exists in Pare Lorentz's *The Fight for Life* (1940). The narrative immediately confronts the spectator with a crisis situation, in which the delivery of a child results in the mother's death. Exposition is delayed until after the event. Then the doctor walks solemnly through the rain, his interior monologue (in voice-over) both asking the relevant questions and stimulating the dramatic progression of the narrative, as the doctors search for safer methods of delivering babies. It is common for documentaries – as for fictions – to *assume,* rather than *initially represent,* a normal, or desirable state of affairs. In this case, the steady state is a society in which maternity is safe for both mother and child.

In *Fires Were Started* (1943), director Humphrey Jennings begins the exposition with explanatory titles, telling the spectator that the film is a story of English firemen during the Nazi bombings of London. Preliminary exposition and the steady state occur simultaneously, apparently during a lull in the bombings. The voice-over introduces us to each of the auxiliary firemen who people the film, while the group gathers around a piano, singing a jolly fireman's song. With the drone of enemy planes overhead and the blasts of exploding incendiary bombs, the firemen's narrative proper begins. Rather than an explicit posing of questions, the raising of questions here is implicit, as in most fiction. The spectator is cued to ask the questions herself. Will the bombing start fires, and will the firemen be able to put them out? What are their methods? How will they hold up in times of extreme danger and stress? Will any of the men be hurt? The formal disruption of the steady state and the epistemological function of raising pertinent questions occur here simultaneously, as the narrative begins its dramatic and epistemological movement, which is eventually brought full circle to a satisfying and symmetrical end.

The beginning of a classical narrative structure, then, serves to catalyze the dramatic movement of the narrative and open the viewer's play of question and answer. But it does more than serve as catalyst for the succeeding narrative elements. It also serves as *exposition,* creating a frame by which the narrative action can be understood. Exposition in the formal narrative documentary serves roughly the same function as it might in fiction. The function of exposition, Meir Sternberg writes, is to

... introduce the reader into an unfamiliar world ... by providing him with the general and specific antecedents indispensable to the understanding of what happens in it. [The reader] must usually be informed of the time and place of the action; of the nature of the fictive world peculiar to the work or, in other words, of the canons of probability operating in it; of the history, appearance, traits, and habitual behavior of the dramatis personae; and of the relations between them.[6]

The spectator of the formally-structured nonfiction film is provided the same sort of information about a projected world presumed to be a model for actuality.

Because its goal is to impart knowledge of the events it depicts, formal exposition tends toward absolute clarity; it thus narrows possible interpretations in favor of the one preferred by the discourse. The formal documentary takes full advantage of the "primacy effect." We are all familiar with the explicit expositional technique of network television documentaries. In the CBS television documentary series, *The Twentieth Century*, which aired from 1957–1966, Walter Cronkite appeared in the prologue of each episode to introduce the subject, explain its significance to the interests of the spectator (assumed to be American, lover of freedom and liberty, anti-Communist, etc.), and imbue the events with a moral import. Such is the typical means of exposition of network documentaries centered around a well-known anchor.

Other methods of exposition include introducing the spectator to important characters through image and voice-over. In the ethnographic film *Dead Birds* (1963), the exposition introduces the spectator to its two major subjects – Wayak, an adult male warrior, and Pooah, a small boy. The voice-over gives the two well-defined psychologies (as they might have were they characters in a classical fiction film), and describes the goals by which they live their lives. When first introduced to Wayak, we hear:

His name means "wrong." For as a child he showed unreasonable rage. As a man he learned to govern his temper, and though neither very rich nor very powerful, he has the respect of all with whom he lives. He is a warrior, a farmer, and leader of a band of men who guard the most dangerous sector of a frontier which divides themselves from the enemy.

In formally structured nonfiction films, exposition often includes spoken or written discourse, since verbal discourse is an efficient and codified means to fix interpretive schemas.

In Chapter Five, I described Meir Sternberg's classification of the various ways exposition may be positioned within a narrative. Because the function of the formal voice is primarily to impart knowledge, exposition tends to avoid "artfulness," and is preliminary rather than delayed, and concentrated rather than distributed. This is the simplest, least mentally taxing approach (for the spectator), but perhaps also the least formally interesting. *The Wilmar Eight* (1980), a Lee Grant film about eight employees of a small Minnesota bank who go on strike, concentrates its exposition before showing the women's ordeal. The first titles urge the political standpoint of the film with a rhyming ditty:

The banks are made of marble
With a guard at every door,
The vaults are stuffed with silver
That the people sweated for.

Over shots of people shovelling snow and the women picketing on a bitterly cold winter's day, the voice-over then explains their situation succinctly and generally:

On December 16, 1977, in Wilmar, Minnesota, eight women, employees of the Citizen's National Bank, walked out of their jobs and went on strike. They walked a picket line for the next year and a half, through the bitter cold of two Minnesota winters, isolated in their own community.

This exposition sets the framework for the entire film. We know both the political sympathies of the narration and how the discourse will represent the struggle (as long, difficult, and lonely). The remainder of the film unfolds the drama of the strike in roughly chronological order.

By *in media res*, Sternberg means a discursive change in the chronological sequence of projected world events. This often entails plunging the discourse into a narrative occasion and the delay of expositional and narrative antecedents. Consider the *in media res* opening of Robert Epstein's *The Times of Harvey Milk* (1984). This film is a narrative history of the political career of Harvey Milk, sometime supervisor of the 5th district in San Francisco and outspoken gay activist. The film begins with news footage showing then-mayor Diane Feinstein announce the shooting of Milk and Mayor George Mosconi. Over a black and white photograph of the two, the voice-over repeats the news of their assassinations. This is succeeded by another photograph, this time of Harvey Milk alone, as the voice-over intones: "Harvey Milk had served only eleven months on San Francisco's board of supervisors, but he had already come to represent something far greater than his office." The film's opening, then, immediately plunges the spectator into the "middle" of the story, creating dramatic interest that will help sustain the narrative history of Milk's career leading up to that crisis point. Even here, though, the plunge is brief and relatively conservative; the spectator is soon given a full account of the gaps in knowledge opened by the beginning. The exposition proper begins immediately following the reports of the murders, and from this point on the discourse parallels the chronological order of projected world events.

To sum up, beginnings in classical structure serve formal, epistemological, and expositional functions. A narrative usually begins with the violation of a steady state, which serves as a catalyst for further actions and events. The epistemological function is to raise the questions that the narrative gradually answers. The opening thus serves as a catalyst both dramatically and epistemologically. The beginning also functions as exposition, creating a frame of reference by which the events of the narrative may be understood.

Endings

The end of the formal narrative documentary has both a dramatic function and an epistemological goal, as does the beginning. The dramatic function is much the same as for the canonical fiction. The end of the classical fiction film typically brings a decisive victory or defeat to the protagonist, or the clear achievement or nonachievement of goals by the major characters. The epilogue often celebrates the stable state achieved by the major characters (reinforcing the tendency to a happy ending) and reinforces the thematic motifs appearing throughout the film.[7]

Because it is also heavily indebted to canonical story formats, formal structure in nonfiction film often shares many of these characteristics. By the end of Raymond Boulting's *Desert Victory*, Rommel and the German armies have been routed in North Africa. The celebration in the epilogue is a patriotic salute to England, including a shot of the British flag. At the end of *Farrebique*, the old patriarch has died, but his eldest son has taken his place, telling his wife that there will always be a new spring and a new beginning. He cuts bread at the family table, as the patriarch previously did at the film's onset, giving the end a strong sense of symmetry. *Target for Tonight* (1941), a Harry Watt film about a British bombing raid over Germany, ends with the success of the mission in the face of incredible odds. The pilots head off to bed, while one ground officer says to another, "Well, old boy, how about some bacon and eggs?" In all of these cases we find strong closure at the level of projected world and the discourse. Also notice the tendency for a happy ending, as in the classical fiction film.

Exceptions to the canonical paradigm exist, of course. The end of *The Silent Village* finds the entire village devastated by the Nazis. Although the end is decisive, it is not happy. The men have been shot, the women and children sent to concentration camps, the town's buildings burned to the ground, and its name taken off the face of the map. Near the end the camera slowly pans across burned items in the smoldering ruins of a house – a sewing machine, a coffee pot, the cracked photograph of a man. After a shot of a burning church, the last image is of broken household items strewn haphazardly in a rocky stream. Although the happy ending is not present here, and although the discourse deems it unnecessary to interpret the projected world events for the spectator, the film works to give a rigorous sense of closure nonetheless.

The *overarching* function of the ending is epistemological rather than dramatic. Formal endings guide the backward-directed activity of the spectator in comprehending the film. The ending may fill in gaps, sum up main points, or suggest a "correct" frame by which the previous data can be interpreted. This backward-directed activity can be achieved by "retrospective additional patterning," by which the end adds to or alters the epistemological framework constructed earlier in the text. Or the end may simply reinforce the frame that has been previously constructed.

For example, in showing the cultural life of the tribe it represents, *Dead Birds* concentrates on the men and their warlike rituals. The epilogue, in voice-over, sums up the film's interpretation of these rituals and what they mean to the culture that practices them: "They kill to save souls, and perhaps, to ease the burden of knowing what birds will never know, and what they as men, who have forever killed each other, cannot forget." War rituals, the voice-over suggests, are a way for this culture to confront their ultimate fate of death. They neither wait for death, nor take it lightly when it comes; instead, they "passion" fate.

The end of the formal narrative documentary parallels the overall epistemological function of the text, providing full, clear, high-level knowledge of the ostensible truth. It accomplishes this by answering salient questions earlier raised, summing up, reinforcing main points, or providing a frame for interpretation. There is a tendency toward a happy ending in films of the formal voice, but more universal is closure, if not in the projected world *and* the discourse, then in the discourse alone. This move toward closure is fitting for the general function of the formal voice – imparting knowledge about the actual world.

Dramatic Structure and Representation

Hayden White observes that historians do not simply *find* stories in the actual world, as though they are there to be plucked, like ripe apples from a tree. If one writes narrative history one must give narrative form to what White calls the chronicle – a simple list of events in chronological order. Real events, White claims, do not offer themselves naturally as stories.[8] We may translate White's claim into my terms; real events may dictate certain characteristics of the projected world of the nonfiction film, but they do not determine the discursive presentation. The historian must choose a beginning, a first event from the infinite number available. Similarly, the narrative must conclude, not merely end. This involves again choosing a last event to depict, and investing it with historical significance. Of the infinite number of events he could represent, the historian must choose what to depict and omit. In addition, the writing of narrative history involves more than establishing a sequence of events; the events must be given a structure of meaning. Every narrative history weights events with a significance for some individual or group, be it a nation, race, or smaller group of peers. Thus, White claims, every narrative history must moralize the events it depicts. A narrative is never a perfect copy of the world in all of its plenitude, but a particular representation from a point of view, given a significance according to the author's perspective at a particular historical juncture.[9]

John Grierson held that the documentary film consists of "arrangements, rearrangements, and creative shapings of natural material."[10] Hayden White offers a provocative account of possible means by which that "natural material" is shaped. All histories, he claims, combine data, theoretical concepts for explaining those data, and a narrative structure; all histories have a deep structural content that is poetic and imaginative. White describes histories as having several levels of conceptualization.[11] In the first instance is the chronicle, a mere list of historical events in chronological order. Next comes the story, through which the chronicle is fashioned into a narrative that features a beginning, ending, and dramatic structure. Within a narrative, data can be explained in various ways; White writes of explanation by emplotment, explanation by argument, explanation by ideological implication, and tropes of discourse. White observes that histories are fashioned in part on broad structural levels, or literary tropes. Here White follows Northrup Frye who, in his *Anatomy of Criticism*, traces five types, or strata, of plot structure in Western literature: myth, romance, comedy, tragedy, and irony. Frye's typology is especially useful for the theorist of historical narrative, White says, because the narrative structures of histories tend to be relatively simple. If one looks closely at narrative histories, one finds that they exhibit one or more or these types of plot structure.

What White says of narrative history also applies to the historical nonfiction film. In narrative films, ordering is not merely chronological sequencing, but investing events with dramatic movement and emotional force according to the perspective of the discourse. The techniques so used foreground, give emphasis, exaggerate, or invest narrative elements with some variety of significance. Although nonfiction stories have their roots in actual events, the stories are not merely "found," "uncovered," and "identified." Invention also plays a part in the operations of the historian and the documentarian.

As I have said, one of the influences on narrative documentaries has been the classical fiction film. In early nonfiction films making extensive use of staged scenes, character and character goals become an important force in the narrative movement, just as they are in the classical fiction film. *Fires Were Started*, about London's auxiliary fire service during the Nazi bombings, follows one group of firemen as they battle a fire after a night bombing. Having been introduced in the exposition to several of the firemen, the narrative is driven forward by their goal of putting out a particular fire. The discourse concentrates on the men as a team rather than on a particular hero, and it is the goal of the team that motivates succeeding actions. The protagonist is a group of men; the antagonist is the fire.

Another sort of classical structure dispenses with characters altogether, at least as they appear in the classical fiction film. In these films, the primary forces set off against each other are broader groups or impersonal agents, such as nations, labor unions, management, farmers, and nature, or natural disasters. Narrative movement in these films progresses according to the actions and goals of these groups or entities. War documentaries provide clear examples of nations as stand-ins for the individual protagonists and antagonists of narrative fiction. The films of the *Why We Fight* series provide an especially apt example. *Prelude to War* (1942) divides the Earth into the "Free World" and the "Slave World," further personifying the "forces of evil" into three nations – Germany, Japan, and Italy – and more specific yet, three leaders – Hitler, Hirohito, and Mussolini. *The Silent Village* presents its narrative as a clear conflict between the Nazis and the townspeople. *The Wilmar Eight* pits a group of women against the management of a bank. The conflict in these films is between groups rather than individuals – groups cast into the roles of protagonist and antagonist.

The narrative movement of many nonfiction films is motivated by the vagaries of nature or history rather than individuals, according to a hypothesized natural or historical progression. In *The Land*, for example, improper farming procedures have caused erosion. Here the antagonist is not a group so much as lack of education and foresight, together with the forces of nature. In this film and also in *Valley Town* (1940), the "growth of mechanization" motivates much of the narrative action. Represented as a natural, irresistible force, however, this growth is never seen as something to be overcome, as a war documentary might see a foreign army. It is seen as a permanent result of natural progression to which human agencies will have to adapt.

In general, the causality attributed to the narrative movement in formally-structured films is based on assumptions about historical progression; history is usually given a teleology. A common feature of the formal voice is the representation of this progression – be it a personal history or broader in scope – as motivated, goal-oriented, and relatively conclusive or interpretable. And although individual characters and their goals may be submerged into those of the larger group, narrative in the formal nonfiction film gives evidence of typical dramatic conventions. The narratives all present conflicts between a force with goals (the protagonist) and an opposing force standing in the way of their achievement. Although the projected worlds of formal nonfiction films differ radically from film to film, then, in the above respects we see a commonality and a continuity.

In addition to these broad structural oppositions, formally-structured films make use of other elements of traditional fictional narrative. For example, it is common for formal documentaries to use devices that create suspense. In *The Sky Above, the Earth Below* (1962), the voice-over stresses the danger of the expedition, as white explorers venture into uncharted areas where humans still live in "the stone age." As the expedition nears a village, the group sees no signs of life; here the discourse encourages suspense by extending the waiting period. Where are the inhabitants? Will they be peaceful or warlike? Will they be cannibals? Are the natives lying in wait, ready to ambush the expedition as it approaches?

In *Target for Tonight* we see that the climactic resolution is another device commonly used in the formal voice. The concern of the film is with the methods and character of the members of the British Royal Air Force during World War II. On the dramatic level, however, the most suspenseful question is whether a British bomber will return safely from its mission over Germany. Men at the airfield wait on the ground in anticipation, hoping for the safe return. The climactic moment occurs when the plane – badly damaged and in thick fog – does land safely. These examples illustrate one means by which events in the documentary are given significance – by traditional dramatic structures incorporated into the nonfiction film.

The epistemological function of the formal voice ultimately determines structure in the narrative documentary. As with beginnings and endings, dramatic movement develops in tandem with a clear rhetorical purpose encompassing the film's narrative development. The exposition poses the salient question or questions. The narrative unfolds in a constant process of answering previous questions, posing new ones, and partially revealing answers that will be answered by the end. In many films this process is explicit. The journalistic television documentary, for example, features an on-screen anchor who explicitly formulates and verbalizes the questions, for example, "Our environment – can it survive a Republican congress?" A more subtle film (or a film of the open voice) might pose these questions only implicitly, relying on the spectator to infer the questions favored by the discourse.

Open Structure

Open structure is a limit case, never found in an absolute form in any nonfiction film. It is a goal or a tendency, limited by the fact that a film must have a perspective, and that its discourse implies a way of viewing the world it projects (it has a voice). Pure open structure would render the projected world formless, as though observation occurred without the direction of the filmmakers, as though someone had set up the camera randomly and had begun and ended filming according to throws of dice. Observation in such a pure form occurs only rarely. Most films with open structure are never purely open, but fall somewhere along the way to withholding epistemic authority, and refusing to form their materials. They lie at various distances from this unattainable limit case (what we might call, in a nod to Platonic Ideal Forms, the "Absolute Open Film"), some closer than others, many mixing formal and open techniques. All of this makes talking about open structure a bit awkward, because open structure often manifests itself in negative terms, as a reaction to formal structure, and as a relative *lack* of structure that never escapes structure altogether.

Werner Herzog's *Huie's Sermon* (1980) comes relatively close to this observational extreme, as it records a minister delivering a spirited homily. Herzog's camera is nearly immobile and is steadily trained on the minister, "Huie," for much of the film. *Huie's Sermon* follows the chronology of the church service quite closely, and provides no background information either through voice-over or titles. We do not learn Huie's surname, the denomination of the church (we assume it is some branch of Protestant Christianity), or the city in which the church is located. While trained on the minister, the camera slowly zooms in and out and moves to follow his actions as his sermon builds to a fever pitch. However, this single take of the sermon allows for no narrational comment and little eliding of time through editing. Some editing occurs at the beginning, as the congregation files into church, and at the end, when the elders bless children and we see baptisms performed. Aside from these shots, the temporal structure of the film is commensurate with the structure of the sermon.

The only overt discursive intrusions occur toward the end of the sermon, and again in the last shot of the film. Towards the sermon's end, Herzog cuts to two tracking shots of the dilapidated neighborhood that is the location of the church. In addition, the last shot is a straight-on view of the now-silent Huie, as he gazes intently into the camera, as though expecting some sign that he may depart. There is little sound, and the minister stands relatively still. The effect is discomforting, because the camera lingers on Huie, refusing to cut away, and because he stares into the camera. Far from the classical summing up and contextualization within a moral or political framework, *Huie's Sermon* ends on this bizarre and enigmatic shot, subject to a wide variety of interpretations.

The uses of open structure are historically determined and malleable. Open structure in the nonfiction film has been heavily influenced by direct cinema and cinéma vérité, both movements of the 1960s. Direct cinema in the United States is partially an outcome of emerging film technologies that enabled less cumbersome means of filming subjects. Filmmakers prodded technicians to develop new equipment, light-weight cameras synchronized with mobile sound recording units, which made possible the "direct" style of shooting. Excited by the possibilities of this new equipment, early users developed an ethos of observation and recording; the function of the filmmaker became to transparently observe the world. Although this style emerged first and foremost as a series of technical and stylistic prohibitions (no voice-over, no influence on the profilmic event, no artificial lighting), it also extended to practices of structure and editing.

However, the observational cinema never settled on a consistent use of structure and editing; filmmakers continued to differ in their approaches to the organization of shots and information. At the extreme, an open structure would consist of uncut footage shot randomly. Any editing or rearrangement of the chronological order of events constitutes a manipulation of the spectator's perception, which is equivalent to the maintenance of authority on the part of the narration. Some proponents of the observational documentary have spoken in favor of preserving the chronological order of recorded events. D. A. Pennebaker, for example, has claimed that he edits his films very little, usually only when the camera malfunctions or he errs in the shooting.[12] And Ricky Leacock has said that he avoids rearranging the chronology of the material "like the plague."[13] Of course, the open documentary cannot record any event in all its plenitude, and the filmmaker must choose elements most relevant to the film's purpose.

Aside from some early and overly enthusiastic pronouncements, filmmakers working in the open voice admit the need to impose order and dramatic structure onto their films. Ordering shots necessarily provides a minimal context and implies an attitude toward the subject. Perhaps the direct cinema filmmaker moving furthest toward formal structure is Robert Drew, who ironically also played a major hand in developing the equipment that made observational filmmaking possible. Drew makes his case as follows:

What we're not doing today is making documentaries which present information and attract people. The only way we have a chance to build our impact is through dramatic development. Verbal development in documentary film is a straight line. It might build a little, but it's not going to build much. But character and life and death and so forth have the potential.[14]

If the observational documentary stands somewhere between respect for the chronology of the represented events and the imposition of a dramatic structure, Drew's films are closer to the latter extreme. Stephen Mamber writes that Drew's films exhibit a "crisis structure" featuring a hero, a contest, a winner, a loser, and a usually positive outcome. Mamber even finds parallels between Drew and Hollywood director Howard Hawks, claiming that the Drew image of the hero is quite Hawksian; a sense of male professionalism predominates the films. Mamber concludes that Drew's films are a mixture of direct cinema techniques and fictional conceptions of character, action, and structure.[15] To say that Drew's conceptions of character, action, and structure are *fictional* goes too far; what is clear is that they conflict with the observational ideal. Despite this, Drew's advocacy of dramatic structure is perhaps not so curious; it simply amounts to a call for a mixture of open and formal techniques – open style (discussed in Chapter Eight) and formal structure.[16]

Even those observational documentaries that avoid *formal* structures, however, have a loose structure that is hardly "neutral" or "objective." Fred Wiseman rarely respects the chronological order of the scenes he shoots. He claims that he selects and orders scenes based on his view of the experience he had while filming:

... your imagination is working in the way you see the thematic relationships between the various disparate events being photographed, and cutting a documentary is like putting together a "reality dream," because the events in it are all true, except really they have no meaning except insofar as you impose a form on them, and that form is imposed in large measure, of course, in the editing. I mean, the limits of the form you can impose are the limits of the raw material you have in your eighty thousand feet or forty hours of film. You finish shooting, but in that framework you can make a variety of movies, and it's the way you think through your own relationship to the material that produces the final form of the film.[17]

Wiseman's films and all open structures have loose, episodic form, more open to various interpretations than classical forms. Indeed, this openness is a conscious goal of many of the filmmakers. As Patricia Jaffe writes, direct cinema, because it is "less formal and more episodic," demands more participation on the part of the audience.[18] Wiseman claims that although his films are structured according to his view of the material, he nonetheless keeps them open-ended to encourage varied responses and interpretations: "Since reality is complex, contradictory, and ambiguous," he says, "people with different values or experiences respond differently. I think there should be enough room in the film for other people to find support for their views, while understanding what mine are."[19] Ricky Leacock repeats the same sort of claim, saying that in watching a direct cinema documentary one "can start to put things together in one's own head and make one's own logic, draw one's own conclusions, and find one's own morality."[20]

Direct cinema has had a strong influence on open structure; we tend to overlook another significant influence, however – the European art cinema. The art cinema emerged after World War II, but is best remembered for the films of the late fifties and the sixties, especially those of Bergman, Fellini, Antonioni, Truffaut, and other well known Western European directors. Jean-Luc Godard, of course, had a fascination for the documentary, and in 1968 came to the United States to make the still unfinished *1 A.M. (One American Movie)* for Leacock-Pennebaker. By that time the art cinema had become known to Americans with the rise of the "art house" and with the accessibility of American theaters to foreign productions.[21] Direct cinema, cinéma vérité, and the art cinema all became recognizable movements in the mid-sixties, and all share a reaction against the classical style. Direct cinema and cinéma vérité were movements opposed to formal methods of documentary filmmaking, whereas the art cinema developed as distinct from the classical Hollywood fiction film.

In its narrative structure, the classical fiction film follows canonical story formats, with clear exposition, linear narrative structure, and a resolution ending the plot line(s) with either a clear-cut victory or defeat for the protagonist. The structure of the art film, on the other hand, is much less predictable, with a meandering plot, a narrative movement seemingly motivated by chance rather than linear causality, and a conspicuous absence of a clear exposition or resolution. By the end of Fellini's *8½* (1963), for example, all but the most supremely confident spectators remain unclear about what has occurred at the level of the projected world. Has Guido shot himself, or has he finally resolved his existential dilemma in some other way? The structure of the art film is often wholly unpredictable, whereas in the most programmatic of classically structured fiction films, one can predict the story's outcome ten minutes into the film. One of the chief characteristics of the art cinema is its adherence to a different conception of reality than that of the classical fiction film – what David Bordwell calls "objective realism." Objective realism is marked by a dedramatization of the narrative, permanent gaps in the exposition, and a tenuous linking of events.[22]

Art films also appeal to the "subjective realism" of character psychology. The protagonist of the classical fiction film is goal-oriented. The protagonist of the art film often undergoes a crisis of identification; he is not directed by a goal, but is searching for one, or in some cases, meandering aimlessly in a world bereft of meaningful action or fraught with contradiction. This makes the choice of any one action impossible or at least uncertain. Where Rick, in the classical film *Casablanca* (1942), determines what is right and acts decisively to effect the escape of Victor and Ilsa Laslow, Guido in *8½* is paralyzed by a lack of focus and by an inability to make decisions. The film in effect becomes less plot-centered and more an exploration of Guido's psyche, illustrating the interest in subjectivity evident in the art film. The art film character, as Bordwell puts it, is "sliding passively from one situation to another."[23] This is sometimes justified as a more realistic portrayal of the human character than the relatively confident, goal-oriented protagonist of the classical film.

What do observational film and open structure have to do with the art cinema? All are reactions to classical means of structuring information. All flourished in the 1960s, and continue to wield significant influence today. All appeal to different conceptions of realism than the classical film. Instead of the imposition of formal structures, we see meandering structures seemingly based on chance rather than causality. Observational films often lack clear exposition, structure information without clear-cut logic or causality, leave out the contextualization of knowledge performed by the "summing up" of the epilogue (if one exists), and leave it to the viewer to make explicit sense of what she sees.

So far I have discussed some historical influences on open structure in the nonfiction film. I now turn to its specific characteristics. Formally-structured films create a clear context and moral/political framework for the viewer, conceptual schemas with which the spectator makes sense of the given information. Much of this work is performed at the beginning and ending of the film. In a "pure" open structure we would expect no preliminary exposition at all. Fred Wiseman's films come relatively close to this limit case. *Law and Order*, a film about the day-to-day experiences of Kansas City police and citizens, begins with its title and a series of mug shots of the faces of men (presumably criminals). It then moves to tales of various people, for example, a man arrested for beating a child, another whose daughter has been raped, an arrested woman, police officers, etc. Nothing but the film's title (and Wiseman's reputation) produce contextual schemas for the spectator, and there exists no preliminary or delayed exposition. Similarly, Tom Palazollo's *Ricky and Rocky* (1974) shows a wedding shower for an engaged couple. The spectator knows what event is being filmed only if he recognizes the depicted practices as those traditionally associated with 1970s Polish-American wedding showers. A spectator from a foreign culture might have no idea what social event occurs in this film, because it provides no exposition.

Although open structures avoid the careful exposition of the formal voice, many open films do employ a "weak" preliminary exposition. This may come in the form of introductory titles that introduce the subject or give information about the film itself. Although filmed in the direct cinema style, *California Reich* (1976) begins with these explanatory titles:

It is estimated that the Nazi Party in America – National Socialist White People's Party – has approximately 2000 members. Nazi units exist in twenty-five cities across the country. Four are in California. *California Reich* was filmed in 1974 and 1975. Its subject is the rebirth of the Nazi Movement in America. There is no narration in this film. It is the filmmaker's belief that the characters' own words are the most eloquent indictment of their racial philosophy.

Notice that this minimal preliminary exposition consists of two parts. The first introduces the subject, narrowing it from the Nazi Party overall to the four units in California. The second gives some background to the film itself, and provides a moral framework – a stance toward the Nazis. Although the discourse remains invisible throughout and is content to observe, it nonetheless calls itself an indictment of the Nazis' racial philosophy.

Several films with otherwise open structures make use of titles or even voice-over as preliminary exposition, giving a modicum of context for the film or its subject. Emile de Antonio's *Point of Order* (1963) begins with a man's voice-over: "Everything you are about to see actually happened. Eight hours a day for thirty-six days, the Special Senate Subcommittee held televised hearings, known as the Army-McCarthy hearings, in the spring of 1954 . . . and the hearings became the greatest political spectacle of its history." Given this sort of preliminary exposition, why is this nonetheless a film of the open voice?

Gauging the epistemological stance of a film is tricky. However, in the open voice, any existing exposition is drastically attenuated. Discursive exposition in the open voice is one or all of the following: relatively uncommunicative, lacking in authority, or lacking in knowledge. Although *California Reich* and *Point of Order* begin with a certain amount of exposition, discourse in the body of the films becomes much less authoritative. In neither film do we hear voice-over or nondiegetic music. The few written titles serve only to give location names and/or dates. Open structures cannot avoid all preliminary exposition, and what exposition does occur is often weak and limited to the film's beginning.

In fact, the conclusion of a nonfiction film is often a stronger clue to its epistemological position. "Absolute Open Structure" offers no explicit epilogue; no voice-over narrator sums up the meaning of the film for the spectator. In Fred Wiseman's *Hospital* (1970), a hospital priest tells worshipers that people are "nothing" before God. The film then ends with a long shot of the hospital, as the camera zooms out to reveal a highway in the foreground. On the soundtrack the parishioners sing, while we see cars driving on the highway in the foreground, and hear the rhythmic clicking of wheels on cracks in pavement. Fade to black. The film offers no explicit summing up, but instead a stark, disturbing ending, subject to multiple interpretations.[24]

In *Point of Order*, a voice-over narrator introduces the subject of the film at the beginning. However, the film ends with no explicit discursive comment, as while the hearings recess and the participants file out, Senator Joseph McCarthy continues to drone on. Like that of *Hospital*, the ending here is again suggestive. It suggests that McCarthy has begun to lose power, as those at the hearing no longer listen to his extravagant warnings about communist infiltration. Films of the open voice, then, may implicitly suggest an interpretation of events, but they cannot offer explicit explanations. Whereas formal structures ask and answer clear questions, open structures may not formulate clear questions, and certainly do not answer them.

The end of *Chronicle of a Summer* suggests a means by which a cinéma vérité film takes the epistemological position of the open voice. At some point during the production, filmmakers Rouch and Morin decide to screen the unfinished film for those people who have been filmed. The discussion that follows shows not only that those persons disagree about the film's merits, failures, and meanings, but that they have begun to quarrel with each other. In the reflexive last scene of the film, the filmmakers discuss the screening and the strategies of the film in general. Rouch does give a weak summation, as he and Morin stroll through an interior hallway: "This film, unlike normal cinema, re-introduces us to life. People react as they do in life. They're not guided, nor is the audience. We don't say, this man is good or another wicked, or nice, or clever. So the audience is bewildered by these people they could actually meet. It feels implicated but would prefer not to be." After these words, the filmmakers wander into the streets. In the last words of the film, Morin says, "We're in for trouble." Immediately following are the end credits (over circus music designed to associate the film with circus-like antics). The film is an experiment, an exploration, and the filmmakers withhold the final authority to explain either the subject matter or the project of the film. Morin's last words express more than hesitancy; they mark his epistemic *doubt*. Although it is never clear what kind of trouble Morin refers to, it is at least plausible that the trouble is one of determining what the film has accomplished.

Exposition occurs in formal structures not only in the beginning, but often is distributed throughout the body of the film. Voice-over typically performs this task explicitly, as language has the capacity to express high-level propositions with efficiency. Films with open structures typically avoid the use of voice-over narration, precisely to forebear the explicit exposition typical of the formal voice. In fact, we see far less exposition throughout the body of films with open structures.

California Reich is organized as a series of personality studies of various neo-Nazis in California. These are interspersed with various events, such as the celebration of Hitler's birthday, and a social gathering during which a group watches football and teaches the children Nazi principles. Although explanatory titles appear at the beginning and end of the film, no explicit discursive presence makes itself known during the body of the film, aside from brief identificatory titles.

After becoming acquainted with the neo-Nazis, the spectator suspects that some suffer from serious mental problems, including paranoid feelings of isolation from society. Where the formal voice might analyze the psyches of the neo-Nazis and *identify* their possible mental disorder(s), *California Reich* refrains from such identification. Where the formal voice might *define* the word "Nazi," or the California brand of Nazism, *California Reich* simply presents us with their words and actions, without such a conceptual framework. *California Reich* does not give the information necessary to constitute an analysis, but merely presents images and sounds. Although the film takes a clear position toward the neo-Nazis, it is nonetheless an observation. Where exposition analyzes and explains, giving explicit information about the various parts of the subject and perhaps their respective functions, observation merely *presents the subject to the senses.*

Similarly, in its account of the Army-McCarthy hearings, *Point of Order* condenses a thirty-six day event into a film of less than an hour in length. Director Emile De Antonio has obviously chosen some of the most heated exchanges between the participants, plus material that reflects poorly on McCarthy. The represented events, however, are linked without benefit of the clear causal structure that would be found in the formally-structured film. Each represented episode is introduced by a title, such as "The Cropped Photo," "President Eisenhower Intervenes," and "The Accusation." The discourse neither implies nor asserts anything about the significance of each episode or its relation to the others. Here the spectator must extrapolate for herself. Permanent gaps in exposition deny the explanations expected of films of the formal voice.

Formal structure is typically unified and coherent, and makes use of strategies of emphasis. Although the open structure is often unified in a weak sense – that is, it is about one subject and not a hodgepodge – it is normally less coherent and less likely to use techniques which ensure emphasis. Coherence is often a matter of order. A logical and conventional system of ordering promotes coherence, and the film using familiar means of discourse ordering – chronological, logical, spatial, etc. – will be more easily comprehended by the Western spectator. A coherent text also makes use of transitions, reminders, repetitions, and "signposts," all of which work to ensure an easy understanding.

Although most open structures are not confusing masses of unrelated parts, they nonetheless exhibit less concern with the precise, linear coherence of their formal counterparts. Wiseman's films, for example, are ordered according to his impressions of the institutions he films. However, they are structured in complex ways which demand a great deal of synthesis on the part of the viewer. A formally structured film about the police in a large city would organize the discourse into neat categories that reflect conventional means of discursive organization. It might first introduce the police, then detail crime problems, then show the interactions between police and the lawbreakers. Or it could deal with jails, the streets, organized crime, and other topics in recognizable groupings. Wiseman's *Law and Order*, on the other hand, is arranged in no such clear ordering system. In an elaborate *mosaic* (to use Bill Nichols' term), we see an interview with a prospective police officer, a man who has been beaten and robbed, roll call at the police station, a domestic dispute, a woman whose purse has been stolen, a man cursing at the police, etc. The spectator eventually gets a sense of the complexity of police work and of the social problems that make police necessary. We might even find a vague structure of sequences showing the police to be alternatively kind and cruel, as Barry Keith Grant says.[25] Although one can interpret a thematic purpose to the structure of sequences, the structure of information is relatively unconventional.

Emphasis is central to the formal film because textual elements attain greater or lesser importance according to the film's epistemological project. The discourse emphasizes through voice-over statements of importance, by the positioning of various elements, by the proportion of time spent on an element, and by repetition and other formal strategies. The open structure must emphasize some events over others; the importance with which spectators invest beginnings and endings makes this unavoidable to a degree. Yet unlike the formal structure, open structure develops no textual hierarchy and allows no clear linear development. In *Law and Order*, for example, no segment is explicitly stated or shown to be more important than another, and no particular scene foregrounded as a key to understanding the film. The roll call scene, in which officers report for duty, is repeated, but only because it is a daily occurrence, and not for any special significance it has. Some scenes are longer than others, but again, the spectator is likely to attribute this to the requirements of the profilmic scene rather than to an emphasis asserted by the film's discourse. The last segment of the film shows a desperate young man pleading for access to his child. This scene takes on a special importance because of its position in the film's structure. The police tell the man that his only recourse is through the courts. Some may interpret this as comment on the inability of the police to solve social problems. Yet again, the film itself does not emphasize this segment by any means other than its position as last segment.

In general, open structures are more episodic, meandering, and idiosyncratic than their formal counterparts, although no film can avoid formal structure altogether. Formal structures are motivated by the requirements of conventions of composition. Open structure may be motivated in various ways, by the filmmaker's associations while filming, by an anthropological experiment or a journey, or by pure chance. Open structures will be less predictable than formal structures. Open structure will always contribute to the voice of the film, and in films of the open voice, it works in tandem with an epistemic hesitance, a reluctance to claim full knowledge.

CHAPTER 8
Style and Technique

Nonfiction film and video obviously depend on technology. The representations possible to the documentarian are limited not only by the imagination, but by the capabilities and availability of many types of machines. If the structure of a nonfiction is somewhat independent of technology, style and technique wholly depend on technological equipment – cameras, film stocks and videotapes, lights, sound recorders, sound equalizers and processors, computers and software, and editing systems. In this chapter we explore the implications of style and technique.

Here I think of film *techniques* as local means of composition in film; obvious examples are editing, camera movement, lighting, and sound. A film's *style* consists of its patterns of uses of such techniques. Style and technique have both a rhetorical and an informational function. Style participates in world projection and the modeling of the real, and thus in the determination of discursive voice. Style transmits information, but its functions extend far beyond this. Like structure, it is also a means to affect the spectator emotionally and perceptually.

The formal voice maintains an epistemic authority toward the world it projects. All of its textual elements – including technique and style – are ordered and unified according to its explanatory or teaching function. Style in the formal voice serves the rhetorical project of the film; it transmits information about the projected world; it helps develop the film's perspective; it elicits the desired perceptual and emotional effects in the spectator. Style is rarely used as an end in itself – as an ornament, but is bridled to the unified functions performed by the film's discourse. Stylistic flourishes may occur, but they remain flourishes in a discourse otherwise marked by a consistent communicative function. Technique, structure, and voice all intermesh in another characteristic of formal style – discourse coherence. A communication is "coherent" when its parts are appropriately organized to facilitate spectator comprehension. In technique, formal style strives for absolute denotational clarity and maximum discourse coherence.

Like open structure, open style is a limit case, and does not exist in a pure form. At the unreachable extreme, open style would withhold any sort of discursive comment or explanation in lieu of mere observation. Yet any use of film technique, and any style in a nonfiction film, must contribute to the perspective of the discourse. Think of open style not as an absolute, then, but in relational terms, as a matter of degree. Open style withholds expression and authority, never absolutely, but in comparison with formal style. Open style moves toward observation and exploration, but cannot entirely escape rhetoric and implication. Open style exists not in a pure form, but approaches that which refuses to explain, analyze, and/or comment on the material it presents.

The observational film manifests one kind of open style – a stylistics of observation. Observational films typically avoid ornamentation in an attempt to capture appearances and sounds. Like formal style, style in the observational film strives for denotational clarity; however, it avoids stylistic techniques that are thought to constitute unwarranted discursive intrusion – music, voice-over, slow motion, etc. The use of hand-held cameras and portable sound equipment results in the trade-mark shaky image and low fidelity sound. Black and white and often high-speed, grainy film stock have enabled filmmakers to work in low-light conditions, although recent improvements in stocks make these characteristics less common. The use of the single camera requires long takes and frequent camera movement, such as zooms in and out and the swish pans used to quickly change camera position. Moreover, as Barry Keith Grant observes, the style of observational films evokes the drama of "the camera's spontaneous search for points of visual interest," which sometimes surpasses our interest in the profilmic events themselves; this accounts for their feel of spontaneity, and their lack of "well-formed" images.[1] In the name of epistemic humility and a confidence in the ability of the equipment to capture the look and sound of a scene, the observational filmmaker avoids stylistic flourishes, but substitutes a stylistics of another sort.

On the other hand, other films of the open voice – for example, Chris Marker's *Sans Soleil* – foreground style as a concomitant factor in an ambiguous presentation of the projected world. In other words, the open voice does not necessarily require observational stylistics, for the ornamental and the expressive can also contribute to epistemic hesitancy or ambiguity. In the films of Les Blank, style is often used to express the filmmaker's exuberant sense of humor, yet it offers no explanations or information. Les Blank's films bear his unique stamp in their celebration of the music and food of diverse ethnic groups. Several of his films have highly reflexive discourse that is overt and expressive, incorporating playful stylistic techniques that call attention to their status as films. For example, *In Heaven There is No Beer* (1984) provides weak exposition for its presentation of Polka music and dancing, but for the most part is content to observe and celebrate eating, drinking, dancing, music, and zest for life. It incorporates some of the nondiegetic stylistic flourishes Blank often uses to comment on the projected world. As the band sings the film's theme song, "In Heaven There is No Beer," Blank gives us a sort of Eisensteinian intellectual montage (without Eisenstein's high seriousness). We see a shot of the statue of an angel with a sad countenance, followed by another shot of an angel – this one with arm upraised, beer can in hand, and a satisfied countenance. Elsewhere, we hear a song about stealing Kiszca (sausage), illustrated by staged shots of a woman stealing a large Polish sausage from a van. Other stylistic marks include graphic matches. One match juxtaposes a shot of a water fountain spurting upward with the spray of a just-opened can of beer. Blank's hand-drawn titles and credits, with their folk-art appeal, mark the films as "small" and "personal" – as Les Blank films.

Blank's films and others fit the epistemological stance of the open voice, yet unlike the observational film, they make use of an ornamental style that becomes a mark of overt discourse and authorship. The open voice does not necessarily require the stylistic minimalism of direct cinema. Expressiveness and the flaunting of style do not necessarily imply a discursive explanatory function, but as in the art film, may serve to flaunt the subjectivity of the filmmaker. Nonetheless, we can make certain generalizations about open style. Although style in the open film may imply attitude, as in Les Blank's films, open style is not used to supply explanations, or to assert high-level propositions about the projected world. In addition, if we take the observational film as the *prototypical* open film, we may add that open style tends toward a stylistics of observation.

Discourse Coherence and Editing

Formal style strives for absolute denotational clarity, or what we might call *coherence*. The coherence or clarity of a discourse resides in part at the global level, the level at which the text makes use of the organizing principles of narrative, rhetorical, or categorical form, plus strategies of beginning, ending, and structuring. But spectators also approach texts at the local level, making sense of elements linked according to conventions and rules of communication. It is this local level, the level of sequences of images and sounds, that I am concerned with here.

Teun van Dijk calls this linkage "discourse coherence."[2] Van Dijk is mainly interested in discourse coherence in relation to the chronological ordering of words and sentences, but we will discuss it in image-related terms as well. For van Dijk, linguistic discourse consists of an ordering of sentences that express sequences of propositions. How do the propositions of discourse combine to form complex meanings? The ordering of propositions, van Dijk says, is constrained by rules or conventions of meaningfulness. Many of these rules are lodged in the preconscious of a particular community of language users. To the extent that the discourse follows these rules, it is considered locally coherent. For example, one common convention is that proposition ordering should reflect the general-to-particular ordering of facts. The example Van Dijk gives is the following:

a. Next month we will be staying in Berkeley.
b. We will be staying with friends.

This sequence of statements is meaningful to the reader because it follows the general-to-particular principle of proposition ordering. When one reverses their order, the sentences' meaning becomes problematic, and their mutual relationship confusing.

In linguistic discourse, the most conspicuous coherence rules hold for the representation of cause/effect or temporal relations between events and actions. Causes will generally be listed before their effects. A succeeding proposition can then function as a specification, explanation, example, comparison, contrast, or generalization with respect to the previous proposition. In addition, Van Dijk writes that discourse coherence is also related to our schemas relating to everyday life. Conventional procedures govern many of our social activities, including, for example, ordering food at a restaurant. When ordering food, we normally follow established protocols. We do not moan loudly to get the waiter's attention, or order a daffodil salad, because we have schemas about polite social behavior and about what foods are served at our culture's restaurants. A coherent discourse assumes and respects similar cultural schemas, allowing the reader/viewer to process information quickly and easily.

Nonfiction film discourse, because it conveys information through images as well as language, cannot be modeled exactly in van Dijk's way. A major parameter of discourse coherence in film is editing. Various styles of editing suggest strategies that are more or less conventional, more or less coherent and easily processed. In the canonical fiction film, certain patterns of editing function this way, allowing for clear spatial and temporal relationships from shot to shot. Within a scene, the first shot will likely be an establishing shot, followed by one of three possibilities: a long shot of a different locale, a long shot of a different view of the same locale, or a closer shot of the same space.[3] Spectators make sense of succeeding shots by fitting their represented space into a cognitive map of the locale often supplied by the establishing shot.

For the most part, nonfiction films are more free-ranging in their use of space and time than classical fiction films. Spaces are often numerous, fleeting, and not as carefully constructed. Where the fiction film often limits a scene or sequence to a single space, the nonfiction film "bounces" around the globe, using whatever images are needed to construct the thread of its linear progression. Moreover, many documentaries make use of stock footage and are limited to however few shots of the subject are available. Since space is often ill-defined in these films, the axis of action is often broken if not wholly ignored; the construction of a well-defined space is of little concern. In "Harvest of Shame," for example, the spectator rarely gets a sense of a unified space in any of the various labor camps and fields in which the laborers work. In nonfiction film, the spatial context can be as broad as the universe itself (as in Errol Morris's *A Brief History of Time*) and the historical framework as all-inclusive as the history of the world. Think of the *Why We Fight* series, for example, with its divisions of the world into "slave" and "free," "evil" and "good." Whereas the classical fiction film maintains unity of time and space within a sequence, the documentary is spatially more fluid, moving from place to place with an ease rarely seen in its fictional counterpart.

Editing in films of the formal voice typically serves the film's rhetoric through the ordering of *propositions* rather than spaces. Paul Messaris calls this "propositional editing."[4] I argued in Chapter Four that images convey propositions in relation to their conventional use, linguistic accompaniment, and context. Messaris further suggests that some of the common propositional uses of editing are to compare and contrast, draw an analogy, infer causality, or generalize. When the formal style uses propositional editing, coherence depends on the same "rules" as as linguistic discourse. The general-to-particular rule and the ordering of cause before effect, for example, function in much the same way.

Editing in the formal style keeps the spectator oriented by maintaining a comprehensible pace of shots, and if space is not carefully defined, it is at least not disorienting. This is accomplished both through conventional cinematographic techniques (discussed below) and cues of continuity editing, such as matches on action and the maintenance of consistent screen direction. In the battle scenes of war documentaries, for example, the guns of the favored army will often aim left to right, while those of the enemy aim right to left, or according to consistent screen directions established by maps or charts. In addition, techniques such as eyeline matches, the use of cut-aways and cut-ins, and shot/reverse shot structures are the norm. Edward R. Murrow's interviews with Secretary of Labor Mitchell in "Harvest of Shame," for example, are staged and cut as in a classical fiction film, although with less variation in their basic editing structures. During the interviews, the camera is typically focused on Mitchell in medium close-up. Interspersed are reverse shots of the interviewer, Murrow, and occasional shots of Mitchell over Murrow's shoulder. Point-of-view shots and eyeline matches are common as well. These are efficient and coherent communicative techniques in part because they approximate a human form of information-gathering.[5] We often look at others to determine what they view, then look at the object of their attention. This exactly follows the sequence of shots in the eyeline match.

Style at the service of information transmission does not preclude poetic interludes and stylistic flourishes, however. The beginning and ending of *The Times of Harvey Milk*, for example, use slow motion montages of shots depicting Milk's political life. Together with the synthesized music, these scenes evoke a dreamlike quality that suggests the importance we often attribute to assassinated leaders. Montage scenes of marchers in the *Why We Fight* series suggest the dance-like lure of regimentation, with their hypnotic rhythms created through sound and editing. And in Disney's *The Living Desert*, informative discourse momentarily halts for a celebration of nature, with a rhythmic montage of courting Scorpions "dancing" the "Stingeree" to country music.

But even with the stylistic flourishes, a primary function of style is to present projected world information, to develop discursive voice, or to cause an effect in the spectator sympathetic to the textual project. In *The Times of Harvey Milk*, the above-mentioned scene clearly preserves the unity of the film's rhetorical emphasis by mythologizing the fight for gay rights in the person of Harvey Milk. In the *Why We Fight* series, the montages of marching serve to illustrate the rigidity and grandiloquence of the fascist regimes. In *The Living Desert*, the musical interludes reinforce the film's depiction of nature as organically unified and fundamentally benign. In films of the formal voice as in the classical fiction film, style is bridled to the drive to full and adequate knowledge. However, that "knowledge" may be communicated by evocative, connotational means as well as those more denotative and straightforward.

I do not imply that maximum discourse coherence is coextensive with maximum realism. Coherence in the *communication about* reality in no way implies *imitation of* reality. What Noël Carroll points out about canonical fiction films also applies to the canonical documentary:

The arresting thing about movies, *contra* realist theories, is not that they create the illusion of reality, but that they reorganize and construct . . . actions and events with an economy, legibility, and coherence . . . which surpass . . . naturally encountered actions and events. Movie actions evince visible order and identity to a degree not found in everyday experience.[6]

Although a coherent discourse sometimes incorporates techniques that mimic human perception, it just as often depends on the exaggeration or intensification of "natural" perception, such that any claims to realism lack credence.

Editing in the formal style is propositional and analytical, directing the spectator to salient details according to the rhetorical project of the film. In Bonnie Klein's *Not a Love Story* (1981), the discourse cuts from an interviewee claiming that pornography eliminates compassion, to a shot of a heavily made-up man beating rhythmically on drums, signifying a return to the primitive – to animal nature – that pornography represents. Such openly rhetorical editing is common, especially in politically-committed works.

In the open style, however, editing can be much looser, and less likely to direct the viewer along a precisely-detailed path of meaning. In Fred Wiseman's *High School*, for example, the camera is restless and continually moving. Sequences often begin with a close-up rather than an establishing shot. Although each sequence occurs in a single space, such as a classroom or gymnasium, the viewer never gets a coherent sense of that space. In one sequence a young teacher leads a typing class. The initial shot shows his face in extreme close-up, moving down to his hands as he prepares his students for a typing drill. Next comes a close-up of a typewriter, followed by a rack focus down a row of typewriters, followed by mostly close-ups of hands on typewriter keys, plaques on the wall, and another extreme close-up of the teacher's face as he reads the tedious passage the students have just typed. No obvious logic – of a spatial, causal, or rhetorical kind – directs these shots. Of the film in general we may say that editing and camera movement often proceed with no obvious motivation other than to observe elements of the profilmic scene.

However, no film can wholly escape the rhetoric of editing; we are again reminded that open style is a matter of degree, not kind. In *High School*, even though specific scenes have editing lacking any clear rhetorical purpose, to say that Wiseman's editing is overall transparent would be to miss much of the artifice of his films. Wiseman edits his films as "theories" about the institutions he observes, and the "theory" is constructed not merely by the order of the mosaic sequences, but through occasional forays into analytic editing within scenes. With regard to *High School*, Wiseman has said that he was interested in showing the gap between an official ideology of freedom and responsibility, and an actual practice of authoritarianism, rigidity, and conformity.[7] Wiseman's editing sometimes presents the teachers in a bad light. For example, in one sequence, an ill-tempered hall monitor walks the halls, humorlessly bullying the students he meets. At one point, he stops to peer through a door. Here Wiseman cuts to a shot of a physical education class in which female students perform a "Simple Simon" routine. Tellingly, the camera lingers on a girl's bottom, suggesting the hall monitor's voyeurism. Wiseman's reliance on editing makes it unlikely that the hall monitor was *actually* watching the girls exercise; the implication fits Wiseman's rhetorical project, however. Given the fact that the film was shot over a period of months, the "hall monitor" and "Simple Simon" sequences were likely filmed on separate occasions.

Image and Profilmic Event

The formal voice allows little room for vagueness and ambiguity, striving instead for absolute denotational clarity. Nonfiction cinematography contributes to this aim. The subject is framed in the center of the composition, or when time for camera set-up permits, according to the "rule of thirds."[8] Camera height is eye- or shoulder-level and the camera angle is straight on. *Variable framing* – the selection of scale (close-up, medium shot, long shot), height, and angle – allows the spectator to pick out the salient detail important to the film's rhetorical project, and to gauge discursive voice and emphasis.

Lighting in the formal style can bear similarities to that of the classical fiction film, especially in films for which scenes are arranged and the production team has time for lighting set-ups. Interior scenes of the films of Humphrey Jennings, for example, show the classical three-point lighting scheme common to Hollywood films. However, "actuality" footage – footage not carefully staged for the camera – often is lit with whatever light is available, either the existing light of the scene or a hastily-set-up lamp carried by a crewmember. This accounts for the raw look of many documentary shots.

Cinematography in the formal style follows a "teaching" logic, making use of central and variable framing to pick out the visual information important to the film. The uses of cinematography in the open style, as one might expect, are looser, tending toward chance observances rather than careful framing to create precise meaning. For example, we see many close-ups in *High School*. In the formal style, one would expect a close-up to reveal a detail of special significance, important to the rhetorical or dramatic project of the film. Such motivations are *sometimes* apparent in *High School*. In one scene the camera humorously zooms in to a close-up of the wagging finger of a gynecologist as he discusses sex, birth control, and pregnancy with an assembly of unusually attentive high school boys.

For the most part, however, close-ups in *High School* seem rhetorically purposeless, lacking clear motivation. In the first sequence, as the teacher reads the daily bulletin, the camera holds an extreme close-up of his mouth and eye. In a later scene, as the discipline officer demands that a student change into his gym clothes, the camera zooms to an extreme close-up of the officer's mouth. One might take these shots as discursive subversions of adult authority, except that the students, with whom the film sympathizes, are subjected to the same treatment. This visual style often condenses the characters into a wiggling finger, a winking eye, a mouth, or a nose. One might attribute this to cramped filming conditions, except that frequent zooms out reveal the possibility of medium and long shots.

For both the formal and open styles, many issues of technique concern using images to reveal information about the profilmic event. One vital difference between formal and open uses of photography has to do with the *physical* or *nominal* depiction of a visible entity.[9] Within its syntactical context, an image physically depicts a dog if it represents a *particular* dog – a Boxer named Bubba, for example. Yet even that same shot can alternatively, in another context, nominally depict a *class* – Boxers, or dogs in general, or dogs that run fast. Such a shot is still *of* a particular dog, but it is *used* as a nominal rather than physical depiction.

As one might expect, nominal depictions are much more common in the formal style than the open. Formal films often make explicit arguments and strictly control local discourse, such that each image fits into a clear rhetorical scheme. When images are used as nominal depictions, they represent a class of entities, and are made to function as a link in a controlled rhetorical chain of meaning. In the *Why We Fight* series, for example, archival images are used as physical depictions only when representing particular Axis leaders, for example, Hitler, Tojo, and Mussolini. More typically, images function nominally. Shots of crowds of Japanese, German, or Italian people are used as nominal depictions of the Japanese, Germans, and Italians in general, as the voice-over narration makes broad claims about national characteristics or the nature of fascism. For example, shots of German soldiers marching, taken from Leni Riefenstahl's *Triumph of the Will,* are used to illustrate fascist regimentation.

Conversely, the open style uses physical depictions. If the open voice observes rather than explains, the representation of particulars takes precedence over classes of entities. *Brother's Keeper* uses images to depict a particular group of brothers, one of whom is accused of murder. *Salesman* depicts a particular group of Bible salesmen, and concentrates on one Paul Brennan. The audience may make inductive generalizations about human nature or salesmen based on the images they see. The images themselves, however, are representations of particular entities. Although there will be exceptions, nonfiction films of the formal style often use nominal and of the open style physical depictions.

An important issue in studies of nonfiction has been the extent and limits of the observational powers of the image. All talk of observation must acknowledge that many nonfiction films manipulate the profilmic event. We often see the use of animation and maps, for example, used to make assertions about the actual world. Some filmmakers interact with their subjects, such that one could hardly claim they attempt to photograph the world as it might be in the absence of the camera. Prominent nonfiction filmmaker Errol Morris manipulates the pro-filmic scene as a matter of course, and actually claims this to be *more* rather then less revelatory. For his *A Brief History of Time*, Morris actually constructed sets to resemble homes and offices, where he was able to conduct interviews in a controlled setting and create the ambiance he desired.

At times, the importance of manipulation or its lack has been overemphasized in discourse about the nonfiction film; in fact, the issue is something of a red herring, when used to deny the recording capacities of photography. Any shot of a subject is from a particular angle, camera height, and perspective, and is but one view of the scene among the many possible. But this fails to negate the informative possibilities of the image. In our everyday life, we also *see* from a perspective; in no way does that endanger our learning from what we see. Similarly, a nonfiction filmmaker may manipulate the profilmic scene in various ways, through lighting, framing, and the placement of the subject. Neither does this counteract the capabilities of the image to give veridical information. Morris's staged interviews with Randall Adams and David Harris in *The Thin Blue Line* are marvelous personality studies, despite Morris's artificial lighting and framing.

A photographic recording of a manipulated profilmic scene is still a photographic recording; it simply requires a bit of critical analysis to understand what information it holds. In gauging what an image can teach us, we must always consider the nature of the profilmic event, its susceptibility to manipulation, and the affect of any suspected or apparent manipulation. When filming an interview, the filmmaker not only may design a set or alter the location, but in addition prods the subject with questions and other cues to elicit the desired response. On the other hand, a filmmaker confronted with a volcanic eruption or a hurricane has little control over what occurs. Some social events, such as a presidential press conference, a college graduation, or a professional baseball game, are designed in part with the presence of cameras and the public in mind. The point is this: the influence of the camera on the profilmic event ranges from substantial to nonexistent. Although the spectator cannot always know how the profilmic event was actually manipulated, she can make educated hypotheses about how the probable influence of the camera affects the meaning of a shot.

To gauge what an image can teach us, we must also consider how the camera is used. When Wiseman and his camera operator investigate an institution, they try to remain as unobstrusive as possible, hoping that eventually they will become unnoticed. In contrast, other filmmakers become intentionally obtrusive, and incorporate themselves and their camera as personae in the body of the film. In Ross McElwee's *Sherman's March,* McElwee frequently appears before the camera, speaking about his film and his mental state. Moreover, he talks to people while filming them, and views the various people in his life through the lens of the camera, which becomes his literal point of view. As he speaks and his hand reaches beyond the lens to touch the face of a tearful friend, the camera films. As he hugs friends good-bye, the camera, perched on his shoulder, films. As he is stung by bees, the camera swings wildly about and we hear his yelps of pain. McElwee's interest in women's bodies is apparent as he films Pat's "cellulite" exercises and slowly tilts up band member Joy's body as she sings and plays.

Of course, despite our best vigilance, photographic images can be used to deceive us. In the early years of newsreels, for example, scenes were often staged or faked, then presented as the original event.[10] These types of deceitful manipulations must be distinguished from the typical influences the camera might have on the profilmic scene. Audiences must never blindly assume that events always unfold just as they would have without the presence of the camera. Yet it is just as naïve to claim that we learn nothing from images. Critical audiences will consider the presence of the camera as a part of the profilmic event. What we can learn about the profilmic scene from a given image depends on complex factors, from clues within the image, to the nature of the profilmic event, to the apparent techniques of the camera crew, to the image in relation to conventional use, linguistic accompaniment, and context. Theory cannot make such a determination in advance.

Voice-Over Narration and the Interview

No discussion of the power of images in communication can fail to ignore the coupling of images with sound. Of all the various sound techniques, documentary voice-over narration has received by far the most attention from film scholars.[11] How does verbal discourse relate to images? Roland Barthes claims that the verbal text accompanying press photographs never simply duplicates the image, but always adds to or narrows the meanings already present. Upon examination, the same holds true for the nonfiction image accompanied by voice-over. All images are polysemous, ambiguous to a certain degree. Independent of its context, the image bears multiple possible meanings. Within the formal style, voice-over carries authority over the meanings gleaned from the images. Barthes and other theorists have found ostensible ideological effects in voice-over narration. Barthes writes that the denotational aspects of the image tend to naturalize the connotational linguistic message (and connotative aspects of the image), causing the text to appear as a phenomenon of nature rather than a constructed, cultural representation: "The connotation is now experienced only as the natural resonance of the fundamental denotation constituted by the photographic analogy and we are thus confronted with a typical process of naturalization of the cultural."[12]

From the standpoint of a psychoanalytic theory of subjectivity, Mary Ann Doane argues that voice-over narration perpetuates "the image of unity and identity sustained by this body [the narrator, the spectator]" and staves off "the fear of fragmentation" in the unconscious of the spectator, thus maintaining the "material homogeneity of the 'body' of the film."[13] This is how voice-over supposedly cooperates in the interpolation of the "bourgeois" homogeneous subject. The voice-over has effects on the conscious spectator as well. Since it comes from outside the diegesis and has no visible body, Doane claims, the narrator is endowed with an authority based on its "radical otherness." Thus the voice seems beyond criticism, and censors questions of origin and identity. The implication is that audiences will uncritically accept what the voice-over narrator claims, because the voice-over is not present as a visible body.

Both of these arguments deserve scrutiny. Both Doane and Barthes imply that the effects they posit are universal, or at least standard for most audiences. However, there is little evidence for these claims, of either an intuitive or empirical kind. Today's audiences are quite suspicious of the media, and do not accept what they see as natural, or the claims of a voice-over narrator as the unproblematic truth. In fact, at the time of this writing, Americans tend to be highly critical, commonly refering to the "bias" of the "liberal media."

Doane points out the diverse relationships possible between voice-over narrators and documentary images. She calls for (1) increasing the number of voices in the voice-over documentary, and (2) changing the relationship of the voices to the image by effecting a disjunction between the sound and its meaning, as Barthes also advocates with respect to vocal music in "The Grain of the Voice."[14] Several documentaries exemplify Doane's recommendations, at least in part. One is

Chick Strand's *Mosori Monika* (1970), a film about a native community in South America. The voice-over in the film is given by two successive female narrators, both of whom are Indian. One has become a nun in deference to the Roman Catholic missionaries who have come to the tribe and who give her sustenance. The other voice-over narrator lives more or less as she did before the missionaries arrived. Neither voice-over is explicitly privileged (although Strand subtly weights the moral center of the film toward the latter narrator) and both give alternative perspectives. Perhaps it is too much to ask that "meaning" be wholly abandoned in nonfiction film in favor of the "grain" of the voice (as Doane seems to advocate), but in *Mosori Monika* meaning is at least made ambiguous and difficult. In this respect *Mosori Monika* employs voice-over narration in the open rather than the formal style.

Another documentary using multiple voices is John Ford's *The Battle of Midway*, though this film maintains a formal style. In representing this World War II battle, the film makes use of four narrators, each bearing a different relationship to the spectator and to the represented events. The first narrator (Donald Crisp) is similar to the omnipotent and impassioned *March of Time* or newsreel narrator. An authoritative patriot, he gets caught up in the excitement, making exclamations such as "Suddenly, the Japs attack!" and "The invasion forces were hit and hit and hit again!" He conveys most of the historical information of the film. The second narrator (Irving Pichel) seems to be a priest or minister, a spiritual and psychological leader. Unlike the first narrator, the second directly addresses the spectator. As the planes return from battle and the airmen disembark, he says: "Men and women of America, here come your neighbors, home from a day's work. You ought to meet them. Here's Jimmy Patch. Seven 'meatballs' on his plane." He also verifies the authenticity of some of the images. As soldiers raise the American flag during a lull in the battle, he claims, "Yes, this really happened." Whereas the first narrator excites warlike emotions, the second is a gentle father or pastor figure. He speaks softly and reflectively. Whereas the first narrator presents factual information, the second enjoys a sort of moral authority.

The third narrator (Jane Darwell) is a particularization of the American mother. She speaks with a definite Midwestern twang. Unfamiliar with the machinery of war, she asks questions that the other narrators answer: "Is that one of those Flying Fortresses?" and "Why, that's young Bill Toomey. He's from my hometown of Springfield, Ohio. He's not going to fly that big bomber?" Her business is domestic. Playing a stereotypical role, she is a nurturer and maintains an authority in this arena. When casualties arrive, she orders the soldiers to "Get those boys to the hospital!"

The fourth narrator, with voice by Henry Fonda, is "one of the boys." A gregarious sort, he speaks to "mother" and also makes comments on some of the pronouncements of the first narrator. In addition, he has the ability to speak to characters in the diegesis. Talking to a pilot, he asks: "How many more today, Skipper?" Skipper holds up four fingers. This narrator, with his inside knowledge and familiarity, interprets the images from within and seconds the pronouncements of the first narrator. As a flyer is rescued and brought aboard ship, this narrator comments: "His first cigarette – boy – that first drag sure tastes good."

Doane argues against what I have called the epistemic attitude of the formal voice, and especially the use of the disembodied voice-over narrator to disseminate information from a position of authority. Among her recommendations is the use of multiple narrators. From this example we see that a multiplicity of narrators does not guarantee a different discursive stance toward the projected world than that which Doane criticizes. Although *The Battle of Midway* makes use of four narrators, and each bears a different relationship to the projected world and to the other narrators, they nonetheless clearly and unambiguously interpret the images for us. The narrators each occupy clearly constructed social positions, and each assumes authority over a carefully-delineated sphere of knowledge. It is clear, then, that what is most important in gauging the relationship of voice-over narrator(s) and image is not their number or gender, but their epistemic relationship to image and referent.

Another lesson of the voice-over narrators in *The Battle of Midway* is that Barthes' functions of anchorage and relay only begin to tap the diversity of functions the linguistic message may have. As Charles Wolfe notes, voice-over in *The Battle of Midway* is not unlike that of other documentaries of the 1930s and 1940s in its awareness "of the distinctions of region, class, gender, or age" and in its definition of "a complex spatial and temporal relation between the assumed sites of vocal enunciation and reception . . . and the constructed space of the diegesis."[15] The voice-over narrator does more than disseminate information or assert authority; he or she may express a wish, advocate, de-

nounce, express solidarity, plead, hesitate, argue, postulate, and rumi-
nate. Even in films with simple, authoritative voice-over narration, the
relationships between voice and image can be highly complex.

Films that avoid voice-overs find other means to supply the information they afford. Sometimes they film persons who are speaking information the film wants to use as exposition. In *Say Amen, Somebody*,
we see a disc jockey talking into his microphone, introducing the event
that becomes one of the centerpieces of the film: "Yes, this is Columbus
Gregory here for KIRL. We'd like to invite you to join us this coming
Sunday, as we gather to honor that legend of gospel singers, Mother
Willie Mae Ford Smith, for her sixty years of gospel singing." Many
films also use interviews to provide exposition.

Interviews are an invaluable resource for the nonfiction artist, and in
their presentation lies one of the great strengths of nonfiction film and
video. We not only benefit from *what* is said, but from the visual and
aural information available in *how* it is said – from facial expression to
gestures to inflections of the voice. For the filmmaker working in the
formal style, the question becomes how to fit the interviews into the
rhetorical project of the film. Each interview has its own perspective,
and the filmmaker wishing to make rhetorical points may want to fit
those perspectives into the larger film's discursive project.

Bill Nichols notes that the use of interviews in documentaries can
lead to problems, for two reasons.[16] First, in the case of films such as
The Wobblies, all of the personal testimonies agree with each other,
creating a facile sense that all personal recollections can be wholly
trusted. The spectator also deduces that the filmmaker has chosen to
interview only people with whom he or she agrees, casting suspicion on
the veracity of the film. A second problem is that the perspective of the
film can become lost behind the interviews, and the spectator can lose
track of the function of the interviews in the film's rhetoric.

Not a Love Story provides a clear illustration of some of these issues.
Not a Love Story does use voice-over narration at times, but whenever
filmmaker Bonnie Klein resorts to the strategy, it is only to present first-
level information, and rarely to reveal her political position. The
rhetorical position of *Not a Love Story* is normally expressed through
other techniques, such as the numerous interviews in the film. Much of
the testimony in agreement with the film's voice gets stylistic support,
while oppositional testimony is sometimes subtly undermined. The testimony of Susan Griffin is accorded more authority than that of Klein
herself, by its temporal positioning and its stylistic treatment. Griffin's

on-screen testimony is positioned at the beginning of the film, immediately following the title sequence, and at the very end of the film, immediately preceding the end credits. Her testimony literally frames the
film, providing moral schemas for the viewer in the exposition (through
the primacy effect), and reinforcing those schemas at the conclusion.
Griffin's voice is given further authority as some of the only testimony
(aside from Klein's) we hear in voice-over, when towards the end of the
film her disembodied summations on pornography play over advertisements and over the scene where Tracy poses for photographs.

Griffin's voice-over accrues authority through stylistic strategies as
well. Her testimonial is supported by sequences of images marshaled as
evidence to support what she says. After the scene in which Linda Tracy protests against pornography in front of the sex club, we see Griffin
talking about pornography's attitude toward women: "Pornography is
like a film that's projected on a blank screen, and that blank screen is
women's silence. Pornography is filled with images of silencing
women." Griffin's voice-over is illustrated by stills – a woman in a
muzzle, a woman chained and gagged, a woman bound to a tree and
gagged. Such illustrative images are afforded other witnesses as they
testify, but not those who oppose the position of the film. David Wells,
editor and publisher of pornographic magazines, is given no such textual support, and in fact, Klein's open (and on-screen) disagreement
with what he says cues the spectator to take his testimony as oppositional. Moreover, the way Griffin's body is framed also adds subtle support to her testimony. We see her only in close-up, a tight shot of her
neck and face, with no cut-aways to listeners. The effect is to fragment
her body and the space from which she speaks, such that her voice becomes akin to the disembodied voice-over narrator of the more traditional documentary.

Oppositional testimony is marked as such in at least two instances.
As Linda Tracy asks questions of the manager of the sex emporium, his
face, unlike hers, is consistently in the shadows. Whether this is a
chance occurrence or a lighting strategy is unclear, but the effect is to
make the man seem especially sleazy. Similarly, at one point Tracy and
Klein talk with three members of the pornographic video industry: an
actor, an actress, and a producer. While the producer defends pornography as a legitimate form of "tripping out," the film cuts to reaction
shots of the raised eyebrows of Klein and Tracy, who obviously take
exception to what he says. Again, the voice of the film makes itself
heard through technical choices.

Another voice of importance is that of Robin Morgan, whose words, like those of Susan Griffith, become wholly coextensive with the film's voice. Morgan's statements on rage and hope in the face of pornography become a centerpiece of the film. Her testimony is supported by its very length, since it is the longest interview; it is also textually supported by its repetition. Of those who oppose the film's position, only Suze Randall, the porn photographer, is shown twice, and then only to illustrate Tracy's feelings of degradation as she poses for the camera. Moreover, Robin Morgan's testimony is given authority through stylistic means. After hearing poet Margaret Atwood read poems about the treatment of women in pornography, we see a still of a woman whose fallen countenance and pose suggest her oppression. The next shot, of Robin Morgan's face, is a graphic match on the face of the woman in this photograph, and lends textual support to Morgan's role as one who speaks for the oppression of women by pornography.

But not all of the sympathetic testimony is supported through temporal positioning and stylistic strategies, and such strategies are not the only means by which the political position of the film is heard. Of course, stylistic strategies don't determine everything; what the witnesses *say* can itself align them for or against the voice of the film. Former pornographic film actor Marc Stevens, for example, says that he was forced to perform acts he found degrading to the women he worked with, and that this is the reason he quit the business. The spectator will fit this testimony into the fabric of the film's voice, since it is supported by so much other textual material. Despite its disparate materials and varied modes of discourse, then, the overall voice of *Not a Love Story* is clear. The strategy of including the testimony of persons affiliated with pornography creates a dense fabric of alternative perspectives, out of which the film weaves a coherent position on pornography.

In the open style, the filmmaker may let oppositional interviews stand, with no attempt to weave them into a unified argument, position, or thread of logical progression. Errol Morris's *Vernon, Florida* (1980), for example, consists almost solely of bizarre interviews with various folks in the small town of the film's title. The film's structure constitutes no argument or narrative, but gives us a pastiche of personality portraits, sometimes cross-cutting between the longer interviews and returning to characters with longer stories to tell (as in the case of the enthusiastic turkey hunter). Similarly, the *Frontline* documentary "L.A. is Burning: Five Stories from a Divided City" (1993), asks five persons to narrate their perspectives on the causes and outcome of the

Los Angeles riots following the Rodney King debacle. The persons interviewed represent diverse ethnicities and points of view, but the discourse makes no attempt to weave their words into a unified account. The film also includes shorter interviews with several other persons. Again, this unwillingness to take sides is a matter of degree, because the film is structured in such a way that the most extreme perspectives – of those who justify the beating of trucker Reginald Deny, for example – are subtly undermined.

Musical Accompaniment

Formal style aims for organic unity. That is, all film techniques finally work together in unity of function. Thus we can ask how music relates to images, to other sounds, and to the text as a whole. Does music assert propositions about the projected world? Does it communicate voice? Does it have an effect on the spectator? What is its communicative function?

For opera, German composer Richard Wagner advocated a total synthesis of drama and music, a synthesis in which musical structure is wholly determined by dramatic action. One manifestation of this is the leitmotif, a musical trademark by which a character is marked and identified. Filmmaker Sergei Eisenstein, in his post-1930 writings, conceived of film music in similar fashion.[17] Eisenstein thought of the wedding of music and picture in relation to *synaesthesia,* the process by which similar sense impressions or other mental states are generated by different perceptual media. Thus a film sequence and a musical segment can be said to have a similar rhythm or tone, for example. Eisenstein's famous example of the combination of music and image according to "fundamental movements" is from the "Battle on the Ice" sequence of *Alexander Nevsky* (1938). Here he finds a correspondence between the movement of the music, considered in abstract, psychological terms, and the movement of the eye over the plastic lines of composition.

Eisenstein's analysis of the use of music and image in *Alexander Nevsky* remains unpersuasive; his concept of "fundamental movement" as applied to music and to images is ambiguous for both media.[18] Nevertheless, his thoughts about syneasthesia are a good starting point for a study of the place of music within filmic representation, for Eisenstein worked along paths which contemporary cognitive studies of music would soon follow. One contemporary psychologist, Terrence McLaughlin, has used the findings of modern physiology to analyze the place of music within communication.[19] His conclusion, in summary, is that music is made up of patterns of tension and resolution corresponding to patterns of tensions and resolution in the brain caused by mental and bodily events. Thus various patterns of music have a fittingness with the mental activity caused by physical action and other human experiences. Whether this process is genetic and/or culturally determined, and whether certain types of music have a natural affinity with our experiences or one based on habit and convention, is a difficult question beyond our present scope. Yet clearly, music carries with it an experiential character; when music is combined with images, this character colors the spectatorial experience by means of a fittingness with other aspects of mental and physical life.

By itself, music provides no factual information, as images can. Neither does it convey propositions or conceptual information about the projected world, as voice-over can. Instead, music provides an experiential, emotional character to the spectator's experience, and thus supports the preferred interpretation of the film's voice. Its primary function is not to assert propositions about the projected world, but to evoke emotion or perceptual activity – to help create the *experiential envelope* in which the spectator views the film. The expression or evocation of emotion is one of its primary functions. *The Battle of Midway* uses familiar songs to evoke pride in both country and armed forces. During the opening credits, we hear a variation on "My Country 'Tis of Thee," and during a lull in the battle, while the flag is being raised, the "National Anthem." After the battle has been won and the enemy vanquished, we hear a medley of the fighting songs of all four divisions of the American armed forces – "The Air Force Song," "Anchors Away," "The Marine Hymn," and "Over There" – in energetic celebration. Thus the film not only relates the events depicted, but makes use of music to represent them with a nationalistic emotional force.

The "experiential envelope" consists in part of created moods. A well-designed musical score contributes a great deal to the mood of the spectator, and to the mental frame she uses to interpret the events of the film. For example, the musical scores of Phillip Glass for Errol Morris's *The Thin Blue Line* and *A Brief History of Time* suggest an air of mystery and fate. The folk singing of the coal miners in *Harlan County, U.S.A.* creates identification between the viewer and the striking miners. The plaintive violin and guitar of Ken Burns' *The Civil War* convey the sadness of the loss of precious human lives.

But the evocation of emotion is only one of many varied communicative functions music brings to film. Music may reinforce the preferred interpretation of a scene in other than strictly affective contexts, lending credence to an assertion or implication about the projected world. In *The Battle of Midway,* we see a short interlude about the "natives" of Midway, not humans but clumsy dodo-like birds with a self-important strut. While the birds waddle humorously, the "whomp, whomp" wails and descending scales of a trombone connote the birds' vainglorious pretensions, as interpreted by the film. Later, the Japanese and Tojo are associated with these "natives" when the camera pans from the wreck of a crashed Japanese plane to a shot of the birds strutting, as though reality has revealed the false pretenses of the enemies' boasting, represented to be as empty as the strut of these birds.

Music may be used ironically, again in tandem with the project of the film. Irony is the dominant device of *Roger and Me.* The spectator who catches on to this takes nothing in the film at face value. Every gesture and facial expression; everything said or shown becomes a new opportunity for subtle (or not-so-subtle) innuendo and a laugh. *Roger and Me* undermines some of what it presents through ironic uses of film technique, often including the juxtaposition of discordant images and music. For example, we hear the Beach Boys' "Wouldn't it Be Nice" while the camera tracks by dilapidated Flint homes and businesses. *Roger and Me* ends at Christmas, but the film uses traditional Christmas music ironically, from the version of "Jingle Bells" barked by a dog, to the choir at the General Motors Christmas celebration, whose singing is used as a backdrop to images of unemployed auto workers as they are evicted from their homes.

Is music used in any special way in formally styled nonfiction films? Because music often implies the authority to interpret events, open style tends to avoid nondiegetic music altogether, as I discuss below. But formal style forges ahead in its use of music to give a perspective toward and assert propositions about the projected world. For example, it signifies emotion, cueing various aspects of the narrative or interpreting narrative events. Music also helps provide unity and continuity. Music in William Wyler's *The Memphis Belle* (1944) provides a fine example. *The Memphis Belle* follows the missions of a "Flying Fortress" as it participates in a particularly ambitious and dangerous bombing mission over Nazi Germany during World War II. Music provides continuity between scenes and unity for the whole project. The music signifies "appropriate" emotions, becoming dramatic during the bombing scene and return to home base, and soft and contemplative as the film shows wounded airmen and damaged planes. When the King and Queen of England appear to congratulate the victorious men, a drum roll signifies the importance of the occasion, and regal music expresses Their Majesties' royal standing.

Music also gives narrative cues. *The Memphis Belle* begins with shots of the England tourists have come to know, with rolling fields and small villages, each with a centuries-old stone church. But things are not as they seem. The voice-over dramatically announces that this is "a battle front." We see a montage of bombers hidden in the landscape, from various angles and distances; the music emphasizes each cut with a loud and dramatic note, as though each shot is meant to drive home the fact that this peaceful English countryside is not the idyll it initially seems to be.

As I said, the open style – especially in observational films – might be expected to avoid music altogether, since it directs the spectator in ways antithetical to the requirements of the open voice. For the most part this is true, but many observational filmmakers cannot resist the inclusion of at least some nondiegetic music, especially in the more self-conscious beginnings and endings of their films. Even the purist Fred Wiseman featured nondiegetic music in *High School*. The opening sequence consists of a series of traveling shots, moving toward the school. We see houses, garages, stores, billboards, and finally the high school itself, looking (as many have observed) much like a factory with its smokestack jutting prominently in front. The traveling shots give the sense of a journey, with the school as the final destination. On the soundtrack we hear Otis Redding's "Sitting on the Dock of the Bay," a song about a man who leaves Georgia in search of a better life, only to find his situation unimproved in San Francisco. Over the black and white shots of the drab city streets, Redding's song tells of inertia and hopelessness. Occupying such a privileged position, the sequence sets a definite tone for the film and establishes an attitude toward the high school. It seems to imply that the high school dooms its students to the intertia and failure that is the subject of Redding's song.

As with voice-over narration, it seems clear that we have only begun to describe the uses of music in the documentary. The relationships between music, image, and text are inventive; each use may be idiosyncratic, such that no prior theoretical account can exhaust their formal possibilities. For the formal style, however, we can make at least the following generalization. Music serves a unifying function in the formal text, helping to develop the projected world and contributing to the rhetorical project of the film. Because the open voice often avoids overt marks of narration, the use of nondiegetic music is rare in such films.

The Formal Voice Returns

The function of formal style is uniform; it supports the film's rhetorical project. In addition, formal style strives for denotational clarity and discourse coherence. Style serves as a conduit through which the discourse asserts propositions about the projected world, and through which its voice can be heard. One of the most important functions of style in the formal voice is to develop the authoritative epistemological stance of the discourse.

Bill Nichols has examined the means by which style makes the discursive voice come forward. As I mentioned, he devised a typology of modes that marshal style and technique in different ways, and create varied forms of discursive voice. Nichols' forms or modes of documentary – expository, observational, interactive, and reflexive – are suggestive because they offer a framework at once historically descriptive and heuristically insightful. The modes are historical because they follow a rough order of chronological development, from Griersonian documentary with its "Voice-of-God" commentary (expository) to direct cinema (observational) to films incorporating interviews and/or the filmmaker's presence (interactive) to films acknowledging their constructedness and foregrounding representation itself (reflexive). On the other hand, the four modes have heuristic value because they represent four alternative styles of nonfiction filmmaking, and four different assumptions about the proper means of constructing textual voice and authority.[20]

Both Nichols and Thomas Waugh find the films of Emile de Antonio to be emblematic of Nichols' fourth mode, the reflexive, or what Waugh calls the new American documentary.[21] Waugh finds fault in observational cinema because although it postures as objective – or critics claim it does – the films in fact take strong attitudes toward their subjects. The new American documentary, on the other hand, openly exhibits a rhetorical and political commitment. Nichols claims that reflexive films also imply a more enlightened attitude toward the world: "De Antonio's films produce a world of dense complexity: they embody a sense of constraint and over-determination. Not everyone can be believed. Not everything is true . . . de Antonio proposes ways and means to reconstruct the past dialectically."[22] Interactive documentaries using interviews may suffer from a diffusion of discursive authority, the sometimes unsuccessful blending of interviewed voices with the overall voice of the film. But de Antonio's films do not accept the testimony of witnesses at face value. In his work, differing and tangential perspectives paint a complex picture of history. Yet in the midst of this complexity, de Antonio asserts his perspective – the voice of the film.

Both Waugh and Nichols, I submit, call for a return to a particular manifestation of the formal voice. Their praise for the new American documentary is primarily based on its openly rhetorical stance, its willingness to make assertions about the actual world, and its simultaneous communication of the world's complexities. But it stops short of the postmodernist rejection of meaning and reference. Waugh expresses contempt for direct cinema in its attempt to observe rather than analyze, for its supposed duplicitous submersion of explicit point of view in its attempts at pure observation. Waugh calls instead for analysis and explanation. He does not advocate "overarching solutions" (to political and social problems, presumably), but nonetheless favors the penetration and unsettling of the "liberal equilibrium." His recommendations imply a preference for discursive authority over hesitant observation, and a simultaneous acknowledgment of the world's complexities.

Nichols claims that the New American Documentaries avoid "the apparent simplicities of an unquestioned empiricism (the world and its truths exist; they need only be dusted off and reported)" and that they "produce a world of dense complexity."[23] Nichols, then, finds de Antonio's films to more *accurately* convey the complexity or magnitudes of the world. Furthermore, in calling for the clear "voice" of the filmmaker in political films, Nichols implicitly advocates explanation over observation, and the formal over the open voice.

Both cases show that the formal epistemic function of nonfiction is not a thing of the past, and not an archaic or discarded relic. On the contrary, it has returned in the "new American documentary," although in a contemporary form. We see it in films such as *Not a Love Story, The Thin Blue Line, Harlan County, USA,* the films of Emile de Antonio, and many others. This form retains the epistemic authority of formal discourse, but unlike some films, reflects or preserves a sense of the complexities and magnitudes of the world. These films move toward knowledge, but present knowledge as difficult, complex, ambiguous – never final and never easy.

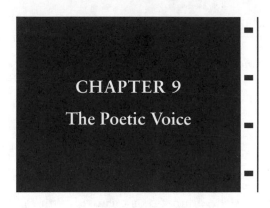

CHAPTER 9

The Poetic Voice

Francis Thompson's *N.Y., N.Y.* (1958) sets its camera on familiar urban street scenes in New York City, but films them with prisms, "funhouse" mirrors, and distorting lenses. Bruce Baillie's *Valentin de las Sierras* (1967) was produced in Mexico, and as the title suggests, is a poetic tribute to the Mexican Sierras, and particularly to the people of Chapala, a small village. It features extreme close-up photography, numerous jump cuts, and a seemingly random structure of information. Chris Marker's *Letter from Siberia* (1957) presents itself as a travelog about Siberia, but spends a disproportionate amount of time on one citizen's pet bear, features silly poems and songs, and includes an animated tribute to dancing woolly Mammoths. Clearly, not all nonfiction films easily fit the open and formal categories. Many fall through the cracks of these broad groupings, and not surprisingly, these can be some of the most creative and interesting films.

An account of the nonfiction film that neglects alternatives to the formal and open voices would be incomplete. Although films of the formal and open voices differ in their methodologies, they both perform a central function of the documentary: providing information through explanation, observation, or exploration. If the nonfiction film is a category with fuzzy boundaries, like the category "game," we would expect to find films with alternate functions. The alternative genres I describe here – the poetic documentary, avant-garde film, parodic documentary, and metadocumentary – tend to foreground aesthetic concerns over teaching, exploit a tension between representation and composition, or alternatively, invert observation or explanation into explicit self-analysis.[1] This isn't a matter of exclusive oppositions. I hope I've made it clear that films of the open and formal voices both depend on aesthetics – that is, structure and stylistics. Similarly, it would be wrong to say that poetic films neither observe, explore, nor teach. (They teach poetry, for one thing). It is simply a matter of emphasis with regard to method and subject matter.

The formal voice has been an exemplar of nonfiction film since the genesis of the documentary. The Grierson school did much to ensure that the documentary would be seen as a form of discourse going beyond observation. Grierson saw the documentary as a means of propaganda, a "bully pulpit" through which the masses could be educated about their complex industrial society. From the poetic documentary he learned that the documentary must be dramatic or creative. With the early sixties and their accompanying social and political upheaval, direct cinema and cinéma vérité seemed the proper response to the cultural and political movements of the time. These films refused to offer conventional explanations, and withheld the epistemic authority of the formal voice. The influence of direct cinema has waned in recent years, and nonfiction filmmakers are again making films featuring the more authoritative voice, in the form of expressive form and structure, if not omniscient voice-over narration.

Films of the poetic voice all have histories that could be traced as well. There are four major groupings of these alternative nonfiction films: the poetic documentary, the avant-garde nonfiction film, the metadocumentary, and the parodic documentary.[2] The poetic documentary perhaps reached its apex during the twenties and thirties with the "city symphony" films, although occasional poetic films have appeared throughout this century (Godfrey Reggio's *Koyaanisqatsi* [1983], for example). The metadocumentary grew important with the rise of ideological self-examination in the sixties and seventies. The fortunes of the avant-garde nonfiction film rise and fall with those of the avant-garde film in general. But common to all of these sub-genres is the fact that they are peripheral to the world of nonfiction film.[3] These types correspond not to logical alternatives to the formal and open nonfiction films; they fit no symmetrical grid designed to exhaust the possible different sorts of films. The sole rationale for discussing these films here is that they represent the major empirical groupings of alternative nonfiction films at this historical juncture. Although these films constitute four separate subgenres, it is not misleading to call them instances of the *poetic voice* in nonfiction filmmaking.

The Poetic Documentary

Poetic documentaries include the so-called city symphonies – *Berlin: Symphony of the City* (*Berlin: Sinfonie der Grosstadt*, 1927), *Only the*

Hours (*Rien Que Les Heures*, 1926), and *Mannahatta* (1921), early Joris Ivens films such as *The Bridge* (*De Brug*, 1928) and *Rain* (*Regen*, 1929), and Bert Haanstra's *Mirror of Holland* (*Spiegel van Holland*, 1950) and *Glass* (*Glas*, 1958). Contemporary examples include Godfrey Reggio's mind-bending *Koyaanisqatsi* (1983) and countless student films and videos produced in production classes throughout the world.

These films represent their subjects as aesthetic objects or events, emphasizing not the dissemination of factual information, but the sensual and formal qualities of their subjects. In *Rain, Berlin: Symphony of the City*, and *Glass*, respectively, rain, the city of Berlin, and glassblowing are infused with the classical aesthetic qualities of symmetry, rhythm, and diversity within unity. The poetic film emphasizes order, clarity, restraint, and harmony of form, appealing to norms established through thousands of years of artistic practice.

Poetic films appeal to classical norms not only in the *presentation* of the projected world, but also in the *nature of* the projected world itself. Making or watching a poetic film may be a process of discovery or observation, but the discoveries and observations emphasize some qualities of the world over others. The poetic film presents a projected world in harmony with classical form and style. The poetic film represents its subject as an aesthetic object.

In *Rain* we see patterns of raindrops on windows, and configurations of umbrellas from the balconies above. We see splashes caused by bicycle tires as they roll through puddles, and trickles and rivulets of water running off the roofs of Amsterdam into the rain troughs, gutters, and streets below. *Berlin: Symphony of the City* concentrates on the rhythms of the city that conform to the cycles of the turning Earth. The city awakens, works, recreates, and sleeps according to the invisible dictates of nature and symmetry. In Bert Haanstra's *Glass*, Haanstra shows us the sensual, rhythmic elements of the craft of glassblowing. With a long metal tube through which he blows, the glass maker fashions his creation out of a steaming mass of molten glass. The film repeats shots of similar actions – the actual blowing, putting the glass blobs into molds, twisting the tubes by hand, and craning the neck to observe the results – and uses matches on movement (together with the jazz score) to develop a dance-like effect. Both the projected world and the discourse presenting it are constructed to heighten this aesthetic effect.

Discourse in the poetic documentary does not simply project a world of sensual and evocative images. It also represents its subject according to conventions of harmony and unity. Thus *Berlin: Symphony of the City* represents Berlin as an organic entity that abides by the harmonious and symmetrical pulses of nature, such as the repeated coming of night and day. *Glass* is structured in another way. Although the film initially sets up an opposition between making glass by hand and the mechanized production of glass, this opposition is eventually dissolved into a new harmony by the film's end.

In *Glass*, the spectator first sees the craft of fashioning glass by hand. This section celebrates glass making with matches on movement, repeated actions, and a jazz score which, with its repetitions and variations, seems to mimic the craft itself. The second section introduces and parodies the mechanical production of bottles on an assembly line. Instead of the jazz score we hear the exaggerated, distorted, and humorous sounds of machinery. At one point the smooth consistency of the production line breaks down and bottle after bottle crashes to the floor and breaks. The short last segment brings mechanization and hand work together in harmony. Shots of the two alternative glass making methods are intercut, as the score quickens and builds to a climax, and both seem to work in rhythm with the same music. The overall effect of the film, then, is to create unity, harmony, organicity – the unification of alternatives and opposites.

Style in the poetic film gives projected world information and reinforces the unifying function of the discourse. Jean Mitry's *Pacific 231* (1944), for example, uses accelerating patterns of editing to contribute to a sense of the building momentum of a locomotive, as it slowly moves from a stationary position to a whirl of powerful motion. Editing plays a particularly important role in *Glass* as well. The individual images of glass-making each have denotational significance, but the film's depiction of the harmony of two ways of glass-making is effected largely through editing strategies. In the segments that celebrate hand-crafted glass, editing also sets up patterns of repetition and variation between the types of shots and movements, effecting a pleasant combination of predictability and surprise, as the dipping and swinging of the glass at the end of the metal tubes create a mesmerizing visual experience. In editing scenes of glass making, Haanstra could have repeated similar sequences of shots, from the shot of a worker's face, to his hands working the tube, to the swinging of the tube as it twists, to the glass at the end of the tubes, to the face, etc. Instead, he sometimes presents shots in this sequence, but elsewhere varies their arrangement and type. In addition, *Glass* often intercuts between different craftsman, often repeating the same type of shot, of hands working the tubes in similar ways, for example. After setting up various sequences of shots, the film also varies their order and shot length, creating variations within repeated patterns. What remains consistent from shot to shot are the constant movement and rhythms of the craftsmen at work, which fit the jazz score on the soundtrack. (In the segment illustrating assembly line glass production, on the other hand, Haanstra creates a rigid and repetitious order, a highly predictable pattern of editing that varies only when the assembly line completely breaks down).

Classical aesthetics also features simplicity and clarity, and indeed, both are common in the poetic documentary. These films feature a high degree of discourse coherence, since what is presented facilitates direct and uncluttered communication from text to spectator. Music expresses a clear theme; the cinematography centrally frames subjects; editing creates symmetrical patterns. Matthew Bernstein has shown how *Berlin: Symphony of a Great City* makes use of classical narrative editing techniques, as it follows the principle of analytical editing and continuity cutting in its patterns of shot articulation and spatial construction.[4] But to say that the poetic documentary manifests discourse coherence is not to say that it communicates information as would the formal voice. Whereas a formal nonfiction film about glass making would teach the spectator factual information about its subject, *Glass* represents it aesthetically, as a "beautiful" craft. *Glass* may also teach, but it teaches us about the sensual aspects of glass-making.

In summary, the poetic documentary forgoes the epistemological function of the formal and open voices in favor of aesthetic representation, styling and structuring its subjects according to classical conceptions of the beautiful and with a concentration on the sensual. In structure and style, the poetic film presents a world of closure, unity, and harmony, and uses style to effect a clear and simple representation of the projected world.

Avant-Garde Nonfiction Film

Avant-garde nonfiction films are often ignored, going almost unnoticed in histories of nonfiction film. They are rarely canonized; nonfiction film criticism, for the most part, relegates alternative films to the fringes and finds "objectivity" and the representation of political and social reality to be central functions. Avant-garde films tend to be the work of individuals working with small budgets in 16 mm film or video. The films are made available by distributors of independent film, such as Canyon Cinema, the Filmmaker's Coop, and by institutions such as the Museum of Modern Art in New York. The Canyon Cinema catalogue, for example, lists dozens of its films under the heading "Documentary." Some of these – Anne Severson's *Animals Running* (1974), for example – are similar to the poetic films I describe above. Others fit more squarely into the avant-garde paradigm. Avant-garde films are normally seen only at museums, special screenings for enthusiasts, and at colleges and universities.

Avant-garde films are *style-centered*. They make use of nonfiction "actuality footage," but manipulate it within a formal system that becomes the organizing principle of the film. They differ from formal and open films in that they not only replace epistemic concerns with aesthetic ones, but make use of an opaque style that is not meant primarily to transmit information, but becomes the primary subject of the film. The avant-garde film foregrounds style to a much higher degree than the poetic film. Moreover, style in the poetic film is classical; in the avant-garde film style is disruptive. In the poetic film, the projected world is infused with classical aesthetic and formal qualities. In the avant-garde film, the discourse itself becomes the primary focus. The viewer concentrates on patterns of form, angle, movement, and color, rather than on a unified projected world.

The poetic film is constructed according to extrinsic norms based on classical aesthetic qualities. The avant-garde film also appeals to extrinsic norms – an appeal to fragmentation, minimalism, and/or perceptual difficulty. Yet the avant-garde film establishes additional and unique intrinsic norms based on stylistic patterning. Norms must be established within the film, because for style to "come forward" it must possess sufficient novelty, redundancy, and internal coherence. For this reason, avant-garde style may even block world projection, creating an opaque surface that is impenetrable. Although avant-garde films project a world, it is partially hidden, obscured by patterns of disruptive stylistic techniques.

The avant-garde nonfiction film encourages an interplay between two ways of viewing the film. On the one hand, the spectator perceives the referent through iconic, indexical images (and perhaps sounds); on the other hand, style makes referentiality difficult, and becomes itself the primary object of interest. When we view an avant-garde nonfiction, we consistently slide between seeing the images as either a window onto the world or a sequence of nonreferential images.

Bruce Baillie's *Castro Street* (1966) illustrates this perceptual interplay. The film is a view of a train yard, trains, and heavy industry through the prism of various expressive techniques. It relies on none of the extrinsic norms common to the various sorts of classicism; it features no narrative, no formal exposition or rhetorical argument, no strong sense of the harmony and order of classical aesthetics. *Castro Street* does apparently confine itself to a single location to establish a unity of place and subject. Nonetheless, it is a world without the temporal ordering strategies that normally enable spectators to make sense of the text. In *Castro Street*, the spectator must turn to other means to make sense of the film. On the one hand, as I will show, formal, stylistic patterns guide understanding. In addition, however, the film's images and sounds also encourage the spectator to view the film as iconic, indexical representation.

The stylistic techniques of the film are many, including a constantly moving camera, negative images, masked images (the iris, for example), images photographed through distorting glass or filters or into mirrors, and the relationships between movement and graphic elements developed through editing and superimpositions. Within its pattern of stylistic techniques we find two tendencies that constitute intrinsic norms: (1) the emphasis on specific textural and graphic elements within the image, and (2) patterns of movement developed through editing and superimpositions.

The images play up the discursive concern with the sensual, formal, and textural more than the realistic. With few exceptions, shots are framed so tightly that their spatial context remains unclear. We see smokestacks, train cars, and the gangly appendages and textured surfaces of machinery, but never an establishing shot. In addition, the camera fragments objects, making them unrecognizable except as abstract forms, lines, and colors. For example, in many of the shots of moving train cars, the camera frames the cars below the horizontal lines of their roofs and above their bases; the effect is of an abstract surface gliding by the camera laterally. The only sustained exception to the pattern of tight framing occurs about midway through the film, when we see a long shot of a Southern Pacific engine on the tracks in a rural field of wildflowers. The camera remains uncharacteristically still as the train slowly rolls right to left, then stops. This shot stands out as a variation on a consistent pattern.

Not only framing, but various distortions and colorations reinforce the discursive concern with surface texture. Many shots are taken through various colors and shapes of glass, and the glass is sometimes moved back and forth and/or up and down to create a bending and distortion of light. We see many superimpositions and negative images. The film's last shot is a negative image of a street sign reading "Castro Street," superimposed over an image bathed in bright red. Split images, mirrors, filters, masks, and irises, create other colorations and distortions of the image.

The above, together with editing and superimpositions, form a clear stylistic system. The strongest patterns of the film are of movements of lines and forms – through camera and subject movement and superimpositions. The camera moves slowly, elegantly, and consistently, usually parallel to the ground but sometimes vertically, as in the tightly-framed tilt up the reds and browns of industrial equipment in the afternoon sun. In addition to the camera movement, the many trains in the film move laterally to the camera in either direction. Moreover, superimpositions create another avenue of movement, sometimes superimposing shots in which camera and subject movement are already present.

Camera movement, subject movement, and superimposition, then, create the possibility of many different directions, speeds, and relationships among movements within the frame. In one segment, the discourse features shots of train cars moving laterally across the frame. The camera slowly pans left to right, while the train cars travel right to left. A train travels right to left, while on a superimposed image a train runs in the opposite direction. The discourse sometimes superimposes lateral with vertical motions, creating a relationship of intersecting motion. Other relationships between movements are more complementary. In one shot, two images of trains moving in the same direction are superimposed, but one is a negative image and travels at a slightly faster rate than the other. In addition, many of the trains are painted with various words or numbers, such as "346," "Loader," "Union Pacific," and "Cushioned Load." The movement of the spectator's eyes from left to right in reading the words adds another dimension of movement. In sum, *Castro Street* creates patterns of movement within the frame and between shots.

Castro Street encourages interplay between two means of viewing the film – as abstract stylistic patterning (parametric narration) or as a unified series of iconic and indexical images and sounds. *Castro Street* cannot be seen as a purely abstract film, and style never becomes wholly dominant. Consider the soundtrack, for example. In contrast with the visual elements of the film, the soundtrack hardly contributes to style-centered discourse. Instead, its motivation is realistic, mimicking the sonic environment of the train yard. We hear no voice-over or music, but instead vague and sometimes muffled industrial and train sounds: large bells ringing, engines chugging, and hissing steam. We also hear the squeaks and moans of heavy machinery. Through its reproduction of ambient train yard sounds, the soundtrack is calculated to produce the "reality effect" and to encourage the spectator to approach the film's images and sounds as at least partially iconic and indexical. The spectator sees the film not only as a stylistic exercise, but also as about the sights and sounds of heavy industry and trains.

Avant-garde nonfiction films are style-centered, and if one attempts simply to look through style to image content, one will miss the fundamental purpose of the films. They encourage an interplay between the image as representation of reality and as a building block in a complex artistic structure. In fact, this is their primary pleasure, in the interplay between iconicity and indexicality, and the expressiveness and pattern-building of style and technique. In encouraging a dual spectatorial activity, an alternation between *seeing through* and *perceiving* the images and style, these films become implicitly reflexive, moving suggestively between representation and discursive opacity, and never ultimately surrendering to either.

Metadocumentary

"Metadocumentary" includes such films as Dziga Vertov's *The Man With a Movie Camera* (1929), and Chris Marker's *Far from Vietnam* (1967), *Letter from Siberia* (1957), and *Sans Soleil* (1983). These films are reflexive *in a specific way*, in that they are fundamentally "about" the documentary and "about" representation itself. Where the avant-garde film is *implicitly* reflexive, metadocumentary is *explicitly* reflexive, drawing attention to its own making at every turn. Unlike the poetic and avant-garde films, metadocumentaries have a primary epistemic function. But they differ from the open and classic styles in their disruptive style and formal intricacy, and in their taking nonfiction representation itself as a primary topic.

The reflexive discourse of the metadocumentary makes it similar to cinéma vérité in a sense. Rouch and Morin's phrase, "cinéma vérité," is a translation of Vertov's *kino-pravda,* or "film truth." However, the metadocumentary also *differs* from cinéma vérité in important respects. First, aside from their reflexivity, the films of cinéma vérité formally and technically resemble direct cinema; they share the attempt to record the surface features of events, but differ in their strategy. For the cinéma vérité filmmaker, the representation of reality is more "true" when the presence and influence of the film crew is provocative during the filming and is acknowledged in the finished film. Cinéma vérité still eschews voice-over narration[5] and the careful lighting of subjects, and favors the spontaneity afforded by the lightweight camera and recording equipment. It also favors the seeming aleatory ordering structures over classical forms of organization.

The metadocumentary, on the other hand, is often formally and technically reflexive, and rarely tries for the "spontaneous" look of cinéma vérité and direct cinema, the look that signifies "reality caught unawares." Metadocumentary plays up montage and the manipulation of the formal elements of image and sound, and the creation of a sense of realism is never a major concern. In cinéma vérité, discourse flaunts itself to get at a truer or "more sincere"[6] representation of reality. Discourse in the metadocumentary parades itself, but does so to examine its *own* nature.

The reflexivity of the metadocumentary is evident at every turn. Vertov was primarily interested in creating a new form of communication appropriate to the post-revolutionary Soviet Union. Of the "kino" eye, he writes:

From now on and for always I cast off human immobility, I move constantly, I approach and pull away from objects, I creep under them, I leap onto them, I move alongside the mouth of a galloping horse, I cut into a crowd, I run before charging troops, I turn on my back, I take off with an airplane, I fall and rise with falling and rising bodies.

Freed from the tyranny of 16–17 images per second, freed from the framework of space and time, I coordinate any and all points of the universe, wherever I may record them.

My mission is the creation of a new perception of the world. Thus I decipher in a new way a world unknown to you.[7]

In addition to its technical experimentation, Vertov's *The Man With a Movie Camera* celebrates the ability of the camera to represent the phenomenal world, and it is that ability that becomes the subject of the film. In its depiction of many facets of life in the Soviet Union of the 1920s, it makes constant visual reference to its own making, beginning with the opening shots of the film, showing an empty movie theater with entering patrons. We see the cameraman setting up his camera. We see the camera in startling locations, on bridges and in cars careening down busy streets. At one point images of children's faces become freeze frames; we then see the same stills as individual frames of film on an editing bench. The camera is even represented as alive, when (through animation) it walks "by itself" on its three-legged tripod.

The fascinating films of Chris Marker deserve a chapter to themselves. Like Rouch and Morin, Marker drew his inspiration from Dziga Vertov. Marker was chief organizer of SLON (Societe pour le Lancement des Oeuvres Nouvelles), a film cooperative responsible for several political documentaries. Among these is *Far from Vietnam* (1967), which Marker compiled from the work of many film makers. He has consistently contributed unique and powerful films, each of which is original in conception and execution. In addition to *La jetee* (1962), an innovative science fiction short consisting of sequences of still photographs plus one shot with motion, Marker has produced several expansive nonfiction films, including *Letter from Siberia, Cuba Si!* (1961), *Le Joli Mai* (1963), *Le Mystère Koumiko* (1965), and *Sans Soleil*. All of the films are reflexive and all self-consciously deal with issues of nonfiction film representation.

In some ways, *Letter from Siberia* functions in a manner similar to *Mondo Cane* (discussed below), in that the discourse encourages spectators to appeal to the conventions of the formal voice – in this case the conventions of travelogs – to make sense of the film. Along the way, however, various cues establish the film instead as a humorous examination of nonfiction representation itself. *Letter from Siberia* sets itself up as an essay of sorts, as the voice-over claims to be "writing this letter from Siberia." We see shots of Siberian hunters, industry, the landscape, reindeer, and most of the other footage we would expect in a film about Siberia. Seriously political in certain respects, the film does not wholly repudiate the teaching function of the formal voice. In one scene, for example, we see workers panning for gold, preferring to work in isolation rather than take a better-paying state job that serves the community. The voice-over criticizes their "stupidity" for valuing individualism beyond all rationality.

However, *Letter from Siberia* soon takes wildly idiosyncratic turns and fanciful meanderings. The pseudoseriousness of the travelogue is often interrupted for scenes such as animated segments of dancing Mammoths, silly poems and songs, and a mock advertisement for reindeer. The narration also presents projected world information that is odd by conventional standards. For example, the film spends an inordinate amount of time on one Siberian's pet bear, which is normally chained in the back yard but is sometimes taken for walks.

The film makes more serious points as well. The best-known scene thrice repeats the same sequence of images of workers smoothing out cement on a city street. With each replay, the voice-over changes its tone and attitude, from pro-Soviet propaganda, to anti-Soviet propaganda, to a playful attempt at objectivity. This segment underscores the power of the voice-over in the interpretation of nonfiction images. In this and in another scene, the voice-over also parodies the time-worn clichés common to travelogs. As a modern automobile passes a horse and buggy in the steppe, the narrator mumbles about the mandatory remarks he should make regarding "the old meeting the new."

Like *Letter from Siberia*, *Sans Soleil* presents itself as something like a letter, or more precisely, a travel diary. A sort of philosophical journalism, the film ruminates on cultural practices in Japan, and on the nature of memory and representation. The structure is free-associational, darting around the world on the seeming whims of the narrator. The images at times resemble those of the most conventional documentary, but Marker also makes use of synthesized video images. Voice-over narration in the film is unique; the traveler (who we assume is Marker) has letters about his journeys read by a woman, Alexandra Stewart. She often reads these letters as they were presumably "written," in the first person, though sometimes she reports their contents in the third person. As though to expand on the film's theme of the vagaries of memory and the inability to communicate transparently, the narration in the film is itself relayed indirectly through a reader, who actually narrates the voice-over narration.

Far from Vietnam, which I here examine more closely, raises other issues regarding voice and especially of voice-over narration. Marker compiled *Far from Vietnam* from sequences contributed by Joris Ivens, Alan Resnais, William Klein, Agnes Varda, Claude Lelouch, and Jean-Luc Godard, among others. As the titles announce, these "technicians" made the film "to assert, in the exercise of their profession, their solidarity with the people of Vietnam in their resistance to aggression." The film, then, is an anthology with a unified rhetorical stance in support of the Vietnamese resistance to the United States' effort in Vietnam. Each of the sequences begins with a title, and several give the name of the filmmaker responsible.

Far from Vietnam makes use of some of the conventions of the formal documentary. Like many rhetorical films, it presents its argument encapsulated at the outset. Making use of the primacy effect, the initial titles construct a rhetorical framework with which the spectator may view the film:

The French artists who created the film you are about to see do not present this as an indictment of the American people, but of American foreign policy. You will see people whom this policy labels "Enemy," but who are rather victims of American interference with people's right of self-determination and progress, by revolution if they choose, a means America herself employed nearly two centuries ago.

Other formal techniques include voice-over narration used to anchor and relay the meanings of images. We see shots of American sailors loading bombs onto jets, and the voice-over says, "This is a rich man's war," relaying the images of advanced war technology to concepts of wealth and riches, and to a war fought for the rich. Over shots of Vietnam and peasants in the fields, it continues: "This is a poor man's war," relaying images of simple farming to being poor and to a war fought by the poor. Further exposition occurs during the segment entitled "A Parade is a Parade," when after scenes of a "loyalty parade" and a protest demonstration, the narration presents a newsreel-like history of the Vietnamese conflict, beginning with the end of French involvement in Vietnam. In several respects, then, the opening sequences of *Far from Vietnam* are typical scenes of the formal voice. Clear exposition gives a history of the conflict and delineates the political position, and style gives projected world information.

The last sequence, "Vertigo," suggests an interpretation that provides order and closure to the film's rhetorical project, but presents it with a stylistic complexity rare in the formal voice. A first impression of the sequence suggests a discursive refusal to make meaning out of the complex events of Vietnam. Flash frames, jump cuts, and quick cuts present a montage of confusing images of America's response to the war. We see anti-war protests, jeering bystanders, shots from Westerns, advertisements, television images, flags, nightclub acts, various American icons, store window displays, Malcolm X, people running in the streets, fights erupting, and shots of more protests. But interspersed between these scenes of confusion and anarchy come shots of Vietnamese people and soldiers. In contrast to the Americans, they move with a measured walk, suggesting unity and consistency. The shots have a calm clarity, unlike the frenzied shots of the Americans. This last sequence represents the confusion and dividedness of the American people, in contrast to the ostensible firm resolve and single-mindedness of the Vietnamese. The film's beginning and the end, then, function classically, introducing global intrinsic schemata and establishing an ideological framework (the United States' effort is racked by moral uncertainty, whereas the Vietnamese are unified in their fight for independence).

However, the overall structure of the film differs radically from the formal paradigm. *Far from Vietnam* lacks a unified and harmonious order of presentation, but is instead structured as a sort of anthology of dissimilar segments. The film allows few conventional transitions, and the ordering within segments is loose and relatively unstructured. It presents the tremendously varied segments themselves in no particular narrative or topical order; they share only a common rhetorical stance.

By far the most stylistically difficult segment is Jean-Luc Godard's, entitled "Camera Eye." Godard in voice-over tells of his being denied permission to enter North Vietnam to make a film, and his response to that disappointment. He comes to the conclusion that "the only thing we can do is to make films. The best that we can do for Vietnam (instead of invading them with a generosity we impose) is to let Vietnam invade us instead." Taking "the scream" as the metaphor for oppression everywhere, Godard concludes that those who are not "true" revolutionaries must "listen and . . . relay all the scream we possibly can." The discourse is very self-conscious. The voice-over, in a consistent self-referentiality,[8] considers the proper response of a filmmaker to the situation in Vietnam. Most centrally, the image track reflexively shows Godard and his camera. The beginning sequence of shots is as follows:

- frontal shot into camera lens (close-up)
- side shot of camera, Godard's head screen right
- frontal shot into camera lens (medium shot)
- side shot of camera (step zooms in)
- frontal shot into lens, Godard's head screen right
- side shot, Godard screen right
- frontal shot, Godard screen right
- side shot, camera light turns off at sound of gunshot
- frontal shot of camera and Godard
- side shot of camera
- frontal shot, with Godard screen right looking into viewfinder
- side shot of camera

- oblique close-up of lens, zoom out to shot of camera in front of a landscape
- full shot of the camera from its back, zoom in to camera light

Reflexive films often intentionally make comprehension difficult, to encourage active mental activity by the spectator; such is the strategy of "Camera Eye." The images described above are accompanied by Godard's puzzling words, spoken in voice-over (and translated into English subtitles):

He read the charge against the woman, a small man in a bleached out uniform pacing before her. A little later, two Thunderchiefs began to circle above us and we could hear them coming in low. We could hear the bombs dropping. And when he . . . , when he got on his feet he had a knife in his hand: the kind of knife that peasants use to open coconuts. Bombers are equipped with machine guns that can fire about six thousand rounds a minute. What terrifying explosions! The peasants stood there motionless watching the spectacle. An F-105 jet whizzed by like a cat meowing over our heads [sound of guns]. It all seemed very strange. The peasants stood there motionless watching the spectacle . . . and it all seemed very strange.

I think if I'd been a newsreel cameraman, a cameraman for a TV network like ABC in New York or San Francisco, or a cameraman for the Soviet newsreel system, that's what I'd have filmed. But I live in Paris and I didn't go to Vietnam. Last year I tried to go to Vietnam.

It seems clear that on first viewing, and even after careful analysis, Godard presents the spectator with a difficult passage to comprehend. Although Godard's later narration is a relatively straightforward account of his reactions as a filmmaker to the war, here the voice-over passage is not introduced and is given no context. Initially, and for several minutes, the spectator is at a loss. What is the discursive perspective toward the states of affairs presented by Godard's words? Is this a fictional passage, or is Godard describing an actual circumstance? Are the events described parts of a single scene, or fragments of descriptions of several different scenes? Do these events occur at one time, or are they fragments of events occurring at different times? The images help very little at first. The fragmented story is accompanied by shots of the camera, a mark for the reflexivity of the passage but no help in understanding the narrative. It is only when the voice-over narrator begins speaking in the first person that the spectator begins to comprehend.

After the opening paragraphs discussed above, the voice-over of the rest of the segment becomes clearer and more conventional, a relatively straightforward rumination on the response of the filmmaker to the war in Vietnam. However, classical style not only makes its voice-over coherent, but also maximizes the coherence and communicativeness of the image track, usually through clear spatial and temporal articulation, analytical editing, and the conventional ordering of shots. Here Godard's segment differs radically from the formal style. In the shot list given above, the shots vary between front and side shots of the camera, with variations in camera distance and camera movement. The image track here *is* coherent, but minimalist – spare and uncommunicative.

The sequence is difficult due to its sound/image relationships. Spectators can process information at various speeds, and the classical style assures that the typical spectator can keep up with the flow of images and sounds. Not so in Godard's segment. The voice-over narration is usually spoken rather quickly, and would require intense concentration even if played apart from the images. During the reflexive scenes, such as the first scene, the images are repetitive and relatively simple, and the spectator may be free to concentrate on the voice-over. Yet at other times the image track becomes complex and difficult.

The following shot list shows a segment of voice-over narration together with the actual words (translated into English) accompanying each image. The voice-over begins here as Godard discusses what he would have done had he been granted permission to travel to Vietnam:

Image	Voice-Over
Tilt down palm tree	"I wanted to show defoliation, spoiled rivers
High-contrast image of two persons kneeling over a prone dog	since, in the
another dog (closer shot)	final analysis,
Sky, unidentifiable object in foreground	we are not fighting gun in hand here. On the contrary, we are very far away.
Pan across dead fish in water	Sure, we say our hearts are bleeding, but this

A dead fish	has no blood relation
Dead birds in water	to the blood of the wounded.
Close-up, dead bird	There was a certain shame in all this. It was like signing peace appeals.
Pan across dead frogs on the bank of a pond	And that's why I think
Frontal view of camera lens	the only thing we can do is to make films. The best that we can do for Vietnam (instead of invading them with a generosity we impose) is to let Vietnam invade us instead
Camera tracks in and toward Asian soldier, then circles him	and find out what part it plays in our everyday lives. It's then you realize that Vietnam is not alone, nor are Africa and South America. We must, then, like Che Guevara says, 'Create two or three other Vietnams.'"

In the formal documentary, the relay and anchorage of the voice-over is straightforward and comprehensible. In the sequence of images listed above, the spectator tries to link sound with image, but is frustrated, as their relationship is ambiguous at best. Godard refuses direct reference of particular sentences to particular images, and disavows the anchorage and relay common to the formal style.

In "Camera Eye" Godard practices the radical disjunction between voice-over and image that I discussed in the previous chapter. Where the formal documentary aims for absolute clarity of reference, Godard encourages ambiguity and contradiction. Part of Godard's aim is to make us wrestle with ambiguities of representation.[9] Although Godard's films may block world projection, they call attention to world projection as an action and as a process.

In its diversity of segments, the diverse sequences of *Far from Vietnam* become a menu of possibilities for the reflexive political documentary, a meditation not only on the Vietnam War, but on the possibilities of nonfiction representation itself.

Mondo Cane and Documentary Parody

A parody of nonfiction film may itself be either fiction or nonfiction. A parody will be nonfiction when it takes an assertive stance toward what it represents. Rob Reiner's *This is Spinal Tap* (1984) and Woody Allen's *Zelig* (1983) parody the nonfiction film, but are themselves fiction. Although they mimic the techniques and exploit the foibles of the documentary, the events represented are in large part fictional. Other films, including Mitchell Block's *No Lies* (1973), Jim McBride's *David Holzman's Diary* (1968), and Michele Citron's *Daughter Rite* (1978), mimic the documentary but feature actors playing roles and a scripted series of events. Although these films may fool the spectator about their status during a first viewing, various textual markers finally reveal the films as fictions that do not claim that the characters portrayed are actual persons, or the events shown occurred unscripted.[10]

Although viewers may find its projected world trivial, demeaning, or sensationalistic, *Mondo Cane* (1961) nonetheless qualifies as nonfiction, because it asserts that the states of affairs it presents actually occurred.[11] Despite its use of irony, bizarre juxtapositions of subject matter, and the discursive mocking of its subjects, *Mondo Cane* nonetheless manages to remain a nonfiction film while it parodies the form itself. To begin with, the subject matter is highly unconventional, the "shocking" and curious from all around the world. Style in *Mondo Cane* is relatively invisible, and the film's voice takes a frankly ironic attitude toward the events it represents, modeling a projected world that is full of cruel spectacle, and that is to be alternatively marveled at, disdained, and pitied.

The voice-over narration is full of double meanings and tongue-in-cheek clichés. One of the recurring themes is human cruelty to animals. Over shots of geese being force-fed (to properly prepare their livers for human consumption), the narrator describes how the animals' feet were at one time nailed to the floor to force the geese to conserve energy. The process now is rare, and the geese's care, the narrator ironically says, is now "humane and civilized." Over shots of wealthy Americans eating ants, beetles, muskrat, and butterfly eggs at a specialty restaurant, the narrator utters dryly: "Here a light lunch costs about twenty dollars, but if you take into account the extreme rarity of the food, the price is generally considered fair." Music is often used ironically as well, with strings, harps, and choruses of singers ("angels") perhaps simulating the evocation of the sublime, but succeeding only in suggesting the ridiculous.

In addition to the overt irony, the discourse sometimes presents various subjects by an unconscious logic of free association, and at other times for pure shock value. In either case, it mocks the sober information-disseminating function of the formal voice, distorting it out of all proportion and ordering information more in the fashion of a wild nightmare. The shocks come with the juxtapositions; of a pet cemetery where Americans mourn the loss of their pet "Fifi," with a Chinese restaurant specializing in fresh dog meat; or from the bust of a young woman attempting to attract American sailors, with a woman in New Guinea breast-feeding a pig. Other sequences are linked only by association. We see an underwater cemetery in Malaysia, in which the sea bottom is covered with skeletons picked clean by sharks. Following this is a sequence on the hunting of sharks, followed by a segment on shark torture, in which fishermen capture live sharks, stuff poisonous sea anemones down their gullets, and release them. Next comes the scene of an Italian religious ritual in which the faithful descend into crypts to dust, polish, and remove nails (!?) from the bones and skulls of the dead. Such "free" and startling associations structure the film.

Parodic documentaries assume spectator familiarity with conventions of formal filmmaking and with "appropriate" or conventional subject matter. If the spectator has seen other "shockumentaries," or has heard or read about the nature of the films, she is already receptive to the subtle and blatant ironies of the text. The better her familiarity with conventional nonfiction forms and subject matter, the more ironies she will see. *Mondo Cane* functions as a comedy in some respects. Henry Jenkins claims that some comedies evoke the surface structures of other genres, then work against those structures, or against schemas of social reality. We approach the text as a serious or realistic work, but comic markers encourage us to revise our expectations. Jenkins writes that it is "only when we displace the original interpretive schemata and begin to read the work in accordance with this new set of rules are we granted permission to laugh at phenomena which before seemed only problematic."[12]

Jenkins' theory well describes our response to *Mondo Cane*. *Mondo Cane* opens with the sort of titles familiar to the nonfiction film spectator. They announce the "authenticity" of the images and cue the spectator to see the film as ostensibly objective and true:

All the scenes you will see in this film are true, and are taken only from life. If often they are shocking, it is because there are many shocking things in this world. Besides, the duty of the chronicler is not to sweeten the truth, but to report it objectively.

In using the words "true," "taken from life," "chronicler," "report," and "objectively," the titles exhort the spectator to approach the film as a serious documentary.

From the start, however, markers frequently cue the spectator to make reference to the conventions of comedy. I've already mentioned the ironic voice-over and the crude, tritely associational ordering of segments. The film's first scene is also telling in this respect. It is Rudolph Valentino's home town in Italy, and hundreds of spectators await the unveiling of a statue in his honor, while an official drones on in vocal tribute. While the voice-over dryly implies that all the young men at the ceremony fancy themselves heirs to Valentino, the camera distorts several of their faces in close-ups taken with a wide angle lens, goes to freeze frame when their eyes have just darted toward the camera, and cuts a split second later in a not-so-subtle dig at their supposed vanity. The film functions in part by constructing a generic framework or mental set with which it can ostensibly be understood, only to represent situations that are radically incongruous with respect to those schemas.

However, *Mondo Cane* is satire, not simply comedy. Comedy presents incongruities for the sake of laughter, whereas satire does that, plus it implies that the conventions from which the representata diverge are somehow deficient. *Mondo Cane* implies that the formal documentary represses the true anarchy, irrationality, and cruelty of the world, imposing a sheen of order and noble purpose. *Mondo Cane* not only satirizes the human race for its cruelty, ethnocentricity, and vanity, but burlesques the function of voice-over narration and of music in the formal style, and, in its blatant appeal to the shocking and "outrageous," mocks the formal voice for its sober and judicious claims to knowledge. In its stead, it offers titillation and voyeurism, the release from high seriousness, and immersion into a cruel, yet darkly humorous world that deserves our contemptuous, uneasy laughter.

CHAPTER 10

Nonfiction Pragmatics and the Limits of Theory

Nonfiction films and videos wield significant power in Western culture. They have a bardic function. They negotiate cultural values and meaning, disseminate information (and misinformation), prompt social change, and engender significant cultural debate. We have so far examined central philosophical problems, such as issues of definition and the nature of photographic communication. We have also discussed the functions of images and sounds, discourse and projected world, various voices of nonfiction film, and structure and style. In this chapter I turn to what some might consider the heart of the matter – a pragmatics of nonfiction films, considering their social uses and significances.

I relegate these issues to the last chapter not because I consider them less important than the so-called technical issues of definition, form, style, and communicative function. Rather, it reflects the intractable nature of these problems, together with my views about the proper means of discovering significances, functions, and effects. Theorists have often been quick to make sweeping pronouncements about issues such as objectivity, reflexivity, and the ideological effects of formal documentaries. But theory alone cannot fully answer all the questions we want to ask. It must often be applied to particular films in relation to their idiosyncratic requirements. In other words, theoretical generalizations need the tempering of specific circumstance. A theory of nonfiction film is most useful in relation to the study of particular nonfiction films, within historical context, for specific audiences. Of course, to comprehend the full extent of particulars in any case is impossible. To the extent that it is possible, however, theory not only can illuminate the issues surrounding particular cases, but the particular case in turn improves and corrects the theory.

A careful theoretical discussion of the nature of nonfiction films contributes to an exploration of broader and more complex cultural problems. The issues that have so far occupied this book are a prolegomena to the following discussions of objectivity, reflexivity, and the purposes, effects, and functions of nonfiction films.

Questioning the Three Voices

In an attempt to eliminate clumsy prose, I have sometimes referred to the formal, open, and poetic voices as categories of nonfiction. However, my aim is not to identify or construct new categories, but to describe strategies of voice, structure, and style. It is *these strategies* that I have labeled "formal," "open," and "poetic." To a degree, a film's voice is a determining characteristic, and a film of the formal voice will often use formal structure and style. However, there exist many films that alternate voices such that parts of the film maintain a formal voice, while others slip into the open or poetic voices. Some films have a voice that never finally settles into one category or another, but rests in that fuzzy area in between. Other films may mix open structure with formal style, or vice versa.

For example, Robert Drew was an early champion of the new direct cinema techniques, and the Drew Unit (including Richard Leacock and D. A. Pennebaker) did much to develop the portable, lightweight equipment that made direct cinema possible. One might expect that the Drew films would completely avoid formal structure and style in favor of the open varieties. However, such is not the case. As I mentioned above, Drew's films give evidence of formal structure and technique at many junctures. They are formed in a "crisis structure," in which Drew focuses on a protagonist whose life events are shaped into a neat dramatic package.[1] Jeanne Hall, similarly, has shown that Drew's films also use what I have called formal techniques. Although the films contain the stylistic marks of direct cinema – the "restless, wandering movements of lightweight, hand-held cameras; the dark, grainy images of fast, monochrome film . . . ," etc., they also feature "(variously) voice-over narration, talking heads, avowed editorials, animated maps, superimpositions, subtitles, nondiegetic music, subjective sequences, matches-on-action – countless conventions of the traditional documentary film and the classical Hollywood cinema. . . ."[2] Drew's films are a complex mixture of formal and open characteristics.

What are the strengths, weaknesses, and ideological effects of the formal, open, and poetic voices? Is the formal voice authoritarian or patronizing? Is the open voice legitimate in view of today's complex world? Is the poetic voice morally defensible, or is it a retreat from responsibility in the face of serious world problems? I begin with the latter question. The discussion of poetic documentary as an inferior subgenre has been prevalent since the 1920s. The concentration of the poetic film on the sensual and the aesthetic has traditionally garnered its criticism as superficial or trivial. A long-standing tradition holds that nonfiction films without social and political content somehow fall short of the form's highest function. Grierson's criticisms of *Berlin: Symphony of the City*, for example, take exception to the film's concentration on aesthetics at the expense of pressing political issues. The eventual rise of National Socialism in Weimar Germany seems to bear Grierson out. Remembering the horrendous events that followed, it seems easy to criticize Walter Ruttman in hindsight for his interest in "mere aesthetics" and for his representation of the city as an organic element of nature. In fact, Grierson was highly suspicious of art itself. He writes, for example, that "the circles devoted to the art of cinema mean well and they will help to articulate the development of technique, *but the conscious pursuit of art carries with it, in periods of public difficulty, a certain shallowness of outlook* [my emphasis]."[3]

Joris Ivens originally produced poetic films, but moved on to works with clear political content. While making *The Bridge*, Ivens writes, he was most concerned with sensual qualities available to the eye:

I learned that when you film repetitive movement such as the action of a counterweight on the bridge, you have to observe this for a longer time and with greater attention than you would think. You will always discover something new, the countermovement of a gliding shadow, a significant trembling as the cables come to a halt, or a more telling reflection at a more subjective angle.[4]

Ivens later came to see the subjects of his poetic films as "less important" than those of his later political films, and sees the early films merely as training for later projects. Of *Rain*, he writes:

The most serious criticism against the film was its lack of "content." In a certain sense this was an exact criticism. I failed to emphasize sufficiently human beings' reactions to rain in a big city. Everything was subordinated to the esthetic approach. In a way I am glad that I laid a foundation of technical and creative perfection before working on other more important elements.[5]

Part of the reason for the critical neglect of the poetic film has been this assumption that the proper subject of documentary is social and political, not aesthetic. Such an assumption has the effect of consigning a considerable body of creative and historically important films to second-class status. It also conjures up images, however inaccurate historically, of puritans with thick-buckled black coats and permanent scowls, ready to squash any signs of pleasure (in this case, aesthetic pleasure) in the name of religious and/or political urgencies. To listen to Grierson and some contemporary critics, poetic filmmakers are akin to Nero fiddling while Rome burns to the ground.

To condemn aesthetic pleasure independent of context is too narrow in outlook. It ignores the fact that much art is capable of a profound political and social function. However, there is also a time and a place for films that "merely" celebrate the grandeur and beauty of nature and art, films that step back from social and political concerns to embrace the joys of life. The question is not whether poetic films are justified *in general*, but when and under what conditions. Certainly there are circumstances in which aestheticism and the poetic film can become an escape from responsibility. But to condemn such films universally, for all contexts, is authoritarian.

The open voice raises other significant issues – about the relationship of the filmmaker to the audience, about reflexivity and objectivity, and about the relative merits of photographic observation. Much of the criticism of the open voice has been slanted toward observational rather than participatory films, that is, toward films where the strategy of the filmmaker is to remain "invisible" to the audience, to record the profilmic scene with as little mediation as possible, and to transparently convey images and sounds in the name of a fidelity to the actual world. Thus the filmmakers of direct cinema, rather than cinéma vérité, have borne the brunt of the criticism. In the rush of excitement about their new equipment and its possibilities, observational filmmakers early on made some brash, and perhaps naive, claims for direct cinema. They talked about objectivity, unmediated truth, the purity of the actual world, and the ability of the filmmaker to recede into the background to reproduce the profilmic scene for the audience.[6] A chief criticism of the observational film, then, is that it pretends to be something that it is not. The discourse of every film must shape its projected world and present it from a point of view. No film can escape a perspective, and under the guise of objectivity or truth, filmmakers have smuggled in subtle and not-so-subtle slants on the subjects they represent.[7]

However fair it may be to say that audiences assume that observational films are objective (and this is a claim I examine below), it isn't right to attribute such notions to the filmmakers themselves. Although some may have embraced overly optimistic notions of their method in the beginning, most consistently rejected the notion that what they were doing was representing reality "just as it is," or "objectively." David Maysles, for example, says that there is no such thing as "being strictly objective in anything that is at all artistic." He goes on: "I don't think we ever strive for that kind of reality. There is no worth in 'this is the way it was – exactly.'"[8] Wiseman has always distanced himself from direct cinema and cinéma vérité, although his films are prototypical examples of the observational cinema. He also rejects the claims of objectivity: ". . . this subjective-objective stuff is a lot of bullshit. I don't see how a film can be anything but subjective. . . . They are not objective because someone else might make the film differently."[9]

What the open voice, in the form of observational cinema, has emphasized are the observational powers of the camera and sound recorder – their ability to record the look and sound of events. Observational cinema has not only revealed what film can do well in this regard, but also what it fails to do. As I argued in previous chapters, the photographic image can bear both an iconic and indexical relationship to the profilmic event. Nonfiction film can thus serve as a witness to events, and as evidence (always problematic and partial) that events occurred in a certain way. The use of images as evidence, though often misunderstood and employed deceptively, has had tremendous importance in this century, from the U.S. Army films of Nazi concentration camps at the close of World War II (which some neo-fascists still claim to be inauthentic), to *The Safer Report* film of G.I.s in Vietnam torching peasant's huts, to the video of Rodney King's beating at the hands of Los Angeles cops, to visual records of the resulting Los Angeles riots and the beating of truck driver Reginald Denny. Having understood the enormous visceral and evidential power of moving pictures, government officials kept cameras away from the battle front in the recent Gulf War with Iraq, to eliminate or strictly control all visual representations of the horrors of war and the power of such images to mold public opinion. The observational film makes full use of the unique strengths of the camera and sound recorder to represent events with a visceral power and veridical authenticity unknown before the invention of motion picture photography.

Yet the ability of the camera to observe is not limited to extreme events such as these, but also extends to films about nature, for example. Words cannot substitute for the photographic representation of animals, plants, and the natural environment. In addition, observation is still valuable in situations where the camera likely has influence. The presence of the camera and filmmaker never renders observation useless; it only makes it problematic. Frederick Wiseman claims that persons act *more* rather than *less* characteristically in the presence of the camera. Few of us are trained as actors, he says. We have a repertoire of characteristic gestures, body movements, and facial expressions, and we're not good enough actors to try out new roles in front of the camera. When confronted with a camera, we revert to characteristic behavior:

I couldn't suddenly start to act like an accountant or affect a factory worker's speech if I didn't know anything about being an accountant or a factory worker – unless, of course, I was a good actor. But most of us aren't good enough actors to suddenly become something or someone we really aren't. . . . My guess is that if people are uncomfortable, they will act in ways which are comfortable rather than increase the discomfort by trying out new roles. This means they will act in characteristic rather than new ways.[10]

Jean Rouch echoes Wiseman's claim, saying that when people are being filmed, ". . . the reactions that they have are always infinitely more sincere than those they have when they are not being recorded."[11] Similarly, in an excellent essay critical of observational cinema in other respects, David MacDougall says that its chief strength is its ability to observe people. As he writes, persons "can behave more naturally while being filmed than in the presence of an ordinary observer, since the cameraperson is preoccupied with his or her job, and this is understood by the subject."[12] When observational films are functioning at their best, he writes, "the people in them seem bearers of the immeasurable wealth and effort of human experience. Their lives have a weight that makes the film that caught but a fragment seem trivial, and we sit in a kind of awe of our own privileged observation of them."[13] More often than not, the open voice resists expressive strategies in deference to the power of the camera to observe, a characteristic that, although fraught with difficulties and ambiguities, nonetheless remains one of the most significant and evocative elements of nonfiction film.

However, although recognizing the revelatory significance of observational films, we can also point to their lack of conceptual development. The open voice, in the form of observational cinema, is content to observe rather than to explain. One might describe this in less favorable terms as the representation of mere appearances and an inability (or a refusal) to deal with underlying causes, motivations, and contexts.

In fact, this has been a significant criticism of direct cinema and cinéma vérité from its beginnings. As William Bluem writes in his history of documentary on television, "vérité has shown us . . . that it can nullify an essentially intellectual message – or impede . . . our appreciation and understanding of it. Because it can interfere with rationality (it is *designed* to do so), the question fundamentally is whether verité is legitimate in News Documentary. . . ."[14]

Observational filmmaking also raises questions about what is actually being observed. MacDougall claims that in ethnographic filmmaking, the observational ideal actually distorts the situation because it implicitly denies the presence of the filmmaker. When the ethnographic filmmaker attempts to make a record of another culture, he neglects the meeting of two cultures that actually occurs – that of the filmmaker and the people he seeks to photograph. If observation is a strength of some films, it can also become a weakness of the ethnographic film: "Its failing lies precisely in the attitude of watching – the reticence and analytical inertia it induces in filmmakers, some of whom feel themselves agents of universal truth, others of whom comment only slyly or by indirection from behind their material."[15]

Observational filmmakers might respond in a number of ways. Wiseman, for example, claims that though his attitude toward his subjects should be clear from his films, they nonetheless allow a *democracy of interpretation*. Rather than explain and preach, they allow viewers to approach events that, although not structureless and unmediated, are subject to multiple interpretations. This captures the heart of the open voice. We have all seen films with stentorian voice-over narrators, confidently making pronouncements about the meaning and significance of the events depicted. The open voice attempts to preserve some of the ambiguity and complexities, or what Bill Nichols calls the "magnitudes," of the world. Whether audiences take these films as objective or unmanipulated reflections of reality, and whether strategies of reflexivity can alter these misperceptions, is another matter. However, "objectivity" and the representation of the world "just as it is" certainly isn't the design of most observational filmmakers. Critics have accused them of all kinds of conceptual crimes, many of which they did not commit.

Last, and certainly not least, we may consider the strengths and weaknesses of the formal voice – the voice many would consider central in the nonfiction film. Noel King argues that like all realist documentaries, *Union Maids* (1976) produces a "'discourse' of continuity which results not in 'the past' but in the effect of a past," a "syntagmatic flow of events, an easy diachronic progression which ensures a working out of all problems, guarantees an increase in knowledge on the reader's part, promises containment and completion." Classical form and style, in sum, smooth over contradictions, fill in gaps, and render the incoherent artificially coherent.[16]

To critique films such as *Union Maids* and *Harlan County, U.S.A.* for producing not the past but the "effect" of the past is, on the face of it, rather odd, as though a successful historical film, through some bag of tricks, would actually bring the past back to life rather than simply represent it (and produce its "effect"). In addition, I am inclined to disagree with King's assessment that *Union Maids* and *Harlan County, U.S.A.*, despite their realist (or what I have called "formal") styles, *do* represent the past as a seamless, effortless, easily understood phenomenon.

Nonetheless, lying behind these criticisms is an assumption that bears further analysis. This assumption is shared by Bill Nichols, when he writes of the inability of conventional documentary methods to represent adequately the complexities, or "magnitudes," of the world.[17] Nichols calls for reflexive, defamiliarizing documentaries that do not deny or disavow complexities. For both King and Nichols, the point seems to be that reflexive, defamiliarizing techniques preserve a sense of the intricacy of reality, whereas classical or what I call "formal" structures and styles cannot do justice to it.

This position correctly assumes a distinction between a discourse and the actual world. If we have no access to extradiscursive reality, after all, then we have no phenomenological ground to claim that classical discourse misrepresents its magnitudes. However, these criticisms make some questionable assumptions about how reality is represented. They make the *imitative form fallacy*, the idea that the form of a discourse must necessarily copy or imitate its real-world subject. I see no reason why, if a subject is complex and contradictory, it cannot be represented as such in a seamless, unified representation that proclaims its complexity. In other words, a film of the formal voice, using classical style and structure, may pay homage to the complexities of the world even while using classical techniques to do so. It doesn't necessarily require a contradictory, meandering discourse to represent events as contradictory and meandering. A film's discourse need not imitate the form of its projected world.

However, the point made by Nichols and King is a good one, if taken as a warning rather than a blanket condemnation of classical style. It is sometimes said that the more one learns, the less one knows, meaning that education teaches us, but also humbles us. Like many discourses, films of the formal voice often make knowledge seem easy by ignoring difficult issues, gaps, controversies, incoherences, etc., that might lead us to question its claims to reveal the truth. Such a false confidence in the extent of that knowledge is a characteristic of some films of the formal voice, and requires vigilance and criticism.

Some followers of the philosopher Michel Foucault assert that all discourse consists not of attempts to tell "the Truth," but as a means of asserting and wielding power. Although not expressly Foucauldian, Jay Ruby expresses similar ideas in the following passage:

The documentary film was founded on the Western middle-class need to explore, document, explain, understand, and hence symbolically control the world. It has been what "we" do to "them." "They" in this case are usually the poor, the powerless, the disadvantaged, and the politically suppressed and oppressed. Documentary films dealing with the rich and powerful or even the middle class are as sparse as are social science studies of these people. The documentary film has not been a place where people explored themselves or their own culture.[18]

If we think of discourse as the mere wielding of power, we could easily see films of the formal voice as authoritarian, since they presume to teach from a position of superior knowledge. Thus E. Ann Kaplan describes criticisms of two realist documentaries, *Joyce at 34* (1972) and *Janie's Janie* (1971): ". . . the cinematic strategies of both films are indeed such as to establish an unwelcome imbalance between author [filmmaker] and spectator. The authors in each case assume the position of one in possession of knowledge, while the spectators are forced into the position of passive consumers of this knowledge. The filmic processes leave us with no work to do, so that we sit passively and receive the message."[19]

Both the passages from Ruby and the criticisms described by Kaplan assume that the spectator of the formal documentary sits passively, merely absorbing the ostensible knowledge imparted by the film. This was once a common assumption of psychoanalytic film theory, although the new interest in cognitive psychology, negotiated and oppositional readings, and discursive communities who use discourses for their own purposes has drawn attention to the fact that spectators are not the homogeneous, passive sponges they were sometimes thought to be.[20]

The larger, and similarly mistaken assumption, is that nonfiction discourse is primarily and necessarily about power relationships, and that documentary films assert hegemonic power over those who are oppressed or marginalized. Such generalizations simply do not stand up to the empirical diversity and disparate uses of nonfiction films. Counterexamples are obvious; *The Thin Blue Line, Harlan County, U.S.A.,* and *Roger and Me* champion the cause of those lacking power – an innocent man convicted of murder, striking coal miners, and unemployed auto workers. Similarly, to reduce all nonfiction discourse to power relationships makes discourse into an easily understood, facile phenomenon. The function of *all* films – of *Vietnam: A Television History, Letter from Siberia, Rain, High School,* and *Say Amen, Somebody* – becomes the simple quest for power. However, the complex functions of discourse cannot be so reduced. The formal voice can become authoritarian, but it isn't necessarily so. Teaching can be highly beneficial, seriously destructive, or benign and uninteresting, depending on subject, audience, and historical context. In its teaching and explanatory functions, the formal voice cannot be condemned *a priori*. To teach from an informed position is an age-old function of discourse.

The poetic, open, and formal voices all have significant capabilities and potential liabilities. However, none is inherently superior to the other; none is necessarily either ideologically progressive or pernicious. These determinations cannot be made by theory alone, but only after considerations of individual instances, in light of a theoretical understanding of nonfiction film. If "Theory" by itself cannot make sweeping ideological judgments about the formal characteristics of film discourse, so be it. Call in criticism, and history, to further the task.

Objectivity and *The Twentieth Century*

In Chapter Two, I claimed that objectivity was a documentary "red herring." By that I meant that "objectivity" has sometimes been thought of as a necessary feature of nonfiction film – in some cases even as the defining feature. I claimed that objectivity, by whatever definition, has no necessary connection to nonfiction film, that many films do not aim for objectivity, and that making objectivity central to nonfiction film unjustifiably marginalizes subjective and expressive films.

That being said, however, it still is true that objectivity and related concepts – fairness, impartiality, balance, etc. – are vital for a nonfiction pragmatics. One of the pervasive uses of nonfictions is to provide information, and in regard to the institutions of film and television journalism, "objectivity" refers to the manner of that presentation. Debates about objectivity reach to the core issues of the representation of reality on film. Here I examine the issue of objectivity and related concepts in more depth than in the second chapter, and in relation to the specific case of the television documentary series, *The Twentieth Century*.

One aspect of the study of nonfiction film and video is the investigation, as Stuart Hall terms it, of "the mediation between broadcasting and power."[21] Broadcast journalists often claim that their work is objective and fair; they often insist upon their freedom from the influence of sponsors, parent corporations, and government agencies. Yet Hall claims that concepts such as objectivity, balance, impartiality, professionalism, and consensus serve as smokescreens for biases and a subtle hegemony. In this section I show the problematic nature of concepts such as "objectivity" and "balance," and then go on to examine possible responses to these problems.

When one examines specific films or programs, one sees that objectivity and similar concepts are not what they claim to be. Consider these concepts as they were played out in *The Twentieth Century*, a major Columbia Broadcasting System (CBS) documentary series that aired on television between 1957 and 1966. The series' producers maintained an apparent autonomy from both the network hierarchy and the sponsors, and remained free of explicit external influences. Nonetheless, the series was oriented wholly within what Hall would call the "hegemonic ideology" of the United States at that time. A brief look at the history of the series reveals its bias toward the status quo of its time, which contradicts its claims for objectivity, fairness, balance, etc.

During the decade spanning the mid-fifties through the mid-sixties, the three major networks relied on two types of nonfiction programming – "news" series like *See It Now*, *NBC White Paper*, and *ABC Close Up!*, and compilation series such as *The Twentieth Century*, *Victory at Sea*, and *Air Power*. *The Twentieth Century* premiered in 1957 as an historical compilation series primarily dealing with the history of World War II. After 1960 it evolved into a more journalistic treatment of contemporary issues. In its longevity and consistent ability to draw large audiences, the series was highly successful. Unlike the compilation series of other networks, *The Twentieth Century* was regularly scheduled, running fifty-two weeks per year, and ran for nine years, from 1957–1966. It had presented 219 programs by the close of the 1965–1966 season.

Of its 219 episodes, more than half (120) are devoted to historical subjects, and most of these are compilation films. Among its histories are thirty-four biographies of famous persons and fifty-four episodes covering war or war-related subjects. Another ninety-four episodes deal with more contemporary issues, for example, seventeen shows on military training and technology, shows on the social problems of the young ("The Delinquents," "Generation Without a Cause"), and thirteen episodes on life in other countries. The series also participates in the cold war rhetoric of the time, with titles including "Brainwashing," "Germany: Red Spy Target," and "Red Ships off Our Shores."

After the 1965–1966 season, producer Burton Benjamin renamed the series, and under its new heading, *The 21st Century*, it was reoriented toward the technology and sciences of the future. It then aired for another four years, making it – under both titles – a series running longer than such popular favorites as *Dragnet* (twelve years) and *The Beverly Hillbillies* (nine years). With the respected and personable Walter Cronkite as host and narrator, *The Twentieth Century* offered both CBS and the series' sponsor, the Prudential Life Insurance Company, a solid prestige production. NBC's *Victory at Sea* was produced and its first run broadcast without a sponsor; it was thus "sustained" by the network. Although it lasted for only one season, *Victory at Sea* eventually became financially successful through residuals – including syndication, sales to foreign markets, etc.[22] In contrast, *The Twentieth Century* enjoyed the firm sponsorship of Prudential for nine years, from its inception until the 1965–66 season. In fact, *The Twentieth Century* owed its genesis to Prudential, because the insurance company had encouraged CBS to develop a new public affairs program after *Air Power* ran its course in 1956–1957.[23] Although public affairs programs reached relatively small audiences, the demographic profile (educated, well-off, male) was thought to make up for their relatively mediocre ratings. Public affairs advertising aimed at the development of a corporate image and only indirectly at the promotion and sales of individual insurance policies.[24]

Stuart Hall claims that the broadcasting institutions of Western democracies are in fact "relatively autonomous," and that the study of "specific 'influences' . . . is an inadequate model for examining the me-diation between broadcasting and power."[25] Hall's claims fit the case of *The Twentieth Century*. No evidence suggests any direct contact, on matters of specific program content, between Prudential executives and the producers of *The Twentieth Century*. Neither did CBS executives interfere with specific documentary or news programming. The show's narrator, Walter Cronkite, for example, maintains that during his 19 years with CBS, he never received advice from CBS Chairman of the Board William S. Paley regarding the content of news programs.[26] Hall suggests that rather than looking to specific influences to determine how power and ideology are played out in the media, we must examine the central concepts that mediate between the media and the "power-ideology complex." It is through such concepts as *balance, impartiality, objectivity, professionalism,* and *consensus,* Hall claims, that the media can at once maintain the appearance of autonomy and preserve domi-nant hegemony.

The producers of *The Twentieth Century* explicitly wore the mantle of objectivity. As producer Benjamin explained, "our function is to re-port on history and not to make interpretations."[27] Cronkite defended what he called the show's "refusal to get up on a soapbox." The series had no business telling people "what they should and should not do." Benjamin preferred to see the series as an historical record of the events of the century, an uncontroversial but compellingly-presented historical documentation. He saw no reason to uncover potentially embarrassing facts or to present controversial material.[28]

Hall claims that concepts such as *impartiality, balance,* and *objectiv-ity* – implicitly invoked by Benjamin and Cronkite – have inherent po-litical implications. *Balance* ensures that journalists will entertain con-flicting points of view, but nonetheless defines the political arena and tacitly maintains the prevailing political order. *Impartiality* can lead to a "false symmetry of issue," a balance between opposing forces that ex-ists only in its journalistic manifestation. Finally, Hall sees *objectivity* as an operational fiction, a pretense of reporting on history and not making interpretations (to rehash Benjamin's claims), which has the ef-fect of making those inevitable interpretations less visible.

In *The Twentieth Century*, the invocation of these concepts masks a definite slant, a strong point of view made increasingly apparent with the passage of time. This is most obvious in the series' treatment of the military. The U.S. military, both in its exploits during World War II and in its contemporary technology and practices, was the most-treated topic of the series. More than seventy shows – roughly thirty percent of the total 219 – have to do with military subjects. Here the series' point of view is clear, however objective it may have appeared to Cronkite and Benjamin. The stance of the series was never merely the neutral observation of war or the growth of military technology. On the contrary, *The Twentieth Century* was uncritically pro-American, and tended to glamorize the U.S. military and its role in world affairs. While episodes such as "Germany: Red Spy Target" spread rumors of the "red menace," *The Twentieth Century* calmed its audience's cold war fears with programs outlining various aspects of American military might, from the training of new draftees to the development of the first solid fuel Intercontinental Ballistic Missiles. The military is portrayed as efficient and well run, and its various component divisions as tight-fitting cogs in a well-oiled machine. Irritating problems such as inefficiency and mismanagement are ignored, as are broader ethical issues about the use of military force and the political and economic motivations behind it.

"Man of the Month: The Draftee" (1966), for example, emphasizes the modernization of the army as it documents the induction and training of new draftees. As clean-cut, enthusiastic trainees parade past the camera, the voice-over narration boasts that the U.S. soldier is "the best-outfitted soldier in the world" and lists the various ways the army had putatively humanized conditions of basic training: "That fixture of another day, the loud-mouthed bully boy platoon sergeant, has been replaced by the somewhat quieter, scrupulously-trained drill instructor." Vietnam is mentioned only briefly in passing, and then only to make the false claim that few soldiers would actually be sent there. That the war and the draft itself had by then become a controversial issue is not recognized.

A similar piece of "objectivity" is the episode "Downrange" (1960), where in the prologue the on-screen Cronkite cheerfully announces: "Today for the first time on television, you will see and hear the story of the air force's 6000 mile shooting gallery. . . ." Cronkite calls them "big birds," but they are better known today as Intercontinental Ballistic Missiles, capable of inflicting almost incomprehensible destruction from long distances. Although this episode gives much technical information, it never alludes to the purposes of these weapons and the consequences of their use. In the view of this episode, and of *The Twentieth Century* in general, the American military ensures not only the safety of the American people, but of the entire "free" world. In the name of objectivity, balance, and impartiality, the show never wavers from this stance.

The military thought a great deal of *The Twentieth Century*, as the numerous awards presented to the series and its staff indicate. The series received the 1961 Department of Defense Outstanding Service Award "for its outstanding service in ably presenting armed forces activities and achievements to the public." Producer Burton Benjamin won two awards, the Department of the Army Certificate of Achievement (1963) and the Navy Meritorious Public Service Citation (1961–62), the latter having been given to only one other civilian – Bob Hope.[29]

In 1971, CBS News aired its documentary "The Selling of the Pentagon," which told of the various ways in which the Department of Defense promoted itself with taxpayer's money. The show caused considerable controversy due to its perceived antimilitary bias. Yet *The Twentieth Century*, an earlier CBS product produced within a different political climate, had promoted the military throughout its nine-year existence, and never (to my knowledge) received any criticism for bias, although its slant, in an opposing direction, was just as clear. *The Twentieth Century* never went so far as to defend the Vietnam War, as did certain Department of Defense films (e.g., *Why Vietnam?* [1965]), but under a guise of impartiality and objectivity, it consistently presented an idealized representation of the U.S. Armed forces and their role in world affairs.

Although our main concern here is objectivity, other related concepts have important implications for representation as well. "Professionalism" is a fourth mediating concept for Hall, a means by which journalists form a defensive barrier that insulates them from issues and forces that threaten to make any program a "sensitive area." Hall claims that the concern with standards, techniques, and good form often supports professional retreatism and the neutralization of content.[30] Professionalism can become a self-validating process by which the media institutions reward themselves for maintaining the standards they set. Again, *The Twentieth Century* is a case in point.

By any industry standard, *The Twentieth Century* was a professional success. By the end of the 1965–1966 season, the series had won 45 awards. Among them were the broadcasting industry's prestige awards – the Peabody, Emmy, and Sylvania – plus special interest group citations, foreign film festival mentions, and so forth.[31] Probably *The Twentieth Century*'s salient "professional" characteristics were on the one hand its flamboyant and energetic formal style, and on the other its tendency to embody its subjects in formal and highly dramatic structures – forms that ensured not only a "good story," but simple clarity and immediate comprehension on the part of the viewer. Producer Burton Benjamin called the historical compilation documentary "living history in its most dramatic form."[32] And although the form may have had shortcomings, lethargic presentation was not among them. The producer's expressed desire was to present the series with "all the showmanship we can."[33] Often the result is a visual and aural extravaganza of lively action and rapid pacing, easily matching the vivacity of a Hollywood screwball comedy. This energetic style extends to all the technical aspects of the production, from sound to image.

Cronkite's voice-over narration tends to give exaggerated significance to its subjects, offering glib observations and mock-solemn analyses. Consider the concluding bit of narration of the 1961 "Sports Cars: The Rage to Race." As Stirling Moss, surrounded by a throng of admirers, accepts the trophy as winner of the Grand Prix de Monaco, an off-screen Cronkite narrates with urgent seriousness, and offers the explanations common to the formal voice:

What is it they seek, that they are willing to face such dangers to achieve? The answer is one that no man can for sure provide for another. It probably is to be found somewhere in the satisfaction of overcoming one's own fears, to tempt danger and defeat, and of joining that small fraternity that has answered the sports car Lorelei, the urge to race.

Cronkite did not do all the talking; he often interviewed "eye-witnesses," persons with special knowledge of or experience with the subject in question. According to William Bluem, the use of the "eye-witness" in the compilation history was "*The Twentieth Century*'s unique contribution to TV documentary."[34]

To complement the histrionics of the voice-over narration, the series contracted composers to create original music that matched the drama and pace of the series' other elements. The series' title sequence for some years consisted of a high angle shot from the point of view of a just-launched rocket, picturing fire and smoke and the rapidly diminishing Earth below. The accompanying music consists of pizzicato notes ascending and descending at a furious pace. The frenzied opening sets the rhythm and tone for the show to follow. In addition to the dramatic use of sound, terse, fast-moving editing created a program that whisks along like a hurried slide show for a restless audience. Professionalism in the journalistic documentary also manifests itself in the imposition of classical form onto history. CBS publicity suggested that producer Benjamin's approach to each episode would be "Aristotelian." Each story "will have a beginning, a middle, and an end, a dramatic conflict." It would also give the viewer, to use a phrase distinctly *non*-Aristotelian, "inside facts combined with nostalgia."[35]

A sample 1960 episode of *The Twentieth Century*, "The Battle of the Bulge," creates suspense, effects a constant ebb and flow of dramatic tension, and builds to an anxious climax. After furious German attacks on the city of Bastogne, Cronkite announces that the "entire town and its gallant [American] garrison will be destroyed unless help arrives." Short on food, fuel, and ammunition, the American troops defending the city desperately need the support of Patton's advancing Third Army and supplies from airforce planes. In an example of classical cross-cutting to create suspense, Patton's army advances while the besieged Americans wait for the relief Patton will bring. Tanks slip and slide on treacherous roads while Cronkite remarks that getting to Bastogne on time "seems impossible." Meanwhile, the air force is unable to supply the men due to bad weather. After we see a plane crash in attempting a take-off, Cronkite intones grimly, "No planes for Bastogne today." The American soldiers in the city – many wounded – look haggard and exhausted. "Where is the air force?" Cronkite asks. Patton and the air force do eventually arrive for the last-minute rescue and the happy ending, a professional technique dating back at least as far as D.W. Griffith.

Clearly, the need to produce an entertaining and dramatic story was of paramount importance in the formula for professionalism specific to *The Twentieth Century*. With an implicit understanding that the series should threaten none of its audience, and that no subject should be explored at a level that would raise uncomfortable questions, professionalism could thus actually become the goal of the production, rather than an appeal to "the need to know," or yet more remote, the need for political and social change.

Hall defines the last significant mediating concept, "consensus," as "the structure of commonsense ideology and beliefs in the public at large." Consensus on any specific issue is fluid, but without some shared beliefs, Hall writes, it would be difficult to broadcast or to govern in democratic societies. Consensus should not be taken as unproblematic "public opinion." Because the majority of people have "little

real, day-to-day access to decisions and information, commonsense ideologies are usually a composite reflection of the dominant ideologies,
operating at a passive and diffused level in society."[36] Here the function
of the media is dual, because while broadcasters must gauge consensus
as a fundamental component of their professional practice, they also
formulate that consensus. As Hall writes, "the media and the dominant
institutions of communication and consciousness formation are themselves the primary *source* of attitudes and knowledge within which
public opinion crystallizes, and the primary *channels* between the dominant classes and the audience."[37]

If Hall is correct in his analysis, the presence of a figure like Walter
Cronkite as friendly host of *The Twentieth Century* would be of the ut-
most significance in the formation of public opinion. Unlike the more
severe and at times controversial Edward R. Murrow, the reassuring
Cronkite earned an almost universal acceptance among his viewers.
Human interest stories appeared in popular magazines with titles befit-
ting the man's benign and fatherly image, such as "The Secret Life of
Walter (Mitty) Cronkite" and "Walter Cronkite: Sports Car Fan."[38] In
its press releases CBS glamorized Cronkite's role as narrator for *The
Twentieth Century*. We learn, for example, that ". . . the CBS News
correspondent regularly tours the United States, commutes to Europe,
and occasionally visits other continents; he goes aloft in planes, goes
down into the sea in subs, crawls under the Arctic ice, and swelters in
the Equatorial sun."[39] Cronkite exudes a combination of friendly trust-
worthiness and professional demeanor that made him important in the
formation of consensus.

In late 1966, producer Burton Benjamin announced the renaming of
The Twentieth Century; the new title would be *The 21st Century*. The
new program would no longer take its subject matter from the past or
the present, but from the future, with developments in medicine, communications, space, and other technologies. The newly-named series
also received a new sponsor, Union Carbide. This change in format can
be accounted for in various ways. What Hall calls the media's "double
bind" is suggestive of the deeper forces that may have been at work.
Hall suggests that in times when consensus begins to disappear – when
intersubjective discourse becomes elusive and a rift in public opinion
about political/moral concerns widens – consensus "ceases to provide
the broadcaster with a built-in ideological compass." When consensus
effectively disappears, the relatively autonomous media "become the
site for the elaboration of hegemonic and counter-hegemonic ideologies

and the *terrain* of societal and class conflict at the ideological level."
The media cannot maintain their credibility, Hall writes, without giving
access to counterhegemonic ideologies, but at the same time, when such
views are aired, the media are open to criticism from those who "attack
broadcasting for unwittingly tipping the balance of public feeling
against the political order."[40]

That this double bind manifests itself most vigorously in times of political turmoil is of special interest to the historian of *The Twentieth
Century*, for at the time the series was being phased out, contemporary
events were fast dividing the United States politically. It was more than
the well-known fact that consensus was disappearing about American
involvement in Vietnam. Relations between the popular press and the
government began to worsen in 1965, when *The Safer Report* showed
film of a marine setting a Vietnamese village on fire. Later that year, the
press wrote of the "credibility gap," a euphemism for outright deception on the part of the federal government. The sponsor could no
longer trust Cronkite to remain the bland figure he'd been throughout
the early sixties. By the mid-sixties, Cronkite had been seriously questioning the reliability of information given to the press; "misleading the
public," he claimed, "has become general armed forces policy."[41]

Under these conditions, the making of *The Twentieth Century*, with
its reliance on a well-defined political consensus, would have become
increasingly difficult. How could the series have maintained its credibility without acknowledging the growth of "counter hegemonic" ideologies? This question looms larger when one remembers that the press itself became an enemy in the eyes of the Vietnam-era military-industrial
complex. It was not merely a question of acknowledging anti-war witnesses and attitudes. Significant members of the press had *become* part
of that movement. The turn to *The 21st Century*, then, effectively by-
passed the potential problems caused by disruptive current events. For
in spite of the Vietnam conflict, significant consensus still existed in relation to issues such as technology, medicine, communications, and
space – the topics of the revamped series.

In *The Twentieth Century*, the concepts Hall considers clearly function in a manner his theory predicts, to mediate the relationship between power and ideology. In itself this is valuable as an historical case
study of the relationship between media and power, a study that seems
to validate and give evidence for Hall's theory. Yet other theoretical issues need raising, especially regarding the implications of such findings.
What are the limits of Hall's model of power in broadcasting? Given

the knowledge that concepts such as objectivity and fairness are not what they seem, what should be our response?

The use of mediating concepts cannot tell the *entire story* of media power and influence. For example, this model cannot account for the existence of bolder media broadcasts such as *See It Now*'s "Report on Senator McCarthy" (1954). In this broadcast, Edward R. Murrow, at great personal risk, stepped out of his institutional role as "objective" news broadcaster to take on the powerful Senator Joseph R. McCarthy and his irresponsible red-baiting. Certainly no hegemonic or institutional forces influenced Murrow to put his career on the line to take on this potent force in American politics. How can Hall's model account for breakdowns in the media/power relationships predicted by his theory? In part, the answer lies in the need to recognize that just as *particular institutions* may operate in relative autonomy from the specific influences of the infrastructure, *individual broadcasters* may operate in relative autonomy from the institutions in which they work. Cultural criticism has recognized that texts are polyvocal, that meaning is unstable, and that the media are open to resistant and subversive interpretations. But if spectators possess a degree of autonomy, why not also producers? In what other way can we account for Edward R. Murrow and Fred Friendly's bold presentation of anti-McCarthy programs for *See It Now*, except in terms of those men's personal agency? An historical analysis based solely on institutional theories of power relationships neglects the importance of personal agency.

Hall claims that specific influences cannot wholly account for the relationship between media and power. However, concepts such as "objectivity" are not solely responsible for a broadcaster's tendency to report news within strictly conventional parameters. In ignoring *all* specific influences, the analyst risks downplaying important factors such as implicit, felt pressures – often unquantifiable and untheorizable except on a commonsense basis, but nonetheless vitally important. These pressures might come from the parent corporation, for example. After Murrow's controversial broadcast, "Report on Senator McCarthy" co-producer Fred Friendly reported that the general feeling among CBS executives was "Good show, sorry you did it."[42] Although they would never accept direct advice from their employers regarding documentary content, CBS journalists knew what CBS executives were after.

Similarly, the needs of the sponsor could never have been far out of the minds of Burton Benjamin and Walter Cronkite as they created episodes for *The Twentieth Century*. The relationship between Prudential and *The Twentieth Century*, although it lasted nine years, was not rock-solid. Prudential was occasionally tempted to abandon the documentary series for more overtly commercial fare and higher ratings. In 1959, for example, Prudential placed an order with CBS for the co-sponsorship of Rod Serling's *The Twilight Zone* and asked the network to "sell" half of *The Twentieth Century* to another sponsor. The deal never came to fruition and Prudential maintained full sponsorship.[43] In March of 1961, Prudential actually announced the end of its affiliation with *The Twentieth Century*, along with the company's "new urge for commercial programming."[44] After screening alternative shows to sponsor, however, Prudential thought better of the change and renewed its commitment to *The Twentieth Century* for a fifth season. CBS reacted like a jilted lover and courted General Electric for sponsorship; in the end, however, CBS "finally decided to take Prudential's money-on-the-line."[45]

This precariousness of sponsorship constituted an implicit, yet specific pressure that no doubt had an enormous impact on the formation of *The Twentieth Century*. Hall is right to point to the mediation of concepts such as balance, impartiality, objectivity, professionalism, and consensus in the interplay between power and the media. But what makes broadcasters beholden to such concepts is in part deference to a sponsor's needs in a world of unspoken assumptions – the cracks between discourse – by which implicit understandings exert explicit and powerful influence.

Finally, and most importantly, we may ask what the purpose of unmasking media institutions is. What political effect can such an activity have, and what response should we have to the slipperiness of concepts such as "objectivity"? For the moment let us assume agreement with Foucault, who writes: "the real political task in a society such as ours is to criticize the workings of institutions which appear to be both neutral and independent; to criticize them in such a manner that the political violence which has always exercised itself obscurely through them will be unmasked, so that one can fight them."[46] Such unmasking is important in the case of *The Twentieth Century* and other media programming, because it brings historical and political understanding. The analysis of *The Twentieth Century* adds more evidence to that claim that as concepts, absolute objectivity, fairness, impartiality cannot be instantiated, and that as practices, they may mask subtle biases and discursive positions that fall within conventional limits to what can and cannot be said.

It is tempting to call for the abandonment of objectivity, balance, and so forth, as media practices, since, as Hall writes, they can work to homogenize the reporting of subjects from diverse perspectives, serving to process the topic within a limited set of interpretations, and masking subtle biases as objectivity. However, what would the journalistic media look like, absent such practices as objectivity, balance, fairness, and impartiality? Suppose that we convinced Western broadcasting institutions to disregard journalistic standards based on these concepts. With no attempt at objectivity, perhaps the particular concerns and perspectives of each broadcast institution would dominate its journalism. With no attempt at fairness, impartiality, and balance, we might see only one side of each issue, that side favored by the journalist in question. In a system featuring equal access to the media this could be an improvement, but in the current situation – in which television networks are owned and operated by multinational corporations – this could result in more biased, hegemonic broadcasting than we currently have. If objectivity masks implicit point of view, throwing out objectivity would make overt bias the rule of the day. The latter is not obviously the better situation.

Concepts such as objectivity, fairness, impartiality, and balance need not be reduced to absolute terms. If we think of objectivity as that which lacks perspective, there can (of course) be no objectivity, because every representation is from a perspective. But given the fact that every representation is relative to a perspective, we still may embrace a *relative* objectivity. As Allan Casebier notes, objectivity "is a matter of degree, not an absolute condition."[47] Such a perspective-relative objectivity may be the only objectivity possible in the journalistic documentary. As Steven Lukes writes, this would not be "'perspective-neutrality,' but rather accounts that are not merely theory, but also perspective-relative, yet constrained by evidence that is as systematic and reliable as possible, and relatable to other perspective-relative accounts."[48] If Absolute Objectivity is unattainable, relative objectivity may nonetheless be possible and desirable.

We might also work with relative versions of concepts such as fairness and balance, for example. Consider the case for and against affirmative action. An account that describes the three most common positions about its desirability and effects is more balanced than one that describes one position, though neither is *absolutely* balanced. Absolute versions of these concepts are unworkable in actual practice, but relative versions have value. It may be that objectivity, fairness, impartiality, and balance are ultimately unreachable. In our attempts to reach them we may attain a beneficial *relative* objectivity, fairness, or balance.

If we were to reject objectivity, balance, and fairness entirely, films such as Emile de Antonio's *Milhouse: A White Comedy* (1971) might become the norm for journalistic documentaries. This film is obviously not meant to be objective in its scathing mockery of Richard Nixon. Yet how many would celebrate this film as a prototype for the new, preferred journalism? The same undermining tactics used against Nixon in *Milhouse* are now used (with less skill) against President Clinton by media conservatives like radio talk show host Rush Limbaugh (whose program is a fine example of "news" free of objectivity, impartiality, and fairness).

Perspective-relative objectivity, balance, and fairness are related to the notion of intersubjectivity. To deny the former is to deny the latter; intersubjectivity is possible only in terms of the consensus of public opinion of which Hall writes. To throw out objectivity could lead to a discursive total war in which social discourse becomes anarchic, unyielding, unconstrained, and polarized. But as Jürgen Habermas claims, the practice of intersubjectivity — human beings in dialogue *with* each other – makes a better foundation for emancipatory social discourse. Thus contemporary journalistic practices, flawed and imperfect as they are, also ensure a greater diversity of voices and opinions than the overt propaganda that could become their substitute.

I see no alternative to an uncomfortable "truce" with relative versions of those concepts, and with the ideal of intersubjectivity. Although they homogenize the news, they also ensure the recognition of at least some diversity of opinion, and some exercise of restraint in the representation of any given topic. Although they fall short of absolute attainment, they remain a worthy goal. Although they may mask perspective, they also bring important advantages to nonfiction discourse. The proper strategy for now is to continue to expose the relative, intersubjective nature of objectivity, balance, fairness, impartiality, and consensus. Thus we can highlight their weaknesses, while preserving the benefits their use brings to a specific type of journalistic discourse.

Illusion and Reflexivity

A pragmatics of nonfiction must consider the possible ideological effects of discourse; contemporary discussions of effect have centered on notions of reflexivity. A reflexive film is one that does more than simply represent its subject – it also examines its own methods and the perspective of its producer(s). Many reflexive nonfiction films are among the most interesting examples of the genre, including *A Thin Blue Line, Man With a Movie Camera, Not a Love Story,* and *Chronicle of a Summer.* The films most consistently and thoroughly reflexive I have called *metadocumentaries.* Reflexive films are often opposed to realist, "illusionistic" films, although reflexivity and realism often coexist within the same text,[49] and the concept of "illusionism," as it has been used, is, to say the least, problematic.

A reflexive film, broadly considered, displays self-consciousness about its methods, its making, and/or its perspective. Contemporary theorists have privileged the reflexive film as superior not only for its aesthetic qualities, but for its political effects, for its effects on the spectator, and for its ability to better represent the complexities of the contemporary world.

The purpose here is to question the centrality accorded to formal and political reflexivity in contemporary scholarship on the nonfiction film. My contention is that reflexive strategies carry no ideological benefits in themselves, when considered apart from the overall perspective and subject matter of the film. Some tend to see reflexive films as the highest step of an evolutionary ladder from innocence to self-consciousness, implicitly valuing the reflexive present as sophisticated and the past as naive. I will argue that the political benefits of reflexivity are overrated, and that considerations of the quality of discourse in a community extend to issues more fundamental than reflexivity and reflexive strategies. The following are several reasons why the calls for political reflexivity are problematic and overstated.

1) *Calls for reflexivity are often based on faulty notions of the nature of nonfiction film.* The first chapter described the means by which some make a distinction between the fiction and nonfiction film. The familiar story goes as follows: "A nonfiction film presents itself as truth based on an uncluttered, unmanipulated reproduction of the real. But whatever its claims may be, a nonfiction film is nonetheless manipulated, and makes use of signifying techniques such as editing, music, lighting, etc., techniques that might properly be termed fictional. A reflexive

nonfiction film makes clear its constructed nature, and renders less harmful the deceptions inherent in nonfiction filmmaking."

This story is misleading, as this book has shown. Nonfiction films both record *and* interpret, and aside from the hysterical proclamations of some direct cinema filmmakers, nonfiction film has never claimed for itself the mere reproduction of the real without the perspective and discourse that accompany it. In the early stages of documentary history, Grierson called the documentary the "creative treatment of actuality," not the reproduction of actuality. There exists no contradiction between the recording function of image and sound and the formative function of discourse; in nonfictions, both inevitably exist simultaneously. The task of the critic or analyst is to examine the parameters of photographic and sonic representation in relation to the creative, rhetorical strategies of a particular film.

In addition, techniques such as editing, music, etc, are not fictional, but *filmic* techniques that can be used in both fiction and nonfiction films. What makes a film nonfiction is not a presumed lack of manipulation of the real, but its assertion that its states of affairs are true in the actual world. The notion that nonfiction films are inherently deceptive is based on unsupported assumptions about the "false claims" that nonfiction films make for themselves. If there is nothing inherently misleading or deceptive about nonfiction films, there is less need for reflexivity in nonfiction filmmaking.

2) *Calls for reflexivity overestimate the illusory nature of texts, and fail to recognize that film texts all are reflexive to a degree.* In the requirements it makes in order to be seen at all, a film loudly announces that it is a text and not a chunk of reality. To see a video or film, we must rent or purchase the video and put it into the tape player, or get into the car to travel to the theater. At the theater we are confronted with the screen and the audience, and while the image is projected with frame edges, scratch marks, and audible audience reactions.

The so-called "suspension of disbelief" never involves the full blocking of our awareness that we are watching a film. Even when we momentarily "forget" where we are and become absorbed in the world of the film, this absorption never constitutes an illusion, because the quality of our response to what we see make evident a background knowledge of our artificial circumstances. In the case of the nonfiction film, this is especially clear. When I see the strike-busting, gun-toting redneck in *Harlan County, U.S.A.*, my response is different from what it would be were I confronted by the man in person. While viewing the film, I never

fear for my safety, since I recognize that what I see is a representation and
not a real man with a gun. In addition, although I do fear for the safety
of those in the film with whom I sympathize, this is nothing like the fear
I would have for them were I witnessing the actual events. The fear is
muted by my recognition – at some level – that what I see is a film, and
that the events depicted either occurred in the past (as in the case of the
nonfiction film)[50] or never actually occur at all (as in fiction).[51]

3) *Calls for reflexive strategies underestimate the critical acumen of
the spectator, and do not differentiate among audiences.* Calls for reflexivity often assume that realist nonfiction films by definition encourage false beliefs on the part of the spectator. For example, E. Ann Kaplan recounts critiques of the realist feminist documentaries, *Joyce at
34* and *Janie's Janie:* "the direct mode of address in both films encourages us to relate to the images of Joyce and Janie as 'real' women, as if
we could know them. Yet, in fact, both figures are constructed in the
film by the processes of camera, lighting, sound, editing. They have no
other ontological status than that of representations." As Kaplan further writes, "the reason we do not realize that each female figure is a
representation is that neither film draws attention to itself as film, or
makes us aware that we are watching a film. Neither film . . . breaks
our usual habits of passive viewing in the commercial cinema."[52]

Three related claims emanate from this position, and all are problematic. The first is that the film spectator mistakes the images and
sounds of Joyce and Janie for real women. The second is that by virtue
of formal realism, spectators at such films automatically accept what
they see as real or true. The third is that since realist films do not draw
attention to themselves as films, they encourage passivity on the part of
the spectator.

Yet it is highly doubtful that spectators mistake the images of Joyce
and Janie for real persons. When viewing a film, we are aware that
what we see is a representation, and not the actual world, as I argued
immediately above in relation to film illusion. More plausibly, prore-
flexivists might be construed to say not that spectators mistake what
they see for the real thing, but that they automatically accept the film's
claims as accurate. But this isn't convincing either. Consider the criticisms leveled at the "liberal bias" of the American news media, for example. Or imagine a realist independent film about UFOs that includes
moving photographs purported to be of alien spacecraft; our skepticism, I submit, would remain in full force. Realism does not guarantee
a dumbfounded, gullible spectator.

Moreover, claims for the importance of reflexivity assert an ordinarily passive spectator, as though spectator mental activity – at least of a critical kind – occurs only in relation to reflexive films. This cannot account for the fact that the realist film spectator often rejects representations with which she does not sympathize. This implies that spectators can be highly active (even oppositional) when viewing realist films. Spectators are not the passive lumps contemporary theory often assumes them to be.

Such broad claims about effect emerge from *ideological formalism*, a formalism that asserts universal ideological effects for certain forms of cinema. The claim is that realist documentaries have negative ideological effects, whereas politically reflexive documentaries encourage self-consciousness and educate the audience. However, such claims downplay historical context, and ignore individual and group differences among spectators. Such claims not only fail to distinguish between spectators on the basis of level of education or critical acumen, but they underestimate the degree to which most spectators are critical of what they see. If most spectators are dupes and simpletons, the need for reflexivity may exist (but never as panacea). If most are critical of what they see, reflexivity is less important. In either case, one could argue that media education is more vital than reflexivity as a strategy for encouraging critical viewing among spectators. The savvy spectator does not require reflexivity to achieve a critical perspective.

4) *Reflexive strategies, apart from considerations of content and perspective, guarantee neither fullness nor complexity of representation.* Just as absolute objectivity is impossible, so is absolute reflexivity. It is impossible for a filmmaker to reflexively examine the entirety of her perspective, or the full extent of the methods used to make the film. In addition to the fact that there is simply too much to reflexively explore in a single work, a fully reflexive film would require an endless regression, as the film constantly folds back on itself to reflexively examine every method, every motivation, each production circumstance encountered, each new scene, each new shot. Whatever reflexive claims or representations the film made would themselves be subject to reflexive examination, because reflexive claims or representations, always only partially reflexive, do not escape the ostensive need for examination any more than the nonreflexive sort.

Michael Moore's *Roger and Me*, for example, is highly reflexive, because the filmmaker reveals his motivations for making the film, tells something of his life history, and appears on camera as he interviews various subjects. The information Moore gives about himself, despite its being reflexive, is still in need of the same examination to which we might subject nonreflexive information. Why does Moore present himself in the way he does? What rhetorical strategies lie behind his reflexive choices? Neither does the film's reflexivity guarantee a full-bodied examination of General Motors and plant closings in Flint. The film leaves many questions unanswered and ignores many topics. What does the state of the American auto industry have to do with the plant closings in Flint? Was it necessary to concentrate on a single individual, Roger Smith, rather than on the institutional and economic influences on General Motors? The point is that reflexivity is always partial, in regard to some aspect of the film's representation, and not in relation to all of the salient possibilities. Reflexivity does not guarantee the representation of the magnitudes and complexities of the world, any more than objectivity guarantees fairness and balance.

5) *Reflexive strategies do not guarantee honesty, integrity, or genuine self-revelation on the part of the filmmaker(s).* A reflexive film can be as manipulative as any other. Reflexive films reveal aspects of the film's methodology and perspective, but nothing guarantees that the revelations of the filmmaker are either presented in good faith or from a position of genuine self-knowledge. In addition, we might ask what the filmmaker has chosen to be reflexive about, and which rhetorical strategies are at work in *this* choice. A wholly honest reflexivity would have required Michael Moore to reveal something like the following: "The events I recount here did not occur exactly as I represent them. I rearranged them for various rhetorical purposes, and due to my need to tell a well-constructed story." Other reflexive films may be less misleading than *Roger and Me*. However, it isn't their reflexivity that makes them so, but their candidness and integrity, qualities that do not necessarily depend on reflexivity.

In addition, we cannot expect a filmmaker to understand fully his or her methods and motivations for making the film. If full self-knowledge is impossible, so is full reflexivity. No technique or formal strategy, including reflexivity, guarantees truth or accuracy in representation. Reflexivity does not guarantee honesty, any more than a recourse to "balance" guarantees a representation of the many sides of any complex issue. However, like conceptions of objectivity, balance, and fairness as relative terms, we might want to preserve some notion of relative reflexivity. In some films, and for some purposes, reflexivity may be an appropriate representational strategy.

Truth-telling: A Conclusion

Quality of discourse in society depends on many factors, from access to the media among diverse groups, to freedom of the press, to a willingness by media producers to investigate issues candidly and boldly, to the willingness of citizens to listen openly to others. It depends on a healthy intersubjectivity, as defined by Habermas. All things being equal, quality of nonfiction discourse also depends on a community dedication to *truth-telling*. Because nonfictions make assertions about actuality, the reliability of those assertions is essential to their usefulness in the community. Only if discourse meets intersubjective standards of truth-telling can it be useful for the diverse functions it performs in a democracy.

In film and literary studies, notions such as Truth, Objectivity, and Fairness are often thought to be bankrupt. Indeed, in today's academic environment, speaking of truth or impartiality sounds archaic indeed. One can see the suspicion of "Truth" in worthy sentiments – in a desire to respect the belief systems of other cultures, ethnicities, and individuals, and to combat the imperialism that has characterized much of Western history. In addition, when we recognize the power of discourse to create social reality, and to influence interaction with our complex world, one can see how claims for truth might actually become strategies in a struggle for power. Richard Rorty, for example, rejects the idea that there are "foundations to serve as common ground for adjudicating knowledge claims," and that discourse is "hooked on to something which demands moral commitment – Reality, Truth, Objectivity, Reason."[53]

Yet it is sometimes too easy to construct and then deconstruct facile versions of "reality," "truth," "objectivity," and other concepts, without examining their more defensible manifestations. Perhaps we have sounded their death knell prematurely. If we think of Truth as an unassailable "Way Things Are," and as the sum total of answers to the "Questions of the Universe," then perhaps human beings can have no access to Truth (with a capital "T"). But can we think of truth in another way? Can we think of "truths" or "approximate truth," always fallible, partial at best, finally inadequate, and subject to revision?

If there exist no truths and no facts of the matter, then we have no basis for disputing the claims or perspective of any nonfiction film, and no basis for choosing one moral or political representation over another, aside from the sheer narcissistic faith that our beliefs or methods are superior. If there is no *actual* order to the events depicted in *Roger and Me*, then it is preposterous to claim that Michael Moore misrepresents their *actual* chronology. If there are no facts of the matter, there can be no misrepresentation. If no truths exist, then on what basis should we take seriously the claims of poor treatment of migrant workers by Edward R. Murrow in "Harvest of Shame"? Investigation and documentation mean nothing if they never uncover truths about a situation or event. Bonnie Klein's *Not a Love Story* claims that pornography causes hatred and aggression toward women. But if this is mere assertion, and not a truth, and if we may disregard evidence for her claims as mere strategies in Klein's rhetorical manipulations, then on what basis should the spectator weigh her claims? If no proximate truths exist, how can a nonfiction film make either accurate or inaccurate claims?

The same might be said of concepts similar to truth. If even relative fairness does not exist in discourse, then on what basis can I claim that a nonfiction film is unfair? Without fairness, all films become equal in this respect. If balance is irrelevant, how may I write about a nonfiction film that ignores an important voice in a controversial issue? If objectivity (in the sense of intersubjectivity) is a sham, how can I appreciate a film that attempts to take diverse perspectives on an issue without unduly slanting the representation toward one perspective or the other? In each of these cases, we must recognize that objectivity, truth, fairness, and balance are problematic concepts – but not discard them altogether. Understand and teach them in all their imperfections, and we can both preserve and encourage whatever is good about our discursive community and teach the critical, informed attitude that makes for savvy, educated spectators.

The actual world, our relationship to it, and the constraints of rational discourse set limits on what we can truthfully and honestly show, say, and imply. The quality of our discourse partly depends on the importance and usefulness of what we choose to say and show. It also depends on our ability and desire, fallible as it is, to distinguish between truths and lies, honesty and deceit. I have written that the nonfiction film is distinguished from the fiction film in part by its assertion that the states of affairs it represents occur in the actual world as portrayed. In weighing these assertions and portrayals, if we cannot distinguish between truths, half-truths, and lies, or between fantasy and actuality, then we have no basis for extending our criticism of nonfiction films beyond purely technical areas of form and style. We could never discuss the relationship of the nonfiction film to its referent, except in formal terms. Such a restriction would severely diminish the value of cultural criticism in relation to the documentary.

That is the dilemma of those who practice ideological formalism. If nonfiction films have no extradiscursive referent, and if their assertions cannot be evaluated on the basis of truth and falsity, objectivity and bias, then we are limited to sterile discussions of formal strategies, into which we invest false ideological significance, and for which we must create a phantom spectator. One critic writes that eventually the nonfiction filmmaker "is going to have to face the possibility of assuming the socially diminished role of interpreter of the world, of no longer being regarded as an objective recorder of reality," and that all films "are created, structured articulations of the filmmaker and not authentic, truthful, objective records."[54] One of the aims of this book has been to show that "interpretation" and "recording" are not necessarily antithetical, and that the fact that a film has a perspective does not necessarily make it inauthentic or untruthful. If every nonfiction film is made from a perspective, and thus interprets, this by no means rules out the recording function of the camera and sound recorder, and it certainly does not preclude the film from asserting truths through its modeling of the world.

If we accept the possibility and desirability of claiming and showing truths, this need not lead to naive and arrogant overestimations of our access to the complexities of the world, nor to imperialistic political practices. We think that our personal beliefs and opinions are true, otherwise why would we hold them? Nonetheless, we may regard them as provisional and tentative, always to be established by the best available evidence and subject to revision. Errol Morris's *The Thin Blue Line* is sometimes showcased as a postmodern rejection of truth, but that is not the intention of its maker. As Morris says:

The Thin Blue Line has been called *Rashomon*-like. I take exception to that. . . . For me there is a fact of the matter, a fact of what happened on the roadway that night. . . . Someone shot Robert Wood, and it was either Randall Adams or David Harris. That's the fundamental issue at the center of all this. Is it knowable? Yes, it is. We have access to the world out there. We aren't just prisoners of our fantasies and dreams. I wanted to make a movie about how truth is difficult to know, not how it is impossible to know.[55]

Perhaps in the end, when examining the potential of the nonfiction film and video to negotiate values, disseminate information, and *show* us aspects of the world as can no other genre or medium, we must respect its tremendous complexity as a medium of communication. The nonfiction film is a conventional means of discourse, making use of rhetorical strategies of structure and style in relation to several channels of information. It is also a recording medium, with an unparalleled ability to give us the look, sound, and "feel" of scenes or events. It is a medium of truths and deceits, recording and manipulation, biases and balance, art and mechanical technique, rhetoric and straightforward information. Nonfiction films are complex representations with an infinite diversity of possible uses. Theirs is a rhetorical and pragmatic complexity that theory alone cannot comprehend; we require the aid of criticism and history. Yet with a clearer understanding of the forms and functions of these works, we move closer to an effective rhetoric and pragmatics of moving picture nonfictions.

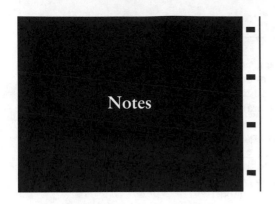

Notes

Introduction

1 *Documentary: A History of the Non-fiction Film* (New York: Oxford University Press, 1993).

2 "Toward a Poetics of Documentary," in M. Renov, ed., *Theorizing Documentary* (New York: Routledge, 1993), 21.

3 See especially David Novitz, *Pictures and Their Use in Communication* (The Hague: Martinus Nijhoff, 1977), and Ernst Gombrich, "The Visual Image," *Scientific American*, 227, 3 (Sept. 72), 82–96.

4 (Minneapolis: University of Minnesota Press, 1993), 1, 3.

5 "Rhetoric." In *Critical Terms in Literary Studies*, 217.

6 If all discourse attempts to gain power, as Foucault claimed, then some contemporary literary theory takes imperialism to a new level. It denies the possibility of truth, but asserts what are ostensibly fundamental truths at every turn. It claims the impossibility of knowledge, but with the tenor of one who knows well. It denies the value of philosophy, but practices philosophy itself. As George L. Dillon writes, "literary theorists have made use of certain elements of rhetoric for their own purposes, which broadly are to isolate, surround, and ingest the discourses of truth and knowledge." See his "Rhetoric," in *The Johns Hopkins Guide to Literary Theory and Criticism*. Eds. Michael Groden and Martin Kreiswirth (Baltimore: Johns Hopkins University Press, 1994), 617.

7 I make this argument at greater length in "Film Theory and Aesthetics: Notes on a Schism," *Journal of Aesthetics and Art Criticism*, 51, 3 (Summer 93), 445–454.

8 "The Documentary Film as Scientific Inscription," in *Theorizing Documentary*, ed. Michael Renov (New York: Routledge, 1993), 37–57. Also see Winston's *Claiming the Real: The Documentary Film Revisited* (London: British Film Institute, 1995).

9 John Tagg imparts a similar broad teleology to the documentary when he claims that the documentary effects a rhetoric of "immediacy" and "truth." It claims, he says, "only to 'put the facts' directly or vicariously, through the report of 'first-hand experience.'" Overall, Tagg argues, the documentary developed in Western European and American history to respond to a "particular moment of crisis." It was aimed at "restructuring the order of discourse, appropriating dissent, and resecuring the threatened bonds of social consent."

One might have confidence in Tagg's claims if they were made on a more local level, and if they showed a more nuanced familiarity with documentary history. For example, like most of us, Tagg takes John Grierson to be a central figure in the development of documentary, but seems unfamiliar with his work or writings. Tagg refers to Grierson as a "film critic," and wholly ignores Grierson's insistence that the documentary, far from transparent truth, is *propaganda* and, in Grierson's phrase, the "creative treatment of actuality." See Tagg, 8.
10   See especially Larry Gross, John Stuart Katz, and Jay Ruby, eds. *Image Ethics: The Moral Rights of Subjects in Photographs, Film, and Television* (New York: Oxford University Press, 1988).
11   The series is to be edited by Jane Gaines, Faye Ginzberg, and Michael Renov for University of Minnesota Press.

1. What is a Nonfiction Film?

1   Throughout this work I use the term "nonfiction film" or "nonfiction" (as short for "nonfiction film") to refer to moving picture nonfictions, be they films or videos, feature-length works, home movies, or snippets of archival footage. I use the designation "nonfiction film" rather than "documentary" because the latter refers to a narrower group of works, as I discuss in the following chapter.
2   I discuss this issue at some length in Chapter Five, "Structure."
3   See *Women, Fire, and Dangerous Things: What Categories Reveal about the Mind* (Chicago: University of Chicago Press, 1987).
4   Glen Collins, "Film Makers Protest to Academy," *New York Times*, 24 Feb. 1990, L13.
5   Charles Fleming, "Oscar Mocks Boffo Docks," *Variety*, 2 March 1992, 1,75.
6   Quoted from Christopher Williams, ed., *Realism in the Cinema* (London: Michael Routledge and Kegan Paul, 1980), 226–227.
7   Neither Wiseman nor the Maysles see this as a problematic aspect of nonfiction filmmaking; in equating manipulation with fiction they draw attention to the positive and creative aspects of their art.
8   "Albert and David Maysles," in Levin, G. Roy, ed., *Documentary Explorations: 15 Interviews with Film-makers* (Garden City, N.Y.: Doubleday, 1971), 276.
9   See Thomas Atkins, "Reality Fictions: Wiseman on *Primate*," in Atkins, ed., *Frederick Wiseman* (New York: Monarch Press, 1976), 50; John Graham, "There are no Simple Solutions: Wiseman on Filmmaking and Viewing," in Atkins, 36. Thomas W. Benson and Carolyn Anderson, in their recent book on Wiseman, *Reality Fictions: The Films of Frederick Wiseman* (Carbondale: Southern Illinois University Press, 1989), follow the director in referring to selection and editing as fictional techniques. Wiseman is not saying that his films cannot accurately be called "nonfiction." The word he is objecting to is "documentary," which has associations (of mere imitation or recording) he wants to break with. What Wiseman does is similar to what *certain* novelists do.
10   Jacques Aumont, Alain Bergala, Michel Marie, and Mark Vernet, *Aesthet-*

ics of Film, trans. and rev. by Richard Neupert (Austin: University of Texas Press, 1992), 77.

11 "From Reel to Real: Entangled in Nonfiction Film," *Philosophical Exchange*, 14 (1983), 23.

12 I do not presume to know *all* of the social functions these films perform. Rather, my argument, which I further below, is that as fiction and nonfiction, they are conventionally used for different purposes.

13 For example, see Dennis Giles, "The Name Documentary: A Preface to Genre Study," *Film Reader* 3 (1978), 18–22. Giles writes: ". . . as filmmakers continue to obscure the classic contradiction between documentary and fiction, as every generic distinction is systematically violated in the theory *and* praxis of cinema, the word *documentary* becomes nonsensical" (18).

14 John Searle, "The World Turned Upside Down," rev. of *On Deconstruction: Theory and Criticism after Structuralism*, by Jonathan Culler, *New York Review of Books*, 27 October 1973, 48.

15 These are, respectively, properties a film *must* have for it to qualify as a nonfiction film (necessary conditions), and/or properties which, if possessed by a film, are sufficient to characterize it as nonfiction (sufficient conditions).

16 The phrase is quoted in Forsyth Hardy's introduction to John Grierson, *Grierson on Documentary*, ed. Forsyth Hardy (Berkeley: University of California Press, 1966), 13.

17 From "First Principles of Documentary," in *Grierson on Documentary*, 147.

18 "The Question of Reality," in Lewis Jacobs, ed., *The Documentary Tradition* (New York: Hopkinson and Blake, 1971), 381.

19 *A Grammar of the Film* (Berkeley: University of California Press, 1959), 289.

20 *Representing Reality: Issues and Concepts in Documentary* (Bloomington: Indiana University Press, 1991), 18, 20.

21 Ibid., 25. Similar arguments have been made by Jeanne Allen, "Self-Reflexivity in the Documentary," *Ciné-Tracts* 1, 2 (Summer 1977), 37, and No'l Carroll, "From Reel to Real: Entangled in the Nonfiction Film," *Philosophical Exchange* 14 (1983), 15.

22 For a thorough philosophical (as opposed to historical) investigation of attempts to define art, see Stephen Davies, *Definitions of Art* (Ithaca: Cornell University Press, 1991).

23 "The Role of Theory in Aesthetics," *Journal of Aesthetics and Art Criticism* 15, 1 (September 1956), 27–35.

24 *Philosophical Investigations*, 3rd ed., trans. G.E.M. Anscombe (New York: Macmillan, 1958), 32.

25 *Women, Fire, and Dangerous Things: What Categories Reveal about the Mind*, 12.

26 "From Real to Reel: Entangled in Nonfiction Film," *Philosophic Exchange* 14, (1983), 5–46.

27 I discuss this element of Carroll's theory in the following chapter.

28 "Defining Documentary: Fiction, Nonfiction, and Projected Worlds," *Persistence of Vision* 5 (Spring 1987), 44–54.

29   See his Works and Worlds of Art (Oxford: Clarendon Press, 1980), or the more accessible Art in Action (Grand Rapids: Erdmans, 1980). A brief formulation of the theory of world projection can be found in "Worlds of Works of Art," *Journal of Aesthetics and Art Criticism* 35, 2 (1976), 121–132.

30   Rather than attempt to explain what states of affairs are, it is more illustrative to give examples. *Stanley Kubrick's being a film director, Clinton's being from Arkansas,* and *Alaska's being the largest state in the union* all are states of affairs. Some states of affairs occur, as in the examples given. Others are possible of occurring but do not, such as *Barry Goldwater's being the president of the United States.* Most simply, a state of affairs is a way something can or cannot be. The world of a work of art, Wolterstorff says, is a state of affairs. For a more extended discussion, see *Art in Action*, 122–155.

31   *Art in Action*, 134.

32   A state of affairs is neither true or false in itself. But when a state of affairs is asserted to occur, that assertion can be evaluated for truth or falsehood.

33   It could be objected here that the claim that we consider states of affairs in fiction, rather than take them as assertions of truth, is vague. I admit a certain vagueness here that stems from the mystery at the heart of our response to fiction itself. When we consider fictional states of affairs, we entertain them not as truths, but as something closer to hypotheses that we know not to be actually true. The fact that such fictions can have such emotional power over us is of course an intriguing conundrum, and a topic of intense speculation in recent work in aesthetics.

34   Thanks to Trevor Ponech for his clarifying suggestions in his essay "Motion Picture Non-Fictions," *Semiotic Inquiry* 15, 1–2 (Spring 1995). Literally speaking, films themselves neither make assertions nor perform any other action. Persons perform actions through or with films (as they do with other means of discourse). However, we may say that a film asserts or shows something as a shorthand expression for what, when often enough repeated, could become a very clumsy expression: e.g., "The filmmaker or filmmakers claim so-and-so through the voice-over narration of the film," rather than "The film's voice-over narration claims . . ."

35   Narrative Comprehension and Film (New York: Routledge, 1992), 193.

36   Dirk Eitzen makes a similar point in "When is a Documentary?: Documentary as a Mode of Reception," *Cinema Journal* 35, 1 (Fall 1995), 81–102.

37   At times social naming may take on political implications. Because words often have distinct and powerful connotations, the label society gives to an entity may become the site of political struggle. For this reason, various social groups advocate words that designate equal status and full respect, such as the use of "woman" rather than "girl" to denote an adult female. But where the conventional use of a term is not the site of political struggle, as in the case of whether to call the toaster a "toaster" or a "club," we call the entity by its conventional name, to facilitate communication among members of a society.

38   *Claiming the Real: The Documentary Film Revisited* (London: British Film Institute, 1995), 259.

39   "When is a Documentary?: Documentary as a Mode of Reception," *Cinema Journal* 35, 1 (Fall 1995), 92.

40   In the parlance of speech act theory, the presentation of texts or of various elements of a text constitutes locutionary acts through which diverse illocutionary and perlocutionary acts are performed.
41   *Film and Phenomenology: Toward a Realist Theory of Cinematic Representation* (Cambridge: Cambridge University Press, 1991), 141.
42   Gary Crowdus, "Getting the Facts Straight: An Interview with Zachary Sklar," *Cineaste* 19, 1 (1992), 29.
43   *New York Times*, 25 Dec. 1991, Sec. 1, 30.
44   "The Making of Alert Viewers: The Mixing of Fact and Fiction in *JFK*," 19, 1 (1992), 14–15.
45   "Motion Picture Non-Fictions."

2. Exemplars and Expression

1   Richard Meran Barsam, *Nonfiction Film: A Critical History* (New York: E. P. Dutton, 1973), 1. The revised and expanded edition (Bloomington: Indiana University Press, 1992) does not make the distinction as explicit, but still assumes a difference between the "social documentary" and factual films, travel films, cinéma vérité, and direct cinema.
2   Brian Winston, *Claiming the Real: The Documentary Film Revisited* (London: British Film Institute, 1995), 8–9.
3   So claims Forsyth Hardy, in his introduction to *Grierson on Documentary*, ed. Forsyth Hardy (Berkeley: University of California Press, 1966), 13. A testament to the protean nature of the genre is that most contemporary observers no longer consider Moana to be nonfiction.
4   "Documentary (1)," *Cinema Quarterly* (Winter 1932), 67–72.
5   "Documentary (2): Symphonics," *Cinema Quarterly* (Spring 1933), 135–139.
6   *Grierson on Documentary*, 135.
7   Ibid.
8   Ibid., 142.
9   Paul Rotha, "Some Principles of Documentary," in Richard Meran Barsam, ed., *Nonfiction Film Theory and Criticism* (New York: E.P. Dutton, 1976), 42; the Rotha selection is from his book, Documentary Film (New York: Hastings House, 1952); William A. Bluem, *Documentary in American Television* (New York: Hastings House, 1965), 14; Lewis Jacobs, ed., *The Documentary Tradition* (New York: Hopkinson and Blake, 1974), 2; Michael Rabiger, *Directing the Documentary* (Boston: Focal Press, 1987), 4; Bill Nichols, *Representing Reality* (Bloomington: Indiana University Press, 1991), 18.
10   The very name of the category, "Best Feature Documentary," suggests potential confusion about whether the award is for nonfiction broadly considered, or for a narrower subgenre such as the Griersonian social documentary or the journalistic documentary.
11   Glen Collins, "Film Makers Protest to Academy," *New York Times* (24 February 1990), L13.

12   "From Real to Reel: Entangled in the Nonfiction Film," *Philocophic Exchange*, 14 (1983), 15.

13   Carroll notes the problem himself in "Reply to Carol Brownson and Jack Wolf," in *Philosophic Exchange: A Journal of SUNY College at Brockport*, 14 (Winter 1983).

14   The film may draw conclusions about some of the matters it discusses; it may at times offer evidence in some sense. However, it doesn't invite us to evaluate those conclusions and that evidence with the same protocols we might bring to a journalistic documentary. For example, the claim that McElwee failed to address "both sides" of Sherman's march to the South strikes us as odd, because McElwee's intention is not to provide a journalistic or historical documentary.

15   John Hartl, "Shutouts," Seattle Times (25 February 1990), L9. I don't mean to imply that the films actually nominated for the 1990 Academy Award for Best Feature Documentary are unworthy. I mean only that some of the most compelling films tend to be ignored. The 1990 winner in this category, *Common Threads: Stories from the Quilt* (Robert Epstein and Jeffrey Friedman), undoubtedly deserves wide recognition.

16   I discuss such arguments at greater length in "Moving Pictures and Nonfiction Film: Two Approaches," in *Post-Theory: Reconstructing Film Studies*, eds. David Bordwell and Noël Carroll (Madison: University of Wisconsin Press, 1996), 307–324.

17   Brian Winston, "Documentary: I Think We Are in Trouble," in Alan Rosenthal, ed., *New Challenges for the Documentary* (Berkeley: University of California Press, 1988), 21–33.

18   "American Direct Cinema: The Representation of Reality," *Persistence of Vision* 3/4 (Summer 1986), 131–156. If we take Barsam's remarks as referring more narrowly to cinéma vérité (or direct cinema), they are more plausible.

19   "The Documentary Film as Scientific Inscription," in *Theorizing Documentary*, ed. Michael Renov (New York, Routledge, 1993), 41.

20   William Guynn, *A Cinema of Nonfiction* (Rutherford: Fairleigh Dickenson University Press, 1990), 18.

21   "Robert Flaherty: The Man in the Iron Myth," in *Nonfiction Film Theory and Criticism*, ed. Richard Meran Barsam (New York: E. P. Dutton, 1976), 213.

22   Ibid., 213–214. Van Dongen notes that even in *Native Land* Flaherty indulges in at least one central staged scene.

23   *The American Newsreel: 1911–1967* (Norman: University of Oklahoma Press, 1972), 310.

24   Raymond Fielding, *The March of Time: 1935–1951* (New York: Oxford University Press, 1978), 239.

25   *Grierson on Documentary*, 145.

26   Ira Halberstadt, "An Interview with Fred Wiseman," in Barsam, *Nonfiction Film Theory and Criticism*, 300.

27   Although I have argued that the assertive stance is characteristic of nonfiction, it is through this stance that the film performs many varied communicative functions. In other words, nonfictions are not limited to merely asserting that the states of affairs it presents actually occur.

28   "Truth Not Guaranteed: An Interview with Errol Morris," with Peter Bates, *Cineaste* 14, 1 (1989), 17.

3. Moving Image Icons

1   *Signs and Meaning in the Cinema* (Bloomington: Indiana University Press, 1972). Peirce's system of signs is immensely complex. The division of signs I describe here is one among many ways of distinguishing various kinds of signs.

2   C.S. Peirce, "The Icon, Index, and Symbol," in *Collected Papers*, 8 vols., ed. Charles Hartshorne and Paul Weiss (Cambridge: Harvard University Press, 1931–1958) II.

3   *Iconology: Image, Text, Ideology* (Chicago: University of Chicago Press, 1986), 40, 90–91.

4   "Ideological Effects of the Basic Cinematographic Apparatus," in *Film Theory and Criticism*, 4th ed., eds. Gerald Mast, Marshall Cohen, and Leo Braudy (New York: Oxford University Press, 1992), 302, 304–305.

5   *Simulacres et simulation* (Paris: Galilée, 1981), 10.

6   "Lucid Intervals: Postmodernism and Photography," in Hugh J. Silverman, ed., *Postmodernism: Philosophy and the Arts* (New York: Routledge, 1990), 157.

7   Like all relativists who assert truths about the world, Baudrillard must explain how he manages to understand the *reality* and *truth* of our ostensive epistemic condition. For if Baudrillard (like the rest of us) is mired in mere simulacra, then how can he make his claims about the "real," "true" nature of the human epistemic circumstance? On the other hand, if his claim is merely that our submersion in simulacra is occasional and partial, and allows for intermittent contact with "the true" (including his own insight), then what he says is hardly new or revolutionary.

8   Certainly many members of the Society for Cinema Studies, a group normally committed to postmodernist/poststructuralist critical analysis, saw the video as clear evidence that an injustice was done. At the 1992 SCS convention, which coincided with the "not guilty" verdict of the Simi Valley jury and the resulting riots in Los Angeles, many signed a petition condemning the jury's refusal to acknowledge the video evidence of police brutality. The defense attorneys' use of the video, the petition states, shows how close readings can incur "misreadings." Certainly the claim of a misreading, or incorrect reading, assumes the possibility of a "correct reading," i.e., a reading that recognizes what the video actually shows about its referent.

9   "Document and Documentary: On the Persistence of Historical Concepts," in *Theorizing Documentary*, ed. Michael Renov (New York: Routledge, 1993), 86.

10   *On Photography* (1977; rpt. New York: Farrar, Strauss, and Giroux, 1989), 87.

11   In Gerald Mast, Marshall Cohen, and Leo Braudy, eds., *Film Theory and Criticism*, 4th ed. (New York: Oxford University Press, 1992), 79–82. In this

chapter, further references to MacCabe's essay will be made parenthetically within the text.

12 MacCabe also embraces Baudry's theories, based on a Lacanian psychoanalysis, on the psychological effects and illusionism of images. My criticisms of Baudry's claims can thus be extended to those of McCabe.

13 "The Ontology of the Photographic Image," in *What is Cinema?* v. 1, trans. Hugh Gray (Berkeley and Los Angeles: University of California Press, 1967), 14–15.

14 "Transparent Pictures: On the Nature of Photographic Realism," *Critical Inquiry* 11, 2 (Dec. 84), 251.

15 "Ideological Effects of the Basic Cinematographic Apparatus," in Mast, Cohen, and Braudy, 302–312.

16 *Languages of Art* (New York: Bobbs Merrill, 1968), 40–43.

17 W. J. T. Mitchell discusses the terms "nature" and "convention" in *Iconology: Image, Text, Ideology* (Chicago: University of Chicago Press, 1986), 75–94. Mitchell argues against Gombrich's claims that images have a "natural" component. However, Mitchell's arguments are unconvincing because they fail to distinguish between the two senses of "natural" and of "conventional" that I have outlined. If the "natural" is defined as "that which is untouched by human culture," it is quite easy to show that any view of photography as natural is wrong.

18 "The Power of Movies," *Daedelus* 114, 4 (Fall 1985), 86.

19 See Gibson's *The Ecological Approach to Visual Perception* (Boston: Houghton Mifflin, 1979). Also see Edward S. Reed, *James J. Gibson and the Psychology of Perception* (New Haven: Yale University Press, 1988), pp. 239–259. David Blinder makes use of Gibson's theory in his "In Defense of Pictorial Mimesis," *Journal of Aesthetics and Art Criticism* 45, 1 (Fall 1986), 19–27.

20 Gibson, *The Ecological Approach to Visual Perception*, 276. In a recent defense of the claim that perceiving cinema images involves epistemic illusions, Richard Allen has claimed that instead of a dual perception of the image as simultaneously two- and three-dimensional, the spectator alternates between seeing the image as one or the other. During those periods when the spectator sees the image as three-dimensional, he suffers an illusion. Although I cannot do justice to Allen's claims here, I believe that Gibson's claims for dual perception better account for our actual response to moving images. If the spectator even occasionally suffered from an illusion that the image were in any sense "real," that would engender a kind of response appropriate to the actual presence of the referent. The fact that we remain in our seats implies a consistent background awareness that what we view is a representation. From top to bottom, our emotional and perceptual response to visual communications differs from our response to events in actual life. This lends credence to the claim that the spectator is *always* implicitly aware of the discursive character of what she sees on film and video, and suffers no ontological illusions. See Allen's "Representation, Illusion, and the Cinema," *Cinema Journal* 32, 2 (Winter 1993), 21–48.

21 I do not believe that spectators identify with the camera as an embodied vision of another person, except in the case of the point of view shot – the view of a character in the world of the film. In the case of the "objective camera" (a view from no particular character's perspective), the audience accepts this "seeing" unproblematically, simply as seeing moving photographs of an event. Thus we need not think of the camera as a body, either literally or metaphorically, to see how the camera can function as a stand-in for human vision.

23   *Narration in the Fiction Film* (Madison: University of Wisconsin Press, 1985), pp. 99–100. Bordwell calls his theory of visual perception "constructivist," because the spectator reworks stimuli, performing mental operations on them, making inferences and assumptions, etc. But the term implies that something is being constructed, and it isn't clear what. Is it the object of perception that is being constructed? Is it inferences in the mind? Or what? Perhaps a clearer name for this view is the "cognitive theory of perception." The contention that cognition is central to visual perception need not require that the mind construct anything aside from its own activities. And does it *construct* those activities, or *perform* them?

23   Ibid., 100–101. A classic example of the type of perceptual theory Bordwell calls "constructivist" is David Marr's Vision: *A Computational Investigation into the Human Representation and Processing of Visual Information* (San Francisco: W. H. Freeman, 1982). Recently Marr's theory, and all of cognitive science, have come under attack by John Searle, who claims that cognitive scientists mistakenly characterize the mind on the model of the computer. See *The Rediscovery of the Mind* (Cambridge: MIT Press, 1992).

24   "Photography, Vision, and Representation," *Critical Inquiry* 2, 1 (Autumn 1975), 152.

25   On this topic see Noël Carroll, *Mystifying Movies*, 138–146.

26   See Michael Coles and Sylvia Scribner, *Culture and Thought: A Psychological Introduction* (New York: John Wiley and Sons, 1974), 67. Also see Stephen Prince, "The Discourse of Pictures: Iconicity and Film Studies," *Film Quarterly* 47, 1 (Fall 1993), 22; Paul Messaris, *Visual "Literacy": Image, Mind, and Reality* (Boulder: Westview Press, 1994), 60–64.

27   Prince, 23. Also see Messaris.

28   I first heard of this research in Arthur Danto's talk, "Animals as Art Historians: Reflections on the Innocent Eye," N.E.H. Summer Institute, "Philosophy and the Histories of the Arts," San Francisco State University, 1991. See Patrick A. Cabe, "Picture Perception in Nonhuman Subjects," in *The Perception of Pictures*, vol. 2, ed. Margaret A. Hagen (New York: Academic Press, 1980), 305–343; "Jumping Spiders React to Televised Images of Spiders as if They Were Real," *Chronicle of Higher Education*, 20 Feb. 1991, A5; R. Zimmerman and J.E. Hochberg, "Pictorial Recognition in the Infant Monkey," *Proceedings of the Psychonomic Society* 46 (1963), abstract.

29   See Stephen Walker, Animal Thought (London: Routledge and Kegan Paul, 1983), 256. The experiment is reported in Hernstein, R.J. and Loveland, D.H. "Complex Visual Concept in the Pigeon," *Science* 146 (1964), 549–551.

30   "Bottlenosed Dolphin and Human Recognition of Veridical and Degraded Video Displays of an Artificial Gestural Language," *Journal of Experimental Psychology-General* 119, 2 (1990), 215–230.

4. Indices and the Uses of Images

1   *Voyages of Discovery: The Cinema of Frederick Wiseman* (Urbana: University of Illinois, 1992), 16.

2   We must take care to distinguish between the indexing of a text (as fiction or nonfiction) and the sign as icon, index, and symbol. Although the potential confusions between *indexing* and the *indexical sign* are significant, the terms have settled into the discourse and are difficult to change.

3   "The Ontology of the Photographic Image," in *What is Cinema?*, vol. I, ed. and trans. Hugh Gray (Berkeley: University of California Press, 1967), 9–16.

4   *The World Viewed: Reflections on the Ontology of Film*, enlarged edition (Cambridge: Harvard University Press, 1979), 23.

5   Joel Snyder and Neil Walsh Allen, "Photography, Vision, and Representation," *Critical Inquiry* 2, 1 (Autumn 1975), 162.

6   Ibid.

7   Andre A. Moeussens, Ray Edward Moses, and Fred E. Inbau, *Scientific Evidence in Criminal Cases* (Mineola, NY: Foundation Press, 1973), 461.

8   Roland Barthes, "The Rhetoric of the Image," in *Image/Music/Text*, ed. and trans. Stephen Heath (New York: Hill and Wang, 1977), 45. Another important essay in the same volume is "The Photographic Message," 15–31.

9   Of course, although shots of the interviews denote facial expressions, gestures, and the type of clothing worn, these also have connotational significance.

10   "Viet War Photo Challenged," *Washington Post* (19 Jan. 86).

11   "'I'll See It When I Believe It': Rodney King and the Prison-House of Video." Unpublished paper, 1994 University Film and Video Conference, Montana State University.

12   J.D. Lasica, "Photographs That Lie: The Ethical Dilemma of Digital Retouching," *Washington Journalism Review*, June 1989, 22. Also see Christopher Anderson, "Easy-to-Alter Digital Images Raise Fears of Tampering," *Science* 263 (21 January 94), 317–318.

13   In response to *Time*'s darkened mugshot of O.J., *Newsweek* editor-in-chief Richard Smith self-righteously declared, "We don't mess around with news pictures." *Time* was happy to note that *Newsweek* had changed a color photo of Los Angeles patrolman Laurence Powell to a grainy black-and-white for a 1993 cover. *Time* spokesman Robert Pondiscio claimed to be "shocked – shocked – that *Newsweek* would mislead people when they say they don't alter cover photos." For details and the rest of the story, see Howard Kurz, "Time to Newsweek: What's Wrong With This Picture?" *The Washington Post*, 24 June 1994, B1.

14   (Cambridge: MIT Press, 1992).

15   "The Documentary Film as Scientific Inscription," in *Theorizing Documentary*, ed. Michael Renov (New York: Routledge, 1992), 55.

16   Grotta, Daniel, and Sally Grotta, "Digital Photography; Evaluation," *Popular Science* 241, 3 (September 92), 62.

17   "The Ontology of the Photographic Image," 16.

18   Mitchell, 224.

19 Ibid., 225.
20 Lasica, 23.
21 Don E. Tomlinson, "Digitexed Television News: The Beginning of the End for Photographic Reality in Photojournalism," *Business & Professional Ethics Journal* 11, 1, 61.
22 See Eisenstein's "Methods of Montage," in *Film Form*, ed. Jay Leyda (New York: Harcourt Brace Jovanovich, 1949), 82.
23 On this issue, see Edward Branigan, "'Here is a Picture of No Revolver!': The Negation of Images, and Methods for Analyzing the Structure of Pictorial Statements," *Wide Angle* 8 (1986), 8–17; Ernst Gombrich, "The Visual Image," *Scientific American* 227, 3 (Sept. 72), 86–87; David Novitz, *Pictures and Their Use in Communication* (The Hague: Martinus Nijhoff, 1977), 85–87.
24 Ernst Gombrich suggests the trilogy "code, caption, and context" in "The Visual Image," 85. Here I translate the terms for more contemporary usage and to fit nonfiction films and videos rather than the still images Gombrich concentrates on.
25 Voice-over quoted from David Bordwell and Kristin Thompson, *Film Art: An Introduction*, 3rd ed. (New York: McGraw Hill, 1990), 245.
26 Barthes, "The Rhetoric of the Image," 40.
27 Novitz, 87.
28 For more about sound in the cinema, see Rick Altman, ed., *Sound Theory Sound Practice* (New York: Routledge, 1992), and Elisabeth Weis and John Belton, eds., *Film Sound: Theory and Practice* (New York: Columbia University Press, 1985).
29 Alan Williams, "Is Sound Recording Like a Language?", *Yale French Studies* 60 (1980), 51.
30 Ibid., 53.
31 Even if we think of a sound in Williams' sense, as an entire volume of air and its vibration, there can still be iconic sound recordings. Say the original sound is a particular volume of air and its vibrations. The sound recording of the original, when played, is another volume of air that vibrates in a certain fashion. Inasmuch as the latter has physical characteristics similar to the former, it can function as an icon of the original sound.
32 James J. Gibson, *The Senses Considered as Perceptual Systems* (Boston: Houghton Mifflin, 1966), 87.
33 Ibid.
34 Also see Jeffrey K. Ruoff, "Conventions of Sound in Documentary," in Altman, *Sound Theory Sound Practice*, 217–234.
35 Robert Parrish, *Growing Up in Hollywood* (New York: Harcourt Brace Jovanovich, 1976), 144–151.

5. Nonfiction Discourse

1 *On Photography* (New York: Farrar, Straus, and Giroux, 1977), 23.
2 These categories are taken from David Bordwell and Kristin Thompson, *Film Art: An Introduction* 3rd. ed. (New York: McGraw Hill, 1993).

3   Seymour Chatman, *Story and Discourse: Narrative Structure in Fiction and Film* (Ithaca and London: Cornell University Press, 1978); Roland Barthes, "Introduction to the Structural Analysis of Narratives," in *Image/Music/Text*, trans. Stephen Heath (New York: Hill and Wang, 1977); Gerard Genette, *Narrative Discourse: An Essay in Method*, trans. Jane E. Lewis (Ithaca: Cornell University Press, 1980); Shlomith Rimmon-Kenan, *Narrative Fiction* (London: Methuen, 1983); David Bordwell, *Narration in the Fiction Film* (Madison: University of Wisconsin Press, 1985).

4   Chatman, 9.

5   Shlomith Rimmon-Kenan, 3.

6   Bordwell, *Narration in the Fiction Film.*

7   Bill Nichols, *Representing Reality: Issues and Concepts in Documentary* (Bloomington: Indiana University Press, 1991), 111–112.

8   Branigan, 1.

9   On *High School* and Wiseman's other films, see Barry Keith Grant, *Voyages of Discovery: The Cinema of Frederick Wiseman* (Urbana and Chicago: University of Illinois Press, 1992). Bill Nichols calls the structure of Wiseman's films a "mosaic" structure. See his *Ideology and the Image* (Bloomington: Indiana University Press, 1981), 210–216. For an interesting analysis of *High School*, see Bordwell and Thompson's *Film Art*, 336–342.

10   Chatman, 28.

11   This information was obtained at Epstein and Friedman's visit to Hollins College and Roanoke, Virginia in 1990.

12   Menackem Perry, "Literary Dynamics: How the Order of a Text Creates it Meanings," *Poetics Today* 1, 1–2 (Autumn 1979), 43.

13   Meir Sternberg, *Expositional Modes and Temporal Ordering in Fiction* (Baltimore: Johns Hopkins University Press, 1978).

14   Ibid., 51.

15   Ibid., 44.

16   See Hayden White, *Metahistory: The Historical Imagination in Nineteenth-Century Europe* (Baltimore: Johns Hopkins University Press, 1973); *Tropics of Discourse: Essays in Cultural Criticism* (Johns Hopkins, 1978); *The Content of the Form: Narrative Discourse and Historical Representation* (Johns Hopkins, 1987).

17   Actually, General Motors had been laying off workers and closing plants since 1974, and continues to do so up to the time of this writing. According to the film's critics, the 1986–87 plant closures resulted in about 10,000 layoffs, not 30,000 as the film implies. Thus one of the film's alleged manipulations is to represent the 86–87 layoffs as a condensed, single event rather than one more step in a long process.

18   White, *Metahistory*, 37.

19   Harlan Jacobson, "Michael and Me," *Film Comment* Nov./Dec. 1989, 25.

20   Gary Crowdus and Carley Cohan, "Reflections on *Roger and Me*, Michael Moore, and his Critics," *Cineaste* 17, No. 4 (1990), 28.

21   Michael Moore, "In Flint, Tough Times Last," *The Nation*, 6 June 1987, 754.

22   This is directly related to my discussion of the possibility of fairness and objectivity in the media. See Chapter Ten.

23   Gerard Genette, 33–160.

24   Bordwell, 80.

25   Rimmon-Kenan, 71.

26   Chatman, 153.

27   I do not mean to imply that the tone or attitude are always univocal and unchanging. Some films may exhibit a changing voice, a voice of ambiguity, or perhaps even contradictory voices. "Voice" does not necessarily assume unity of purpose or function, although in many cases one finds such unity.

28   "The Voice of Documentary," in *Movies and Methods*, v. 2, ed. Bill Nichols (Berkeley: University of California Press, 1985), 260–261.

6. Voice and Authority

1   Bill Nichols, *Representing Reality: Issues and Concepts in Documentary* (Bloomington: Indiana University Press, 1991), 32–76.

2   Ibid., 33.

3   Ibid., 266.

4   Ibid., 34,38.

5   Ibid., 36.

6   David Bordwell and Kristin Thompson, *Film Art: An Introduction*, 3rd Ed. (New York: McGraw Hill, 1990), 54–104.

7   *Narration in the Fiction Film*, 150.

8   "The Power of Movies," *Daedelus* 114, 4 (Fall 1985), 98. It could be argued that Carroll overstates the case here, implying that classical narratives leave no salient questions unanswered, leave nothing to the imagination. At the very least, however, this is a tendency among classical films, and one that some of the more interesting films may avoid.

9   David Bordwell, Janet Staiger, and Kristin Thompson, *The Classical Hollywood Cinema: Film Style and Mode of Production to 1960* (New York: Columbia University Press, 1985), 38–39.

10   Bordwell, 49.

11   Noël Burch, *Theory of Film Practice*, trans. Helen R. Lane (New York: Praeger, 1973).

12   Steven Lukes makes a similar distinction between primary and secondary theory in "Relativism in its Place," *Rationality and Relativism*, eds. Martin Hollis and Steven Lukes (Cambridge: MIT Press, 1985), 265.

13   *Narration in the Fiction Film* (Madison: University of Wisconsin Press, 1985), 160.

14   The open voice is usually present in what Umberto Eco calls the "open work." See his *The Open Work*, trans. Anna Cancogni (Cambridge: Harvard University Press, 1989).

15   "Jargons of Authenticity (Three American Moments)," in Michael Renov, ed. *Theorizing Documentary* (New York: Routledge, 1993), 119.

16   See Brian Winston, "Direct Cinema: The Third Decade," in *New Chal-

lenges for the Documentary, ed. Alan Rosenthal (Berkeley: University of California Press, 1988), 518. In making this distinction, I do not share the implicit assumption that while cinéma vérité is philosophically sophisticated, direct cinema is naïve in its claim to capture reality directly. As William Rothman says, the direct cinema filmmakers are typically not guilty of the simplistic views sometimes attributed to them. See his *Documentary Film Classics* (Cambridge: Cambridge University Press, forthcoming). Brian Winston assumes that direct cinema "hides" its processes of production. We need not share Winston's hermeneutics of suspicion to recognize the value of the distinction between direct cinema and cinéma vérité. As I use the distinction, it refers to two methods of approaching the profilmic scene, with no presumption that one method is superior to the other.

17   Quoted in James Blue, "Thoughts on Cinéma Vérité and a Discussion with the Maysles Brothers," in *Film Comment* 2, 4 (1964), 27, 29.

18   Quoted in B. Roy Levin, "Fred Wiseman," in *Documentary Explorations*, ed. G. Roy Levin (Garden City, New York: Doubleday, 1971), p. 318. As I write in the introduction to *Ordered Images*, Brian Winston claims that the aura of science accompanying the reception of visual images contradicts the filmmakers' disavowals of objectivity, and that spectators will necessarily view such films as the unproblematic truth. See "The Documentary Film as Scientific Inscription," in M. Renov, ed., *Theorizing Documentary*, 37–57. I take issue with Winston's position in "Moving Images and the Rhetoric of Nonfiction: Two Approaches," in *Post-Theory: Reconstructing Film Studies*, eds. David Bordwell and Noël Carroll (Madison: University of Wisconsin Press, 1996), 307–324.

7. Structure

1   See Bill Nichols, *Representing Reality: Issues and Concepts in Documentary* (Bloomington: Indiana University Press, 1990), 134–137.

2   *The Classical Hollywood Cinema: Film Style and Mode of Production to 1960* (New York: Columbia University Press, 1985).

3   An exception is Alan Rosenthal's *Writing, Directing, and Producing Documentary Films* (Carbondale: Southern Illinois University Press, 1990).

4   W. Hugh Baddeley, *The Technique of Documentary Film Production*, 3rd ed. (New York: Hastings House, 1975).

5   (Boston: Focal Press, 1987), 170.

6   Meir Sternberg, *Expositional Modes and Temporal Ordering* (Baltimore: Johns Hopkins University Press, 1978), 1.

7   Bordwell, *Narration in the Fiction Film*, 159.

8   Hayden White, "The Value of Narrativity in the Representation of Reality," in *On Narrative*, ed. W.J.T. Mitchell (Chicago: University of Chicago Press, 1981), 1–24.

9   I do not mean to imply that the ubiquity of perspective signals absolute freedom of expression for the historian. Athough histories are perspective relative, they still must follow rules of evidence-gathering and historical reasoning. It is in the formation of data into a narrative that creative work occurs.

10   John Grierson, *Grierson on Documentary*, ed. Forsyth Hardy (Berkeley: University of California Press, 1966), 146.
11   Hayden White, *Metahistory* (Baltimore: Johns Hopkins University Press, 1973), 1–42.
12   G. Roy Levin, "D.A. Pennebaker," in *Documentary Explorations*, ed. G. Roy Levin (Garden City, New York: Doubleday, 1971), 257–258.
13   Quoted in James Blue, "One Man's Truth: An Interview with Leacock," in *The Documentary Tradition*, ed. Lewis Jacobs (New York: Hopkinson and Blake, 1971), 410.
14   Quoted in Peter Biskind, "Does Documentary Have a Future?", *American Film* 7 (1982), 63.
15   Stephen Mamber, *Cinéma Vérité in America* (Cambridge: MIT Press, 1974), 115–116.
16   For an account of Drew and his career, see P.J. O'Connell, *Robert Drew and the Development of Cinéma Vérité in America* (Carbondale: Southern Illinois University Press, 1992).
17   Quoted in John Graham, "'There are no Simple Solutions': Wiseman on Filmmaking and Viewing," in Thomas R. Atkins, ed., *Frederick Wiseman* (New York: Monarch Press, 1976), 36.
18   Patricia Jaffe, "Editing Cinéma Vérité," *Film Comment* 3, 3 (1965), 43.
19   Quoted in Alan Westin, "'You Start Off With a Bromide': Fred Wiseman on Film and Civil Liberties," in *Frederick Wiseman*, 50.
20   Quoted in James Blue, "One Man's Truth: An Interview with Leacock," in *The Documentary Tradition*, ed. Lewis Jacobs (New York: Hopkinson and Blake, 1971), 406.
21   David Bordwell, *Narration in the Fiction Film* (Madison: University of Wisconsin Press, 1985), 228–233.
22   Ibid., 205–207.
23   Ibid., 207.
24   Barry Keith Grant, for example, calls the end here a "comment on contemporary alienation and indifference." See *Voyages of Discovery: The Cinema of Frederick Wiseman* (Urbana: University of Illinois Press, 1992), 63.
25   Ibid., 64.

8. Style and Technique

1   *Voyages of Discovery: The Cinema of Frederick Wiseman* (Urbana: University of Illinois Press, 1992), 13.
2   Teun A. van Dijk, "Semantic Discourse Analysis," in *Handbook of Discourse Analysis, ed. Teun A. van Dijk* (London: Academic Press, 1985), 103–136.
3   David Bordwell, *Narration in the Fiction Film* (Madison: University of Wisconsin Press, 1985), 112.
4   *Visual Literacy: Image, Mind, and Reality* (Boulder: Westview Press, 1994), 106–112. Messaris's book is in general an excellent discussion of the issue of visual literacy, visual communication, and the degree to which various parameters of visual communication are culture-bound or universal.

5   Messaris, 74–85.

6   Noël Carroll, "The Power of Movies," *Daedelus* 114, 4 (Fall 1985), 86.

7   Alan Westin, "'You Start off with a Bromide': Fred Wiseman on Film and Civil Liberties," in *Frederick Wiseman*, ed. Thomas Atkins (New York: Monarch Press, 1976), 54.

8   The "rule of thirds" is a convention of framing in which the image frame is (imaginatively) divided both horizontally and vertically by two parallel lines, parcelling the frame into nine equal rectangles. According to the rule of thirds, visual centers of interest should be placed along one or more of these imaginary lines, rather than symmetrically in the middle of the frame.

9   Noël Carrol, "From Real to Reel: Entangled in the Nonfiction Film," *1983 Philosophical Exchange*, 14, 26–31.

10   Raymond Fielding, *The American Newsreel: 1911–1967* (Norman, OK: University of Oklahoma Press, 1972).

11   A very useful study of the parameters of voice-over is Sarah Kozloff's *Invisible Storytellers: Voice-Over Narration in American Fiction Film* (Berkeley: University of California Press, 1988).

12   Roland Barthes, "The Photographic Message," in *Image/Music/Text*, 26.

13   Mary Anne Doane, "The Voice in the Cinema: The Articulation of Body and Space," *Yale French Studies* 60 (1980), 33–50.

14   Roland Barthes, "The Grain of the Voice," in *Image/Music/Text*, pp. 179–189.

15   "Voice-over in the 'Classical' Documentary Film," Unpublished paper, Society or Cinema Studies conference, May 1991.

16   *Representing Reality: Issues and Concepts of Documentary* (Bloomington: Indiana University Press, 1991), 44–56. Nichols draws a helpful distinction between four kinds of interviews: (1) conversation, (2) the "masked" interview, (3) pseudo-dialogue, and (4) the common interview. See 51–52.

17   Sergei Eisenstein, "Color and Meaning," in *The Film Sense*, ed. and trans. Jay Leyda (New York: Harcourt Brace Jovanovich, 1975), 150.

18   For an interesting critique of Eisenstein's thought on this issue, see Hans Eisler, *Composing for the Films* (London: Dobson, 1946), 65–71.

19   Terrence McLaughlin, *Music and Communication* (London: Faber and Fager, 1970). Interesting recent work on the psychology of music includes J. Sloboda, *The Musical Mind: A Cognitive Psychology of Music* (Oxford: Clarendon Press, 1985), and J. Dowling, *Music Cognition* (Orlando: Academic Press, 1986).

20   Bill Nichols, *Representing Reality: Issues and Concepts in Documentary* (Bloomington: Indiana University Press, 1991), 32–75.

21   Thomas Waugh, "Beyond Verite: Emile de Antonio and the New Documentary of the Seventies," in *Movies and Methods*, v. 2, ed. Bill Nichols (Berkeley: University of California Press, 1985), 233–258.

22   Bill Nichols, "The Voice of Documentary," in Movies and Methods, v. 2, 268. Linda Williams comes to similar conclusions in her recent "Mirrors Without Memories – Truth, History, and the New Documentary," *Film Quarterly* 46, 3 (Spring 1993), 9–21. She claims that films such as *Shoah* and *The Thin Blue Line* show "that there can be historical depth to the notion of truth" (20).

23   Ibid. 265.

9. The Poetic Voice

1 For an investigation of historical relationships between documentary and the avant-garde, see Charles Wolfe, "Straight Shots and Crooked Plots: Social Documentary and the Avant-Garde in the 1930s." In Jan-Christopher Horgath, ed., *Lovers of Cinema: The American Avant-Garde Before 1945* (Madison: University of Wisconsin Press, 1995).

2 Like all film genres, these are not groups with essential characteristics and clear boundaries, but fuzzy categories with prototypical examples or exemplars, and membership gradients.

3 One could argue that the poetic documentary (including some of Flaherty's films) once occupied a central place in documentary practice, at least before Grierson criticized its lack of explicit social engagement.

4 Mathew Bernstein, "Visual Style and Spatial Articulations in *Berlin: Symphony of a Great City*," *Journal of Film and Video* 36, 4 (Fall 1984), 5–12.

5 One should note, however, that the majority of Rouch's films have almost nonstop voice-over narration and thus are not the exemplars of cinéma vérité that *Chronicle of a Summer* is.

6 See "Jean Rouch," in *Documentary Explorations*, ed. G. Roy Levin (Garden City, NJ: Doubleday, 1971), 135.

7 Quoted in P. Adams Sitney, ed., *Film Culture Reader* (New York: Praeger, 1970), 362.

8 Although Godard's work here is self-referential, one might ask whether the sequence explores the forms and functions of documentary, or merely refers to them.

9 See Bordwell, 311–334.

10 In Daughter Rite, for example, I would claim that although the film is meant to encourage the spectator to mistake what is presented as fiction for nonfiction, it ultimately indexes itself as fiction with end credits that list character and actor. Thus we should see the film in retrospect not as one that asserts that which it depicts (women discussing their relationship with their mother) actually occurred, but that mimics such an assertion. What actually occurred in the profilmic scene was not women discussing their relationship with their mother, but actresses playing women discussing such a relationship.

11 What makes it nonfiction is that it purports to tell truths, albeit truths with an ironic slant.

12 Henry Jenkins, III, "The Amazing Push-Me Pull You Text: Cognitive Processing and Narrational Play in the Comic Film," *Wide Angle* 8, 3 & 4, 40.

10 Nonfiction Pragmatics and the Limits of Theory

1 Stephen Mamber, *Cinéma Vérité in America* (Cambridge: MIT Press, 1974), 115–140. For a biographical account of Robert Drew's career, see P.J. O'Connell, *Robert Drew and the Development of Cinéma Vérité in America* (Carbondale: Southern Illinois University Press, 1992).

2 Jeanne Hall, "Realism as a Style in Cinéma Vérité: A Critical Analysis of Primary," *Cinema Journal* 30, 4 (Summer 1991), 29.

3 John Grierson, *Grierson on Documentary*, ed. Forsyth Hardy (London: Faber and Faber, Ltd., 1966), 185.

4 Joris Ivens, *The Camera and I* (New York: International Publishers, 1969), 28.

5 Ibid., 40.

6 See Brian Winston, "Direct Cinema: The Third Decade," in Alan Rosenthal, ed., *New Challenges for the Documentary* (Berkeley: University of California Press, 1988), 517–529; see also Winston's "Documentary: I Think We Are in Trouble," in Rosenthal, 21–33.

7 See Thomas Waugh, "Beyond *Vérité*: Emile de Antonio and the New Documentary of the Seventies," in Bill Nichols, ed., *Movies and Methods*, v. 2 (Berkeley: University of California Press, 1985), 235.

8 Quoted in James Blue, "Thoughts on Cinéma Vérité and a Discussion with the Maysles Brothers," *Film Comment* 2, 4 (1964), 29.

9 Quoted in G. Roy Levin, "Fred Wiseman," in *Documentary Explorations*, ed. G. Roy Levin (Garden City, New York: Doubleday, 1971), 320,322.

10 Quoted in Ira Halberstadt, "An Interview with Fred Wiseman," in *Nonfiction Film Theory and Criticism*, ed. Richard M. Barsam (New York: E.P. Dutton, 1976), 300.

11 From James Blue, "Jean Rouch in Conversation with James Blue," *Film Comment* 4, 2&3 (1967), 84.

12 David MacDougall, "Beyond Observational Cinema," in *Movies and Methods*, v. 2, 287.

13 Ibid., 279.

14 A. William Bluem, *Documentary in American Television* (New York: Hastings House, 1965), 128.

15 MacDougall, 282.

16 Noel King, "Recent 'Political' Documentary: Notes on *Union Maids* and *Harlan County, U.S.A.*," *Screen* 22, 2 (1981), 9.

17 See his *Representing Reality: Issues and Concepts in Documentary* (Bloomington: Indiana University Press, 1991).

18 Jay Ruby, "The Image Mirrored: Reflexivity in the Documentary Film," in Rosenthal, 72.

19 E. Ann Kaplan, "Theories and Strategies of the Feminist Documentary," in Rosenthal, 87.

20 See Janet Staiger, *Interpreting Films: Studies in the Historical Reception of American Cinema* (Princeton: Princeton University Press, 1992).

21 Stuart Hall, "Media Power: The Double Bind," in Alan Rosenthal, *New Challenges for the Documentary*, 357–364.

22 See Vance Kepley, Jr., "Documentary as Commodity: The Making and Marketing of Victory at Sea," *Film Reader* 61 (1985), 103–113. Also of note is Kepley's "The Origins of NBC's *Project XX* in Compilation Documentaries," *Journalism Quarterly* 61, 1 (Spring 1984), 20–26.

23 "Prudential Recalls History of Ad 'Firsts' in Marking 90th Birthday," *Advertising Age*, 7 April 1958, 10.

24 *Broadcasting*, 5 July 1965, 27. In the sixties many insurance companies

gravitated toward public affairs advertising. See *Printer's Ink*, 10 March 1961, 56; *Broadcasting*, 5 March 1962, 52–53; 17 September 1962, 44; *Advertising Age*, 14 February 1966, 2.

25 Hall, 357.

26 "William Paley: Tribute to a Broadcasting Giant," CBS News Special, 31 October 1990.

27 Quoted in Robert Higgins, "The First Eight Years of *The Twentieth Century*," *TV Guide*, 5 June 1965, 7.

28 Higgins, 8–9.

29 "Nine Year Report: 1957–1966," Burton Benjamin Papers, Wisconsin State Historical Society Archives. Madison, Wisconsin.

30 Hall, 362.

31 "Nine Year Report," Burton Benjamin Papers.

32 Burton Benjamin, "The Documentary Heritage," in *The Documentary Tradition*, ed. Lewis Jacobs (New York: Hopkinson and Blake, 1971), 304.

33 CBS Press Release, 12 December 1958, Burton Benjamin Papers.

34 Bluem, 169.

35 CBS News Press Releases, 24 July 1957 and 16 December 1958, Burton Benjamin Papers.

36 Hall, 362–363.

37 Ibid., 363.

38 Lewis Lapham, *Saturday Evening Post*, 16 March 1963, pp. 65–67; *TV Guide*, 25 February 1966, 64.

39 CBS News Press Release, 20 October 1960, Burton Benjamin Papers.

40 Hall, 363–364.

41 Walter Cronkite, *The Challenges of Change* (Washington, D.C.: Public Affairs Press, 1971), 85. In 1968 Cronkite traveled to Vietnam and upon his return told television audiences that in his opinion, the best the U.S. military could do in that country was a stalemate. See "Cronkite Takes a Stand," *Newsweek*, 11 March 1968, 108.

42 Fred Friendly, *Due to Circumstances Beyond Our Control* (New York: Random House, 1967), 59.

43 *Variety*, 1 April 1959, and 10 February 1960, 28.

44 *Variety*, 8 March 1961, 56, and 15 March 1961, 31.

45 *Variety*, 29 March 1961, 17.

46 "Human Nature: Justice Versus Power," in *Reflexive Water: The Basic Concerns of Mankind*. Ed. Fons Elders (London: Souvenir Press, 1974), 171.

47 Allan Casebier, *Film and Phenomenology: Toward a Realist Theory of Cinematic Representation* (Cambridge: Cambridge University Press, 1991), 143.

48 Steven Lukes, "Relativism in its Place," in Martin Hollis and Steven Lukes, eds. *Rationality and Relativism* (Cambridge: MIT Press, 1982), 305.

49 Robert Stam, Robert Burgoyne, and Sandy Flitterman-Lewis, *New Vocabularies in Film Semiotics* (New York: Routledge, 1992), 201–203.

50 The phenomenal and emotional qualities of viewing live video require further investigation.

51 See my "Affect, Cognition, and the Power of Movies," *Postscript* 13, 1 (Fall 1993), 10–29.

52   E. Ann Kaplan, "Theories and Strategies of the Feminist Documentary,"
op. cit., 87. Kaplan is recounting these criticisms of the realist documentary
and is not necessarily invoking them as her views.
53   Richard Rorty, *Philosophy and the Mirror of Nature* (Princeton: Princeton University Press, 1980), 316–317.
54   Jay Ruby, op. cit., 75.
55   "Bill Moyers Talks with Errol Morris," PBS, recorded 26 April 1989. Linda Williams argues that Morris's film embodies "postmodern truth." However,
postmodern epistemology typically denies the existence of truth. The idea that
the truth can be partial, contingent, ambiguous, and complex was not born
with postmodernism. See "Mirrors Without Memories – Truth, History, and
the New Documentary," *Film Quarterly* 46, 3 (Spring 1993), 9–21.

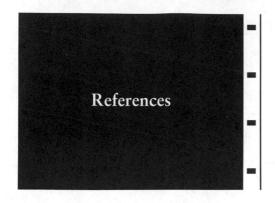

References

Allen, Jeanne. "Self-Reflexivity in the Documentary." *Ciné-Tracts* 1, 2 (Summer 1977), 37–43.

Allen, Richard. "Representation, Illusion, and the Cinema." *Cinema Journal* 32, 2 (Winter 1993), 21–48.

Allen, Robert C., and Douglas Gomery. *Film History: Theory and Practice.* New York, Alfred A. Knopf, 1985.

Altman, Rick, (ed.) *Sound Theory Sound Practice.* New York: Routledge, 1992.

Anderson, Christopher. "Easy-to-Alter Digital Images Raises Fears of Tampering." *Science* 263 (21 Jan. 94), 317–318.

Andrew, Dudley. *Concepts in Film Theory.* Oxford: Oxford University Press, 1984.

Arnheim, Rudolph. *Film as Art.* Berkeley: University of California Press, 1957.

Arthur, Paul. "Jargons of Authenticity (Three American Moments)." In *Theorizing Documentary.* Ed. Michael Renov. New York: Routledge, 1993, 108–134.

Atkins, Thomas, ed. *Frederick Wiseman.* New York: Monarch Press, 1976.

Aumont, Jacquie, Alain Bergala, Michel Marie, and Mark Vernet. *Aesthetics of Film.* Trans. and rev. by Richard Neupert. Austin: University of Texas Press, 1992.

Baddeley, W. Hugh. *The Technique of Documentary Film Production,* 3rd ed. (New York: Hastings House, 1975).

Barsam, Richard Meran. "American Direct Cinema: The Representation of Reality." *Persistence of Vision* 3/4 (Summer 1986), 131–156.

———. *Nonfiction Film: A Critical History.* Rev. and Expanded. Bloomington: Indiana University Press, 1992.

———, ed. *Nonfiction Film Theory and Criticism.* New York: E.P. Dutton, 1976.

Barthes, Roland. *Image/Music/Text,* ed. and trans. Stephen Heath. New York: Hill and Wang, 1977.

Bates, Peter. "Truth Not Guaranteed: An Interview with Errol Morris." *Cineaste* 14, 1 (1989).

Baudrillard, Jean. *Simulacres et simulation.* Paris: Galilée, 1981.

Baudry, Jean-Louis. "Ideological Effects of the Basic Cinematographic Apparatus." In *Film Theory and Criticism.* 4th ed. Eds. Gerald Mast, Marshall Cohen, and Leo Braudy. New York: Oxford University Press, 1992, pp. 302–312.

Bazin, André. *What is Cinema.* Vol. I. Trans. Hugh Gray. Berkeley and Los Angeles: University of California Press, 1967.

Benson, Thomas W., and Carolyn Anderson, *Reality Fictions: The Films of Frederick Wiseman.* Carbondale: University of Southern Illinois Press, 1989.

Bernstein, Mathew. "Visual Style and Spatial Articulations in Berlin: Symphony of a Great City." *Journal of Film and Video* 36, 4 (Fall 1984), 5–12.

Biskind, Peter. "Does Documentary Have a Future?" *American Film* 7 (1982).

Blinder, David. "In Defense of Pictorial Mimesis." *Journal of Aesthetics and Art Criticism* 45, No. 1 (Fall 1986), 19–27.

Blue, James. "Jean Rouch in Conversation with James Blue." *Film Comment* 4, 2 & 3 (1967), 84–88.

———."One Man's Truth: An Interview with Leacock." In *The Documentary Tradition,* ed. Lewis Jacobs. New York: Hopkinson and Blake, 1971, pp. 406–419.

———. "Thoughts on Cinema Verite and a Discussion with the Maysles Brothers." *Film Comment* 2, 4 (Fall 1964), 22–30.

Bluem, William A. *Documentary in American Television.* New York: Hastings House, 1965.

Bordwell, David. *Narration in the Fiction Film.* Madison: University of Wisconsin Press, 1985.

Bordwell, David, and Kristin Thompson. *Film Art: An Introduction.* 3rd ed. New York: McGraw Hill, 1990.

Bordwell, David, Janet Staiger, and Kristin Thompson. *The Classical Hollywood Cinema: Film Style and Mode of Production to 1960.* New York: Columbia University Press, 1985.

Branigan, Edward. "'Here is a Picture of No Revolver!': The Negation of Images, and Methods for Analyzing the Structure of Pictorial Statements." *Wide Angle* 8 (1986), 8–17.

———. *Narrative Comprehension and Film.* London and New York: Routledge, 1992.

Burch, Noël. *Theory of Film Practice.* Trans. Helen R. Lane. New York: Praeger, 1973.

Cabe, Patrick A. "Picture Perception in Nonhuman Subjects." In *The Perception of Pictures.* Vol. 2. Ed. Margaret A. Hagen. New York: Academic Press, 1980.

Carroll, Noël. "From Real to Reel: Entangled in the Nonfiction Film." *1983 Philosophic Exchange* 14, 5–45.

———. *Mystifying Movies: Fads and Fallacies in Contemporary Film Theory.* New York: Columbia University Press, 1988.

———. "Nonfiction Film and Postmodernist Skepticism." In *Post-Theory: Reconstructing Film Studies.* Eds. David Bordwell and Noël Carroll. Madison: University of Wisconsin Press, 1996, pp. 283–306.

———. *Philosophical Problems of Classical Film Theory.* Princeton: Princeton University Press, 1988.

———. "The Power of Movies." *Daedelus* 114, 4 (Fall 1985), 79–104.

Casebier, Allan. *Film and Phenomenology: Toward a Realist Theory of Cinematic Representation*. Cambridge: Cambridge University Press, 1991.

Cavell, Stanley. *The World Viewed: Reflections on the Ontology of Film*. Cambridge: Harvard University Press, 1979.

Chatman, Seymour. *Story and Discourse: Narrative Structure in Fiction and Film*. London: Cornell University Press, 1978.

Cole, Sylvia, and Scribner. *Culture and Thought: A Psychological Introduction*. New York: John Wiley and Sons, 1974.

Collins, Glen. "Film Makers Protest to Academy." *New York Times* 24 Feb. 1990, L13.

Crowdus, Gary. "Getting Facts Straight: An Interview with Zachary Sklar." *Cineaste* 19, 1 (1992).

Crowdus, Gary, and Carley Cohan. "Reflections on Roger and Me, Michael, Moore, and his Critics." *Cineaste* 17, 4 (1990).

Davies, Stephen. *Definitions of Art*. Ithaca: Cornell University Press, 1991.

Doane, Mary Anne. "The Voice in the Cinema: The Articulation of Body and Space." *Yale French Studies* 60 (1980), 33–50.

Dowling, J. *Music Cognition*. Orlando: Academic Press, 1986.

Eco, Umberto. *The Open Work*. Trans. Anna Cancogni. Cambridge: Harvard University Press, 1989.

Eisenstein, Sergie. "Color and Meaning." In *Film Sense*. Ed. and trans. Lay Leyda. New York: Harcourt Brace Jovanovich, pp. 113–156.

Eisler, Hans. *Composing for the Films*. London: Dobson, 1946.

Eitzen, Dirk. "When is a Documentary?: Documentary as a Mode of Reception." *Cinema Journal* 35, 1 (Fall 1995), 81–102.

Fielding, Raymond. *The American Newsreel: 1911–1967*. Norman: University of Oklahoma Press, 1972.

———. *The March of Time: 1935–1951*. New York: Oxford University Press, 1978.

Friendly, Fred. *Due to Circumstances Beyond Our Control*. New York: Random House, 1967.

Genette, Gerard. *Narrative Discourse: An Essay in Method*. Trans. Jane E. Lewin. Ithaca: Cornell University Press, 1980.

Gibson, J.J. *The Ecological Approach to Visual Perception*. Boston: Houghton Mifflin, 1979.

———. *The Senses Considered as Perceptual Systems*. Ithaca: Cornell University Press, 1966.

Giles, Dennis. "The Name Documentary: A Preface to Genre Study." *Film Reader* 3 (1978), 18–22.

Gombrich, Ernst. "The Visual Image." *Scientific American* 227, 3 (Sept. 72), 82–96.

Goodman, Nelson. *Languages of Art*. New York: Bobbs Merrill, 1968.

Graham, John. "'There are no Simple Solutions': Wiseman on Filmmaking and Viewing." In Atkins, Thomas, ed., *Frederick Wiseman*, pp. 33–46.

Grant, Barry Keith. *Voyages of Discovery: The Cinema of Frederick Wiseman*. Chicago: University of Illinois Press, 1992.

Grant, Barry Keith, and Jeannette Sloniowski, eds. *Documenting the Documentary*. Detroit: Wayne State University Press, forthcoming.

Grierson, John. "Documentary (1)." *Cinema Quarterly* (Winter 1932), 67–72.

———. "Documentary (2): Symphonics." *Cinema Quarterly* (Spring 1933), 135–139.

———.*Grierson on Documentary*. Ed. Forsyth Hardy. London: Faber and Faber, 1966.

Grotta, Daniel, and Sally Grotta. "Digital Photography: Evaluation." *Popular Science*, 241, 3 (Sept. 92), 62.

Guynn, William. *A Cinema of Nonfiction* Rutherford: Fairleigh Dickenson University Press, 1990.

Halberstadt, Ira. "An Interview with Frederick Wiseman." In *Nonfiction Film Theory and Criticism*. Ed. Richard M. Barsam. New York: E.P. Dutton, 1976, pp. 296–309.

Hall, Jeanne. "Realism as a Style in Cinéma Vérité: A Critical Analysis of Primary." *Cinema Journal* 30, 4 (Summer 1991), 24–50.

Hall, Stuart. "Media Power: The Double Bind." In Rosenthal, *New Challenges for the Documentary*, pp. 357–364.

Hartl, John. "Shutouts." *Seattle Times*. 25 February 1990, L9.

Hernstein, R.J., and D.H. Loveland. "Complex Visual Concept in the Pigeon." *Science* 146 (1964), 549–551.

Hollis, Martin, and Steven Lukes, eds. *Rationality and Relativism*. Cambridge: MIT Press, 1982.

Ivens, Joris. *The Camera and I*. New York: International Publishers, 1969.

Jacobs, Lewis, ed. *The Documentary Tradition*. New York: Hopkinson and Blake, 1971.

Jacobson, Harlan. "Michael and Me." *Film Comment* (Nov/Dec 89), 16–26.

Jaffe, "Editing Cinema Verite." *Film Comment* 3, 3 (1965), 43–47.

Jenkins, Henry, III. "The Amazing Push-Me Pull You Text: Cognitive Processing and Narrational Play in the Comic Film." *Wide Angle* 8, 3&4.

Jones, Rebecca, Edward S. Reed, and Margaret A. Hagan, "A Three Point Perspective on Pictorial Representation: Wartovsky, Goodman, and Gibson on Seeing Pictures." *Erkenntnis* 15 (1980), 55–64.

Kaplan, E. Ann. "Theories and Strategies of the Feminist Documentary." In Alan Rosenthal, 78–102.

Katch, M. Ethan. *The Electronic Media and the Transformation of Law*. Oxford: Oxford University Press, 1989.

Kepley, Vance, Jr. "Documentary as Commodity: The Making and Marketing of Victory at Sea." *Film Reader* 61 (1985), 103–113.

———. "The Origins of NBC's Project XX in Compilation Documentaries." *Journalism Quarterly* 61, 1 (Spring 84), 20–26.

King, Noel. "Recent 'Political' Documentary: Notes on *Union Maids* and *Harlan County, U.S.A.*" *Screen* 22, 2 (1981).

Kozloff, Sarah. *Invisible Storytellers: Voice-Over Narration in American Fiction Film*. Berkeley: University of California Press, 1988.

Kracauer, Siegfried. *Theory of Film: The Redemption of Physical Reality*. Oxford: Oxford University Press, 1960.

Lakoff, George. *Women, Fire, and Dangerous Things: What Categories Reveal About the Human Mind.* London: University of Chicago Press, 1987.

Lasica, J.D. "Photographs that Lie: The Ethical Dilemma of Digital Image Retouching." *Washington Journalism Review* (June 89), 22–25.

Lesage, Julia. "The Political Aesthetics of the Feminist Documentary Film." *Quarterly Review of Film Studies* 3, 4 (Fall 1978), 507–523.

Levin, G. Roy, ed. *Documentary Explorations: 15 Interviews with Film-makers.* Garden City, N.Y.: Doubleday, 1971.

MacCabe, Colin. "Theory and Film: Principles of Realism and Pleasure." In *Film Theory and Criticism.* 4th Ed. Eds. Gerald Mast, Marshall Cohen, and Leo Braudy. New York: Oxford University Press, 1992, pp. 79–92.

MacDougall, David. "Beyond Observational Cinema." In *Movies and Methods,* v. II. Ed. Bill Nichols. Berkeley: University of California Press, 1985, pp. 274–286.

Mamber, Stephen. *Cinéma Vérité in America.* Cambridge: MIT Press, 1974.

Marr, David. *Vision: A Computational Approach.* Cambridge: MIT Press, 1982.

McLaughlin, Terrence. *Music and Communication.* London: Faber and Faber, 1970.

Messaris, Paul. *Visual "Literacy": Image, Mind, and Reality.* Boulder: Westview Press, 1994.

Mitchell, W.J.T. *Iconology: Image, Text, Ideology.* Chicago: University of Chicago Press, 1986.

Mitchell, William J. *The Reconfigured Eye: Visual Truth in the Post-Photographic Era.* Cambridge: MIT Press, 1992.

Moore, Michael. "In Flint, Tough Times Last." *The Nation* (6 June 87).

Nichols, Bill. *Blurred Boundaries: Questions of Meaning in Contemporary Culture.* Bloomington: Indiana University Press, 1994.

———. *Representing Reality: Issues and Concepts in Documentary.* Bloomington: Indiana University Press, 1991.

———. "The Voice of Documentary." In *Movies and Methods.* Vol. II. Ed. Bill Nichols. Berkeley: University of California Press, 1985, pp. 258–273.

Novitz, David. *Pictures and Their Use in Communication.* The Hague: Martinus Nijhoff, 1977.

O'Connell, P.J. *Robert Drew and the Development of Cinéma Vérité in America.* Cabondale: Southern Illinois University Press, 1992.

Parrish, Robert. *Growing Up in Hollywood.* New York: Harcourt Brace Jovanovich, 1976.

Peirce, C.S. *Collected Papers.* 8 vols. Eds. Charles Hartshorne and Paul Weiss. Cambridge: Harvard University Press, 1931–58. Volume II.

Perry, Menackem. "Literary Dynamics: How the Order of a Text Creates its Meanings." *Poetics Today* 1, 1–2 (Autumn 1979).

Plantinga, Carl. "Affect, Cognition, and the Power of Movies." *Post Script* 13, 1 (Fall 1993), 10–29.

———."Defining Documentary: Fiction, Nonfiction, and Projected Worlds." *Persistence of Vision* 5 (Spring 1987), 44–54.

————. "Film Theory and Aesthetics: Notes on a Schism." *Journal of Aesthetics and Art Criticism* 51, 3 (Summer 1993), 445–454.

————. "Moving Pictures and the Rhetoric of Nonfiction Film: Two Approaches." In *Post-Theory: Reconstructing Film Studies*. Eds. David Bordwell and Noël Carroll. Madison: University of Wisconsin Press, 1996, pp. 307–324.

Ponech, Trevor. "Motion Picture Non-Fictions." *Semiotic Inquiry* 15, 1–2 (Sept. 1995).

Prince, Stephen. "The Discourse of Pictures: Iconicity and Film Studies." *Film Quarterly* 47, 1 (Fall 1993), 16–28.

Rabiger, Michael. *Directing the Documentary*. Boston: Focal Press, 1987.

Reed, Edward S. *James J. Gibson and the Psychology of Perception*. New Haven and London: Yale University Press, 1988.

Renov, Michael, ed. *Theorizing Documentary*. New York: Routledge, 1993.

————. "Re-thinking Documentary: Toward a Taxonomy of Mediation." *Wide Angle* 8, Nos. 3–4, (1986), 71–78.

————. "Toward a Poetics of Documentary." In *Theorizing Documentary* 12–36.

Rimmon-Kenan, Shlomith. *Narrative Fiction*. New York: Methuen, 1983.

Rorty, Richard. *Philosophy and the Mirror of Nature*. Princeton: Princeton University Press, 1980.

Rosen, Philip. "Document and Documentary: On the Persistence of Historical Concepts." In *Theorizing Documentary*. Ed. Michael Renov. New York: Routledge, 1993, pp. 58–89.

Rosenthal, Alan, ed. *New Challenges for the Documentary*. Berkeley: University of California Press, 1988.

————. *Writing, Directing, and Producing Documentary Films* (Carbondale: Southern Illinois Press, 1990).

Rotha, Paul. *Documentary Film*. New York: Hastings House, 1952.

Rothman, William. *Documentary Film Classics*. Cambridge: Cambridge University Press, forthcoming.

Ruby, Jay, Larry Gross, and John Katz, eds. *Image Ethics: The Moral and Legal Rights of Subjects in Photographs, Film, and Television*. New York: Oxford University Press, 1988.

Ruby, Jay. "The Image Mirrored: Reflexivity and the Documentary Film." In Alan Rosenthal, *New Challenges for the Documentary*, pp. 64–77.

Ruoff, Jeffrey. "Conventions of Sound in Documentary." In *Sound Theory Sound Practice*, ed. Rick Altman. New York: Routledge, 1992, pp. 217–234.

Searle, John. "The Logical Status of Fictional Discourse." *New Literary History* 6, (1974), 319–338.

————. *The Rediscovery of the Mind*. Cambridge: MIT Press, 1992.

————. "The World Turned Upside Down." *New York Review of Books* (27 October 1973), 48.

Simon, Art. "The Making of Alert Viewers: The Mixing of Fact and Fiction in JFK." *Cineaste* 19, 1 (1992), 14–15.

Sitney, P. Adams, ed. *Film Culture Reader.* New York: Praeger, 1970.

Sloboda, J. *The Musical Mind: A Cognitive Psychology of Music.* Oxford: Clarendon Press, 1985.

Snyder, Joel, and Neal Walsh Allen. "Photography, Vision, and Representation." *Critical Inquiry* 2, 1 (Autumn 1975).

Sobchack, Vivian. "Inscribing Ethical Space: Ten Propositions on Death, Representation, and Documentary." *Quarterly Review of Film Studies* 9, 4 (1984), pp. 283–300.

Sontag, Susan. *On Photography.* Rpt. New York: Farrar, Strauss, and Giroux, 1989.

Spottiswoode, Raymond. *A Grammer of the Film.* Berkeley: University of California Press, 1959.

Staiger, Janet. *Interpreting Films: Studies in the Historical Reception of American Cinema.* Princeton: Princeton University Press, 1992.

Stam, Robert, Robert Burgoyne, and Sandy Flitterman-Lewis, *New Vocabularies in Film Semiotics.* New York: Routledge, 1992.

Sternberg, Meir. *Expositional Modes and Temporal Ordering in Fiction.* Baltimore: Johns Hopkins University Press, 1978.

Stam, Robert, Robert Burgoyne, and Sandy Flitterman-Lewis. *New Vocabularies in Film Semiotics.* New York: Routledge, 1992.

Tomasulo, Frank. "'I'll See It When I Believe It': Rodney King and the Prison-House of Video." Paper presented at the 1994 University Film and Video Conference.

Tomlinson, Don E. "Digitexed Television News: The Beginning of the End for Photographic Reality in Photojournalism." *Business and Professional Ethics* 11, 1 (1990), 51–70.

Tuchman, Gaye. "Objectivity as Strategic Ritual: An Examination of Newsmen's Notions of Objectivity." *American Journal of Sociology* 77, 4 (Jan. 72), 660–679.

van Dijk, Teun A. "Cognitive Processing of Literary Discourse." *Poetics Today* 1, 1–2 (1979).

———. "Semantic Discourse Analysis." In *Handbook of Discourse Analysis*, ed. Teun A. van Dijk. London: Academic Press, 1985, pp. 103–136.

"Viet War Photo Challenged." *Washington Post* (19 Jan. 86).

Walker, Stephen. *Animal Thought.* London: Routledge and Kegan Paul, 1983.

Walton, Kendall. "Transparent Pictures: On the Nature of Photographic Realism." *Critical Inquiry* 11, 2 (December 1984), 251–273.

Warren, Charles, ed. *Beyond Document: Essays on Nonfiction Film.* Hanover and London: Wesleyan University Press, 1996.

Waugh, Thomas. "Beyond Vérité: Emile de Antonio and the New Documentary of the Seventies." In *Movies and Methods.* Vol II. Ed. Bill Nichols. Berkeley: University of California Press, 1985, pp. 233–258.

———. *Show Us Life: Towards a History and Aesthetics of the Committed Documentary.* Metuchen: Scarecrow Press, 1984.

Weis, Elisabeth, and John Belton, eds. *Film Sound: Theory and Practice.* New York: Columbia University Press, 1985.

Weiss, Allen. "Lucid Intervals: Postmodernism and Photography." In *Postmodernism: Philosophy and the Arts*. Ed. Hugh J. Silverman. New York: Routledge, 1990.

Weitz, Morris. "The Role of Theory in Aesthetics." *Journal of Aesthetics and Art Criticism* 15, 1 (September 1956), 27–35.

Westin, Alan. "'You Start off With a Bromide': Fred Wiseman on Film and Civil Liberties." In Atkins, ed., *Frederick Wiseman*, pp. 47–66.

White, Hayden. *Metahistory: The Historical Imagination in Nineteenth-Century Europe*. Baltimore: Johns Hopkins University Press, 1973.

———. "The Value of Narrativity in the Representation of Reality." In *On Narrative*. Ed. W.J.T. Mitchell. Chicago: University of Chicago Press, 1981, pp. 1–24.

Williams, Alan. "Is Sound Recording Like a Language?" *Yale French Studies* 60 (1980), 51–66.

Williams, Christopher, ed. *Realism in the Cinema*. London: Routledge and Kegan Paul, 1980).

Williams, Linda. "Mirrors Without Memories – Truth, History, and the New Documentary." *Film Quarterly* 46, 3 (Spring 1993), 9–21.

Wilson, George M. *Narration in Light: Studies in Cinematic Point of View*. Baltimore: Johns Hopkins University Press, 1986.

Winston, Brian. *Claiming the Real: The Documentary Film Revisited*. London: British Film Institute, 1995.

———. "Direct Cinema: The Third Decade." In *New Challenges for Documentary*. Ed. Alan Rosenthal. Berkeley: University of California Press, 1988, pp. 517–529.

———. "The Documentary Film as Scientific Inscription." In *Theorizing Documentary*, ed. Michael Renov, 37–57.

———. "Documentary: I Think We Are in Trouble." In *New Challenges for the Documentary* 21–33.

Wittgenstein, Ludwig. Philosophical Investigations. Trans. G.E.M. Anscombe. New York: Macmillan, 1958.

Wolfe, Charles. "Straight Shots and Cooked Plots: Social Documentary and the Avant-Garde in the 1930s." In *Lovers of Cinema: The American Avant-Garde Before 1945*. Ed. Jan-Christopher Horak. Madison: University of California Press, 1995.

———. "Voice-Over in the "Classical" Documentary Film." Unpublished paper. Society for Cinema Studies Conference, USC, 1991.

Wollen, Peter. *Signs and Meaning in the Cinema*. Bloomington: Indiana University Press, 1972.

Wolterstorff, Nicholas. *Art in Action: Towards a Christian Aesthetic*. Grand Rapids: Erdmans, 1980.

———.*Works and Worlds of Art*. Oxford: Clarendon Press, 1980.

———. "Worlds of Works of Art." *Journal of Aesthetics and Art Criticism* 35, 2 (1976), 121–132.

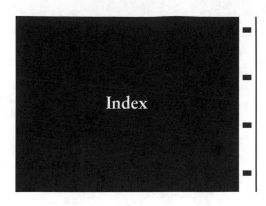

Index